T0333854

THE SOCIAL STRUCTURE OF THE USSR

Recent Soviet Studies

THE SOCIAL STRUCTURE OF THE USSR

Recent Soviet Studies

Edited with an introduction by
MURRAY YANOWITCH

M. E. SHARPE, INC.
Armonk, New York

Second Printing

Copyright © 1986 by M. E. Sharpe, Inc.

Russian texts are translated by arrangement with VAAP, the USSR
Copyright Agency.

Available in the United Kingdom and Europe from M. E. Sharpe,
Publishers, 3 Henrietta Street, London WC2E 8LU.

Published simultaneously as vol. xxiv, nos. 1, 2, and 3 of
Soviet Sociology.

Translated by Liv Tudge

Library of Congress Cataloging-in-Publication Data

Main entry under title:

The Social structure of the USSR.

   Translations from the Russian.
   ''Published simultaneously as Soviet sociology, vol. xxiv,
no. 1–3''—T.p. verso.
   Bibliography: p.
   1. Social classes—Soviet Union—Addresses, essays, lectures.
2. Social structure—Soviet Union—Addresses, essays, lectures.
3. Soviet Union—Social conditions— 1945-   —Addresses, essays,
Lectures. I. Yanowitch, Murray.

HB530.Z9S645   1985   305.5'0947   85-18322
ISBN 0-87332-362-9
ISBN 0-87332-468-4 (pbk.)

Printed in the United States of America

Table of Contents

Introduction

MURRAY YANOWITCH

With one exception, the materials included in this volume originally appeared in Soviet publications during the early 1980s (the
one exception, selection 4, was published in 1977). An earlier
collection of Soviet writings on social structure, which I edited
jointly with Wesley Fisher,[1] acquainted Western readers with
some of the principal Soviet studies in this field of the late 1960s
and early 1970s. Although in most respects the final years of the
Brezhnev regime and the period immediately thereafter (the years
in which the selections which follow originally appeared) hardly
strike most observers as particularly "innovative," the professional literature in sociology in this period—and social stratification and mobility research, in particular—developed an intellectual momentum of its own. The result is that, while staying
largely within the boundaries laid down in the formative period of
Soviet sociology (as represented by the studies included in the
earlier collection referred to above), the more recent studies
included here have gone beyond the earlier ones in a variety of
ways. To put it more directly, we may observe here both a basic
continuity and a partial break with the limits of earlier studies.
The remainder of this introduction will provide a few illustrations
of this theme.

1. Like those in earlier years, the more recent studies present
abundant empirical evidence of inequalities in earnings, status,
and educational attainments and opportunities within Soviet society. Now, however, the range of occupational groups included and
the particular types of inequalities disclosed have been extended.

In the late 1960s and early 1970s the more serious studies
by Soviet sociologists moved beyond the earlier, simplistic three-
fold division of Soviet society (into the working class, the collective-farm peasantry, and the intelligentsia) to eight or nine "socio-occupational groups" (ranging from unskilled manual
workers to "organizers of production collectives"); today, we
have available measures of the relative economic status and degree of managerial authority and job autonomy for more than 70
occupational titles (see selection 4, particularly Table 1). Not
only is the range of inequality between the extremes of the occupational hierarchy thereby extended, but the legitimacy of intro-
ducing such occupational groups as party functionaries and army
officers into studies of social structure is implicitly affirmed. The
readiness to compare the value of "property" holdings (presumably consumer durables and perhaps the value of private household plots and vacation homes) for a limited range of occupational groups (see selection 6) is another novel feature of the recent
Soviet literature on social structure.

2. Quite apart from disclosing additional empirical evidence
of social and economic inequality, recent studies also provide
some illustrations of changes in the concepts and ideas commonly
relied on in Soviet discussions of this subject. For example,
although the familiar notion that the Soviet Union is moving
toward "full social homogeneity" continues to be reiterated (see
selections 4 and 5), it is now explicitly recognized that socialism
may also generate new forms of social differentiation—new strata
and social groups—and that it is just as important to study this
process as to look for signs of movement toward the ultimate goal
of "social homogeneity" (see selection 3).[2] Furthermore, while
"egalitarianism" (*uravnilovka*) remains a term of opprobrium, it
has also become possible to criticize—at least obliquely—unjusti-
fied inequalities in real income, that is, inequalities in access to
consumption opportunities which do not correspond to inequalities in labor contribution. This appears to be the significance of
Ovsiannikov's critical observation (see selection 6) concerning
the relatively high value of "property" held by households with

family members employed in the trade network and "management organs." The theme of "excessive inequalities," particularly those associated with the receipt of certain types of non-labor incomes (incomes derieved from "bribery, speculation, encroachment on social property") has been carried further in the writings of sociologist V. Rogovin. Even those forms of non-labor income that are legal (for example, those derived from the inheritance of monetary savings and personal property) but which contribute to the "excessive advantages" of particular social groups, have come under fire recently. Thus Rogovin has proposed revamping the tax system with the aim of "the effective taxation of excessively high incomes," a return to the kind of inheritance taxes that were in effect during the early years of the Soviet regime, as well as the establishment of a legal maximum on per capita family income.[3] Is this the initial phase of an explicit examination of "privilege" in the Soviet sociological literature?

3. Similarly, Titma's stress on the importance of studying the differing "social interests" of distinct strata represents a potentially significant step in a new direction (see selection 3). Needless to say, in the Soviet view the existence of distinct group interests does not signify an "antagonism" or "fundamental differences" in interests such as prevail under capitalism. Nonetheless such group interests, for Titma, are directed toward retaining or changing the group's position in society. Hence the need to study "social interests" as an aspect of "the reproduction of the social structure." Recent Soviet writings have explicitly acknowledged the role of group interests (of ministerial authorities, for example) in blocking the transfer to lower-level economic units of functions ordinarily performed by central authorities. This issue has been posed most sharply in T. I. Zaslavskaia's discussion (published too recently for inclusion in this volume) of the obstacles to implementing decentralizing and market-oriented economic reforms. For Zaslavskaia it seems obvious that the attitudes of various social groups toward the prospect of such reforms will differ depending on their "position in the hierarchical system of managing the economy." More specifically, au-

thorities at the industrial ministry level stand to lose (and hence are a source of resistance to the reforms) while managerial personnel at the enterprise level stand to gain. Perhaps the most promising aspect of Zaslavskaia's analysis is her readiness to affirm the applicability of concepts like "contradictory interests" and "collision of interests" to group relations in the Soviet Union.[4]

4. Some of the more recently published selections included here (for example, selections 1 and 2) embody a particular kind of "reformist" strain not usually found in earlier studies. Gordon and Nazimova provide a highly useful analysis of census data on the changing socio-occupational structure of the Soviet work force, with special emphasis on the comparatively slow decline in the proportion of low-skilled jobs in recent years. This slow decline, when considered jointly with the rapid increase in educational attainment levels and the more ambitious occupational aspirations which increased education generates, has had a negative impact on work attitudes and is admittedly a source of "social tensions." The solution, in the view of Gordon and Nazimova, does not lie merely in continued technological advance—the traditional solvent of economic and social problems in the Soviet view—but in changes in "production relations," in increased opportunities "for the participation of working people in management," and in increased scope for "self-realization, self-activity, self-organization." Is this the kind of rhetoric that substitutes for reform or does it help prepare the ground for genuine reform? In any case, it has begun to permeate Soviet studies of social structure.

5. One sign of the growing maturity of Soviet sociology, and of the literature on social structure in particular, is the readiness of Soviet scholars to draw on analytical techniques commonly employed in Western studies. Some illustrations of this may be found in the selections on social mobility in Part III (particularly selection 9, in which the Soviet authors explicitly acknowledge their reliance on the work of Blau and Duncan). Somewhat less welcome, and perhaps grating to Western readers, is the occasional need which some Soviet sociologists still have to celebrate

the greater "openness" of their society compared to capitalist society. However strong this need may be, it should not obscure the readiness of Soviet scholars to disclose and document the processes through which social inequalities continue to be transmitted across generations (see page 178 below): "The children of workers and collective farmers embark upon socially useful work, as a rule, by taking an educational 'shortcut'—after completing school or a secondary specialized educational institution. Representatives of the intelligentsia and employees, for their part, encourage the younger generation to proceed on to higher education."

6. There is one area that has remained almost completely "off-limits" to Soviet sociologists: the serious study of power. Inequalities in income, prestige, educational opportunities, "property," gender inequalities—all these are regarded as appropriate areas of study, as the essays in this volume demonstrate. But insofar as we can judge, no progress has been made toward legitimizing genuine intellectual discourse on the phenomenon of distribution of power in the sociological literature. This is surely the most serious limitation of what is still a comparatively new intellectual discipline under Soviet circumstances.

Notes

1. Murray Yanowitch and Wesley A. Fisher, editors, *Social Stratification and Mobility in the USSR*, White Plains, N.Y.: International Arts and Sciences Press, Inc., 1973.

2. See also, N. A. Aitov, "Some Debatable Questions in the Study of the Soviet Intelligentsia," *Sotsiologicheskie issledovaniia*, 1979, 3, pp. 32–33.

3. V. Rogovin, "Social Justice and Some Questions of Improving Distributive Relations," *Politicheskoe samoobrazovanie*, 1985, 6, pp. 50–51.

4. T. I. Zaslavskaia, "Economic Structure Through the Prism of Sociology," *EKO*, 1985, 7, pp. 3–22. See also A. Prigozhin, "On the Potential of an Experiment," *Kommunist*, 1985, 5, pp. 35–36.

Part I

Socio-occupational Structure

1. The Socio-occupational Structure of Contemporary Soviet Society

Typology and Statistics*

L. A. GORDON and A. K. NAZIMOVA

**The study of socio-occupational structure
on the basis of official statistical materials**

The development of the occupational structure is a central feature of Soviet society's economic and social progress in the contemporary context. It is an organic part of the restructuring of all social relations that typifies the phase of mature socialism. Realignments in the occupational structure are part and parcel of the decisive economic processes of our day, as the socialist economy adopts a course of intensive growth and absorbs the attainments of the revolution in science and technology. Indeed, these processes serve as the objective basis for the party's thrust toward "higher production efficiency and the intensification of production."[1] In historical scope and consequences, they have much in common with other profoundly important transformations, such as industrialization. Concurrently, progress in the occupational composition of society is also linked to profound changes in our country's social structure, the nature of which was pointed out in Iuri V. Andropov's report, *Sixty Years of the USSR*.[2] The evident corollary of the conclusion reached at the Twenty-sixth Party

*Russian text © 1983 by "Progress" Publishers. "Sotsial'no-professional'-naia struktura sovremennogo sovetskogo obshchestva: tipologiia i statistika," *Rabochii klass i sovremennyi mir*, 1983, No. 2, pp. 61–73

Congress—that a classless structure of society will be essentially established within the historical framework of mature socialism—is that there will be a certain shift in the "center of gravity" in social structure and social policy. As class differences are eroded, certain distinctions within society which transcend the class framework will become central. In particular, the relative importance of many occupational divisions will increase substantially, and the occupational structure of society will accordingly gain in significance.

This being so, the need to study the social aspects of the development of occupational structure naturally increases. The "social aspects of occupational structure"—the socio-occupational structure, in the true sense—is here taken to mean not the totality of occupational groups and the links among them, but, rather, a certain portion of that totality. More concretely, we refer to the system that comprises those occupational groups, membership in which automatically defines not only the organizational and technical specifics of productive activity but also the essential traits of working people's social profile—the salient peculiarities of the conditions and nature of their work, daily life, culture, social psychology, and mode of life.

Having established this understanding, it follows, of course, that our discussion of the socio-occupational structure can only cover fairly broad—and therefore necessarily amorphous—groups. People's social profile can hardly be much affected by adherence to individual occupational-technical categories. Distinctive features may logically be sought by juxtaposing, say, working people in industrial and agricultural occupations, or those doing extremely simple manual work, and those performing complex mechanized work, but certainly not by comparing turners and milling-machine operators, combine operators and tractor drivers, or internists and surgeons.

The socio-occupational structure has always commanded the attention of Soviet social scientists.[3] Until recent years, however, most studies in this field dealt with the socio-occupational structure at individual enterprises or in certain economic branches or geographical areas, examined at a given moment of time. Only in a few studies was the sociological analysis done longitudinally, over time, and even these normally involved the comparison of data predominantly gathered within a fairly limited time-span (the findings of chronologically contiguous censuses, for instance).

However, it now appears possible to combine cross-sectional analysis with the disclosure and interpretation of long-term trends that reflect the principal processes of socio-occupational development in society as a whole. The accumulation of official statistical data—primarily the release of materials gathered in the four All-Union population censuses (1939, 1959, 1970, 1979) and several special occupational surveys—is of paramount significance here. The published materials contain listings of jobs held by the employed population, with an indication of the number of people in any given job at the time of the survey. Thus they provide the statistical groundwork for a study of changes in the occupational composition of Soviet society from the 1940s to the 1970s.

Hence, the ultimate goals of this paper are, first, to shed light on the composition of consolidated occupational groups whose social profiles exhibit common traits (i.e., elements of the socio-occupational structure as previously described), and, second, to trace changes in the size and relative importance of these groups over the past two, three, or even four decades, i.e., to describe the direction and approximate quantitative indices of development of the socio-occupational structure of Soviet society during the establishment and optimization of mature socialism within that society. The preliminary condition for the attainment of these goals is a sound definition of the grounds upon which a multitude of specific jobs may be reduced to a relatively small number of major socio-occupational groups. The immediate tasks of this paper must, therefore, incorporate a typological analysis of official employment statistics as the first step toward a socio-occupational classification. Accordingly, the greater part of what follows is an examination of typological and classificational issues.

Socio-occupational groups differing in terms of the nature and complexity of work performed

When applying ourselves to the construction of a socio-occupational typology of jobs in a statewide statistical framework, it is appropriate to emphasize at the outset that a typology of this sort which is in any way complete, or at least suitable for applied sociological research, can hardly be based on a single foundation. An excessive multiplicity of foundations, however, would deprive it of that generalizing focus which alone makes any typology meaningful. This, then, leads us to search for two or three foundations that would permit us to identify several sets of occupational groups in which the distinctive features of working people's social profile, stemming from the singular features of their occupational position, are revealed in a fairly complete and at the same time fairly generalized manner.

It should be observed that certain of the crucial foundations of socio-occupational classifications have already been studied in detail by Soviet social scientists and are therefore taken for granted. Primary among these is the distribution of occupations according to the complexity of the work associated with them. Disparities in the complexity of work processes determine, to a significant extent, the existence of groups and categories of occupations that differ in the nature and substantiveness of their labor activity, and the relative importance of routine and creative functions involved. On the other hand, these disparities are also linked with the social efficacy and payment of labor, and hence with workers' well-being. Finally, variations in occupational complexity presuppose differences in occupational and general educational training, which affect, in one way or another, a worker's entire mode of life.

One proviso is in order here. Our classification estimates complexity and level of training for work in the given occupation according to the objective technical/technological demands of the type of production within whose framework and structure that occupation predominates. It is obvious, however, that although a worker's actual occupational training, skills, and even the existing complexity of his work approximate technically prescribed conditions, they by no means always conform totally to normative requirements.

Clearly, in analyzing the socio-occupational structure at a social level, if one may so phrase it, it seems advisable to consider only a few of the more essential categories of objective complexity of occupations.

There is a sense in which some idea of the dimensions of these categories is given by the distinction between occupations involving predominantly physical work and predominantly mental work. It should be recognized, however, that in the context of developed socialism a simple dichotomous division is overly reductive, and in some instances simply impressionistic. In reality, it is by no means always possible to distinguish between the two. It is more appropriate here to consider this division as part of a more general division of labor according to the degree of work complexity. In this approach, among the jobs traditionally associated with physical labor we may single out the category of extremely simple work which may be performed with virtually no occupational training before taking up employment (nonspecialist agricultural hands, common laborers, etc.) and the category of complex occupations that require occupational training, usually in a vocational-technical educational institution (the basic occupations in industry, construction, transport and trade, machine-operating occupations, etc.). At the present time the group of more highly complex occupations within this latter category that require specialized training in a technicum, a technical training school, and so forth (equipment service and maintenance technicians, instrument technicians, repairmen in many fields, computer operators) is growing.

The occupations predominantly involving mental work, taken overall and with respect to the above-named categories, rank as among the more complex.

In the final analysis their particular social character has derived in the past, and to a significant extent still derives, from this greater complexity. Yet it is obvious that occupations involving mental work, which in contemporary Soviet society account for a very sizable proportion of the population (over 25%), are far from identical in level of complexity, length of required training, and the social profile of the people associated with them. In a socio-occupational classification covering society as a whole they must be segmented into at least two categories of complexity— highly skilled mental occupations requiring specialized higher or secondary education (engineer, technician, teacher, doctor, scientific worker), and other occupations in relatively simple mental or, more precisely, nonphysical work (drafting, bookkeeping).

This is not an arbitrary division. It is predicated upon an objective blurring of socio-occupational boundaries in the contemporary production process. Today, working people in many occupations that have traditionally been considered as occupations of physical or relatively simple mental labor are so similar in their social profile—and as regards the actual nature of their work activity, for that matter—that the distinctions between them are in many respects less marked than the distinctions between these groups and individuals doing simple physical work, on the one hand, or doing complex mental work, on the other.

This is essentially a reflection of the integrative processes associated with the restructuring of occupational and skill relationships which is leading the way, in a socialist context, to the establishment of a classless social structure. As these processes continue the mental worker/physical worker division becomes less clear cut, less rigid. Gradually this dichotomous split gives way to a system of less abrupt divisions related above all to the complexity of the work involved. This leads to a broadening of intermediate groups, where the work is transitional in nature, neither explicitly mental nor explicitly physical. In this situation strictly physical labor is typically associated only with the simplest, least skilled occupations. In the work activity of those employed in the more complex occupations that are generally considered to be physical jobs, sheer physical effort is no longer a preponderant element. For the most part, the work is becoming jointly mental and physical in nature. Automation and integrated mechanization in the production sphere is accelerating this process. In level of complexity and level of productive culture this kind of work is in no way inferior to many varieties of simple mental work, and sometimes even surpasses them in these respects. These two categories—complex physical or combined mental/physical work and less skilled nonphysical work—are tending to take on identical socio-occupational traits. (We note in passing that statistical practice unmistakably reflects this process. In every census conducted over the past quarter-century, more and more nonphysical service occupations—that is, the less-skilled mental jobs—have been combined with the "classical" skilled physical occupations.)

At the same time, however, working people in highly skilled mental occupations still differ substantially, both in the nature of their labor activity and in many other features of their social position, from all other working people. These differences are seen above all in the larger share of complex mental work, the relative absence of routine, the presence of creative elements, the level of culture, the lifestyle traits implicit in all this, and so forth. The social profile of those employed in complex jobs is also affected by the fact that a significant proportion hold executive posts in the production sphere or in community life. They are in leadership positions at various levels. We note that insofar as leadership activity entails decision making and responsibility for the implementation of decisions, it can be considered as especially complex work: leadership occupations thus occupy a special position among the occupational categories distinguished by their level of objective complexity.

Overall, the enumerated categories give a fairly complete picture of that facet of socially significant occupational divisions which is predicated upon differences in job complexity. Accordingly, once the majority of specific occupations listed in official statistics are distributed among these categories, it is no difficult matter to calculate the quantitative indices of development of this

Table 1

Distribution of Employed Population, with Occupations Classified According to Nature and Complexity of Work (in %)

Occupational category	Late 1930s	Late 1950s	Late 1960s	Late 1970s
1. Employed in simple, predominantly physical work requiring no occupational training prior to commencement of work activity	64	52	35	29
2. Employed in complex physical and mental/physical work requiring occupational training prior to commencement of work activity	19	29	38	41
including: employed in physical and mental/physical work of greater complexity, requiring specialized occupational training (in a technicum or technical training school following a secondary education)* prior to commencement of work activity	negligible	(1–2)	(3–4)	(6–7)
3. Employed in relatively simple, predominantly mental (nonphysical) work requiring a certain level of general education prior to commencement of work activity	8	4	4	5
4. Employed in complex mental work requiring specialized higher or secondary education prior to commencement of work activity	9	15	23	25
including: executives (work involving leadership of collectives)	2	4	5	5
Total employed population included in this classification	100	100	100	100

* Estimate.

facet of the socio-occupational structure. If the nature of the work, the typical occupational training required, and relevant expert evaluations are factored in, it is feasible to calculate the quantitative indices for jobs covering some 90% of the employed population from the 1940s to the 1970s (see Table 1).[4]

The resulting picture of changes in relative importance of occupational groups differing in the nature of work performed and occupational training required, although it represents only one aspect of socio-occupational development, apparently offers considerable food for thought. It becomes obvious that recent decades have seen some momentous changes in the occupational composition of society. Only a quarter-century ago more than half of this country's employed population was concentrated in occupations of relatively simple physical labor and had never had any modern occupational training. Today, approximately two-thirds of working people are employed in complex, skilled occupations of the modern type. The majority of the working class and a significant portion of the peasantry are employed in such occupations. Personnel with higher or specialized secondary education now comprise a major stratum of working people, far outnumbering the peasantry. They now make up the bulk of the intelligentsia. There has been a conspicuous development of a completely new socio-occupational category, that of worker-specialists, who are objectively in a position to become one of the working class's most advanced groups, combining the best sociopsychological traits of both workers and intelligentsia. The Soviet people's socio-occupational potential (as evidenced by data on the distribution of the employed population according to work complexity) has risen to a fundamentally new level.

No less germane to an assessment of the opportunities offered by a generalized analysis of government statistics is the fact that the data showing growth in the relative share of complex jobs within the occupational structure also reveal some rather important contradictions associated with the socio-occupational development of Soviet society. Specifically, when matched against data on the Soviet people's rising educational level, the indices of increased complexity in social labor provide an insight into some of the acute socioeconomic problems of the present day. This comparison shows that between the 1940s and the 1970s—and especially in the last ten years of this period, when, for various reasons, changes in the composition of the employed population began to slacken—the rise in the general educational level was significantly more rapid than the development of the occupational structure.

This difference in growth rates created a kind of imbalance

between the distribution of occupations according to their complexity, on the one hand, and working people's occupational am-
bitions, on the other. It is a fact that relatively simple physical
occupations—mostly involving a preponderance of not overly
skilled, predominantly manual work—generally meet the needs
of people with little education (especially when these comprise
the majority, or a significant portion, of the population). But
well-educated people find such jobs unattractive. Their orientation is toward the more complex and substantive occupations,
toward up-to-the-minute skills gained through specialized instruction whose prerequisite is, as it happens, a good general
education. Moreover, when well-educated people are in the majority, their occupational orientation becomes a social norm,
which influences the occupational self-appraisal of all working
people, including those with a low level of education.

For this very reason, only 20 to 25 years ago this country had
no particularly urgent problem associated with unattractive, extremely simple, low-skilled work, despite the fact that a far greater share of the work force was employed in low-skilled occupations than now. In those days this share accounted for over half of
all employed persons. But at that time there were even more
people with only an elementary education or less—57%, according to the 1959 census.[5] Thus the number of people who were
readily satisfied with low-skilled kinds of work exceeded the
number of corresponding jobs available.

In the 1960s the number of low-educated workers was almost
halved—to 35% in 1970—as a result of the rapid rise in educational levels.[6] But during this same period the number of those
employed in extremely simple varieties of work, predominantly
involving manual labor, also fell to 35%. Although this exact
numerical correspondence is, of course, a mere coincidence
(since our entire classification does not presume to be anything
but a provisional, approximate estimate), there can be no doubt
that there was an approximate congruence during this period
between the number of low-skilled jobs available and the number
of less-educated working people. True enough, the evolution of a

well-educated majority in this country (in 1970, 65% of the employed population had attained an incomplete secondary education or more) could not fail to affect the occupational aspirations of many poorly educated working people. Accordingly, society began to experience the problem of the unattractiveness of extremely simple, low-skilled labor, though at this point it was perceived more as a scientifically formulated prediction than as a practical economic issue.[7]

The relative share of extremely simple, low-skilled occupations continued to fall in the 1970s, though more slowly than in previous years. Specifically, employment in the simplest kinds of work fell during the 1970s by only six percentage points, from 35% to 29%. But mass education burgeoned at the same rate as before, so that the proportion of people with only an elementary education or less dropped to 19% in 1979.[8] This disparity in growth rates created a situation that had never before existed. For the first time society had far more low-skilled jobs available than working people of the appropriate cultural type (who in the past had been readily on hand) to fill them. An increasing portion of these jobs must today be filled by young people with ten or eleven years of schooling. This kind of work is not infrequently a source of social distress for these people, and for society it generates economic and social tensions. Documents of the Twenty-sixth CPSU Congress quite rightly regard low-skilled manual work as a substantial stumbling block "on the way to transforming work into a prime living need," and as one of the reasons why some young people, their occupational training notwithstanding, exhibit "an insufficiently responsible attitude toward labor."[9]

The unattractiveness of low-skilled manual work becomes a social problem, not when such work predominates, but rather, precisely when (and if) the gradual decline in this kind of work does not keep pace with the growth of education. Such is the state of affairs at this time. Accordingly, this problem has taken on a practical dimension. The urgency of accelerating the reduction in unattractive, low-skilled occupations is heightened by the increasing scarcity of labor resources and the need to utilize them more efficiently in the period of transition to intensive forms of economic growth.

The divergence between the growth rates of public education and the rise in the relative share of complex occupations within the employment structure has a broader implication. The former process is organically linked to an increase in social requirements and the latter with an upsurge in the social productive power of labor, which is the decisive means of satisfying those requirements. The disharmony between these two processes implies that although the almost two-fold reduction in the number of those doing the simplest kinds of work over a twenty-year span reflects some truly historic advances, an occupational structure in which one-quarter to one-third of the employed are concentrated in the simplest kinds of labor activity is certainly not one that conforms to the requirements of mature socialism.

It is natural that the party considers a further reduction in low-skilled, physically taxing manual work, and the enhancement of work content to be among the goals of its socioeconomic strategy for the 1980s.[10]

The development of the socio-occupational structure generated by changes in technological types of production

For a typological analysis designed to shed light on central developmental tendencies in a virtually boundless multiplicity of figures and lists of jobs, divisions according to the nature and complexity of the work are a necessary but not sufficient condition. It is also vital to consider at least one more basis for classification—a differentiation of occupations according to the technological type of production with which they are associated and hence the type of occupational structure to which they belong. In the long run scientific and technical progress follows what could be called a step-pattern. It is linked to changes in the type of production and its material and technical base and in technological relations—all of which lead to the disappearance of many old occupations and the gradual appearance of new ones, while in the occupations that remain, the nature, content, and conditions of work change. Accordingly, the movement of the occupational structure, perceived as a historical process, represents not only realignments in the relative importance of simple and complex labor within a given range of occupations, but also a gradual modification in the whole range of occupations, until ultimately one type of occupational structure is replaced by another. The type of production with which an occupation is associated, as well as the complexity of the work performed, has a profound effect upon workers' social profile. In this sense the association with a type of production is a discrete facet of the socio-occupational structure.

To understand this facet of the socio-occupational structure it is advisable to turn to the Marxist-Leninist theory of development of technological modes of production, of technical modalities. As we know, each sociohistorical formation is associated with a maximally appropriate type of production. However, in historical reality, and especially in epochs of transition from one sociohistorical formation to another, types of production that are identical from the technical/technological perspective may be found in societies with differing social structures. Similarly, the development of the productive forces presupposes that transitions to qualitatively new technical/technological conditions and the ensuing changes in technological relations can occur within the bounds of a single formation. These stages of productive organization, which are predicated upon technical progress, take the form of technological modes of production, technical modalities, and types of production.[11]

Their role in the movement of the social structure is smaller than that played by formations, social modes of production, and socioeconomic modalities. However, the divisions that derive from types of production are themselves an important element of the socio-occupational structure: while the social mode of production determines the basic classes and social groups that typify any given society, the technological mode of production that develops within the bounds of a particular socioeconomic mode of production is the basis upon which socially significant occupational distinctions take shape. To be sure, modifications in the latter are still contingent upon the nature of class relations, within whose framework the technological type of production functions.

The classic example of changes in technological modes of production within the framework of a single social system— which simultaneously serves as an example of the way in which the social identity of occupations is contingent upon technological types of production—is the stage-like development of capitalism in industry from capitalist cooperation, to manufactories, to plants (large-scale machine-based production). Soviet scholarly publications have shown that in the more economically developed countries, the original manufacturing modality is transformed into a technological mode of production wherein social labor is principally organized around the assembly line. With the development of the scientific and technical revolution, the assembly-line mode of industrial production is gradually replaced by a technological type of production that is based upon the transformation of science into a directly productive force and the automation of mass-production methods.[12]

In the socialist context, likewise, the productive forces pass through stages of development that may be represented as a gradual transition from one technological type of production to another. To be sure, this movement is inseparable from the entire social development of Soviet society. All the conclusions that follow, except as otherwise specified, are therefore meant to refer exclusively and solely to processes occurring under socialism.

In applying the concept of technical modalities to the development of the socio-occupational structure of contemporary Soviet society, however, it is important to take the following circumstances into account. When socialist construction began in the USSR, the productive forces were developed to the point where large-scale machine-based industry already existed in this country, and the issue was to transform it into the predominant type of production. From this point of view it is not absolutely necessary to distinguish premechanical technical modalities in order to understand socio-occupational change in recent decades. During this period the rapid pace of socialist industrialization resulted in a situation where the factory-industrial and assembly-line types of productive organization have become so closely commingled that they have essentially come to form a single technical modality that does not lend itself to subdivision. But it is clear that the contemporary occupational structure in the USSR will remain unintelligible unless it is realized that in many spheres of the national economic complex, a scientific-industrial production type, closely linked to the scientific and technical revolution, is taking recognizable shape.

In sum, it is possible to subject the occupational structure of Soviet society to a typological analysis that is based on a differentiation of occupations and jobs corresponding to three technical /technological types of production: 1) premechanical, preindustrial, and early industrial production; 2) developed industrial or assembly-line industrial production; and, 3) scientific-industrial production. Each of these types confers upon its characteristic occupations certain common traits that influence many facets of people's working conditions and daily lives. This is what makes such a grouping of jobs essential in order to gain an understanding of the factors and tendencies of change in the socio-occupational structure.[13]

We must, it is true, begin with a disclaimer: the correlation of occupations and types of production (especially in a secondary analysis of generalized statistical material) cannot claim to be as precise as the classification of jobs according to work complexity. Aside from the fact that this problem has not been so thoroughly studied, certain objective features of the development of occupational structure (arising as a result of changes in technological modes of production) also come into play here. The point is that in this process of change the complete substitution of one type of production by another takes place only over a very lengthy historical span. At any given moment the national economy is seen to accommodate elements of diverse technological types of production, which are interwoven and intermingled. This kind of coexistence has been strikingly apparent throughout the Soviet economy's development. In the push to build socialism rapidly, when it was imperative to bring every strength to bear upon the task immediately at hand, the impact of technical progress was felt most strongly in the key branches of the national economy.[14] Progress was skewed, in the sense that the widespread dissemination of the most advanced techniques in certain branches and technological processes ran parallel with the retention of early industrial and preindustrial (premechanical) technological types of production in others. The occupational composition of the working population that evolved under those conditions, and exists in part to this day, is a complex miscellany that contains ranges of occupations typifying diverse stages of technical progress.

A researcher would need to do a special study, drawing upon material that describes in detail not only each occupation but each available workplace, in order to establish a strict correlation between the occupations within that miscellany and any given technological type of production. An approach of that kind is scarcely practical in any attempt at a societywide analysis. Aggregated statistics, which provide the factual basis for such an analysis, necessarily provide only a very general characterization of the conditions and content of work in specific occupations. Moreover, the same occupational designations are frequently attached to job positions that are associated with the most dissimilar—though chronologically coexistent—technical modalities. (A baker, for instance, might work in an automated, multiple-line bakery or a small bakeshop where everything is done by hand.) It is even more problematic to establish a precise connection between technological modes of production and those occupations that are only indirectly connected with machines and technology. In the final analysis, the transition from one technological mode of production to another affects all components of the socio-occupational structure. Sooner or later there is a change in the content and nature of work not only in the occupations where these elements are directly determined by technical progess, but also in the jobs that are far removed from material production proper (those held by managerial staff, say, or cultural employees, or health workers). But changes in the social profile of such occupational groups come about gradually, not abruptly, which means that an unequivocal correlation between these occupations and the technological modes of production is virtually impossible to achieve.

Clearly, given the present state of our knowledge, it is preferable to abandon our attempts to classify jobs directly according to technological modes of production, and turn instead to more indirect and approximate methods. The use of particular secondary, indirect indicators typical of occupations associated with a given technical modality becomes decisive here. We trust that these indirect criteria will enable us to identify job groups that, though not perhaps corresponding precisely to types of production, will at least exhibit an approximate correspondence and, by displaying certain elements of the relevant facet of the socio-occupational structure, will enable us to assess the processes developing therein.

Socio-occupational groups distinguished by degree of mechanization of labor

Among the indirect indices that reflect the link between various jobs and types of production, precedence must go to the degree of mechanization of labor that typifies a particular occupation. Actually, one wonders about labeling this an ''indirect'' indicator: as things currently stand, mechanization and automation are, in fact, crucial factors in the transition from one technological mode of production to another. We should, rather, call this an incomplete or partial indicator, because it is certainly not applicable to all occupations. The degree of mechanization as a yardstick of the relative state of development of an occupation is meaningful only for those jobs in which the content of labor activity depends—directly and fairly extensively—upon the technical state of the implements of labor used by workers. It is pertinent only when classifying occupations such as these. In particular, there is every reason to believe that a grouping based on the extent of mechanization of labor will serve to show how physical and mental/physical occupations where people are directly engaged in processing or reworking raw materials or finished articles, in constructing or repairing buildings or other structures, in freight transport, and so forth, are distributed according to types of production.

Of course, the classification of such jobs—embracing only one sector of the occupational structure, comprising the totality of workers' occupations that are, broadly speaking, of an industrial nature—gives only an incomplete and fragmentary picture of the relative importance of socio-occupational groups associated with diverse technical modalities. But workers' occupations of an industrial nature encompass a very large and growing portion of the employed population (slightly over half), and one that is growing not only in the industrial branches (industry, construction, transport) but in virtually all economic spheres. In point of fact, these occupations encompass the industrial core of the working class, which, with the emergence of a classless structure, is becoming the social and productive core of the Soviet people.[15] The leading socioeconomic and socio-occupational processes typical of mature socialism are developing more rapidly and more visibly here than anywhere else.

The relative precision of the correlation between industrial jobs and types of production—a correlation derived from the level of mechanization in those jobs—is predicated upon the fact that within the framework of this category a fairly reliable degree of equivalence is found to exist between the majority of occupations involving automated labor and today's highest types of production (the scientific-industrial type of production), and also between the majority of occupations involving mechanized labor and the mass-based industrial assembly-line type of production.

It is true that the connection between types of production and the remaining nonmechanized and nonautomated occupations is more complex. Although most manual work clearly relates to premechanical, preindustrial—or, at the very least, early industrial—production, to declare an unconditional equivalence would be to grossly oversimplify the issue: manual work also has a place—a wholly justified place from the technological viewpoint—in later technological stages. In this connection it seems advisable, when classifying industrial jobs (especially those involving manual work), to consider not only the degree (or absence) of mechanization in workers' jobs typical of the given occupation, but also to observe the broader picture—the level of mechanization of the entire production process that embraces the bulk of workers in any given occupation.[16] (For the sake of simplicity we shall henceforth call this the "generalized index of mechanization.")

Within the framework of this approach it becomes immediately apparent that occupations involving equipment maintenance, service, and repair cannot be counted as manual jobs. The mass-based character of such occupational groups obviously does not derive from their association with the kind of production in which manual labor dominates. They are rooted in mechanized and automated technology. From this point of view—and also by virtue of their required level of occupational training and their general sociocultural traits—workers in the above-named occupations have more in common with workers in automated production than with other occupational groups. Therefore these people, like those who are actually employed on complex automated equipment, may be regarded as among the range of occupations associated with scientific-industrial production.

Furthermore, in the light of the generalized indices of mechanization it is obviously advisable to distinguish between industrial jobs involving the "classic" manual occupations and manual occupations associated with flow-line or assembly-line organization of production. In the first case the worker's activity has no direct or immediate attachment to machine-based technology, while in the second case it is intimately associated with that technology, even if the individual may be performing mostly manual operations. Manual workers on an assembly line are indistinguishable, in terms of their standing, from people doing mechanized assembly-line work, or, in point of fact, from the majority of those who work with machinery and mechanical devices. From this it follows that all these workers belong to occupational groups involved in the industrial assembly-line type of production.

Overall, the generalized indices of mechanization may be used to divide workers' occupations of an industrial nature into three categories corresponding to the basic technical/technological types of production that exist in today's economy.

First, there are the manual industrial occupations that are not directly connected with flow-line production, or with equipment maintenance, service or repair (such as common laborers, loaders, carpenters, tinsmiths, etc.). Viewed in historical perspective, it is appropriate to call these the classical, traditional manual occupations. It should, however, be remembered that their "traditional" nature is not absolute. In principle, these groups typify the premechanical type of production, but in today's industrial branches premechanical production is not so much a discrete entity as a kind of technological appendage, a supplement to industrial-mechanical production. Both types are often found in more or less developed sections within the same enterprises. From this point of view, very nearly the majority of premechanical-type occupations are actually a manual appendage to mechanized labor.

Second, there are occupations associated with the control and servicing of machinery and mechanical devices, as well as the manual occupations associated with work on flow lines and assembly lines. This covers the majority of industrial workers' occupations—for instance, machine-tool operator and assembler in processing industries, concrete worker and installer in the construction industry, driver and machine operative in the transport industry. Under present circumstances these occupations conform to the industrial assembly-line technological type of production.

Third, there are occupations associated with work on automatic, semi-automatic, and highly mechanized equipment, and occupations involving equipment maintenance, service, and repair—for instance, computerized machine-tool turner, rolling machine operator, machinery operator in the chemical industry, automatic machine-tool turner, and machine-tool and automatic machinery service technician. In most cases these occupations now represent the industrial sphere of the scientific-industrial technological type of production.

It is not our intention to overstate the precision of this classification. The generalized criterion of mechanization makes it possible to differentiate repairmen and maintenance technicians from workers in premechanical manual labor, but when aggregated statistics are used that criterion is of little help in distinguishing those in the former group who work with automated machinery from those who do not. Thus, our allocation of all repairmen and maintenance technicians to the scientific-industrial type of work is a provisional approximation. Nevertheless, it seems obvious that the generalized criterion of mechanization of labor is useful in singling out among industrial jobs those categories which unquestionably contain occupations that are most typical of a particular technological type of production (the "classic" jobs for that production type, as it were), and clearly contain no occupations that are "classically" typical of other types.

The occupational categories that are distinguished according to the generalized level of mechanization can quite easily be matched (much as we did after having grouped occupations by work complexity) against the listings of jobs and information on their numbers provided by government statistics. We merely note that only a portion of the population is involved here, which means that the rather broad assumptions which must be made will have stronger repercussions on our results. It seems appropriate, therefore, to limit our calculations to a shorter period of time—beginning, say, in the late 1950s. In practical terms, these calculations can be applied to cover workers in occupations of an industrial nature, which accounts for 40%–45% of the entire employed population and about 65% of the working class of the USSR (see Table 2).

Table 2

Distribution of Workers Employed in Work of an Industrial Nature, with Occupations Categorized According to Degree of Mechanization (in %)

Occupational category	Late 1950s	Late 1960s	Late 1970s
1. Employed in predominantly manual work not associated with flow-line production or with equipment maintenance or repair (predominantly premechanical-type work or the nonmechanical type of work which is a technological appendage of industrial production)	52	38	35
2. Employed in mechanized and flow-line work (work of the industrial assembly-line type)	38	49	52
3. Employed in automated work or in equipment maintenance or repair (predominantly work of a scientific-industrial type)	10	13	13
Total employed in workers' occupations of an industrial nature included in this classification	100	100	100

Our calculations result in a quantitative measure of socio-occupational realignments occurring in the industrial core of the working class under the influence of changes in technological types of production, which supplements the depiction of changes associated with the rising share of complex occupations. It seems that even the most cursory glance at these results will serve to show that, with this supplementary information, it is now possible to focus more closely upon those facets of the development of occupational structure which are not accessible to an analysis based solely on data for work complexity. The figures thus obtained demonstrate that in recent decades the former preponderance of early industrial types of jobs among industrial workers has given way to a preponderance of developed industrial jobs.

They also confirm that the process of transition from an early industrial type of occupational structure to a developed industrial occupational structure is not yet complete, not even in the worker's own milieu. Finally, these same figures give us some indication of the scale of new problems engendered by the urgent need to speed up the transition to scientific-industrial production and by the fact that the relevant socio-occupational groups as yet account for only about one-tenth of the working class' industrial core.[17]

A two-dimensional classification of working-class socio-occupational groups by complexity and degree of mechanization of labor

From the methodological standpoint (which is of major importance here), the crux of the matter is not that calculations based on a classification of occupations by level of mechanization can supplement calculations based upon a classification of occupations by complexity. More to the point, all the previously described elements of both classifications can be organically combined to form the basis of a two-dimensional typology of industrial occupations that takes into account both the complexity of any given job and the link between it and a particular technological type of production (see Chart 1). In addition, since the original typological criteria were derived from the very start from available statistical materials, a determination of specific parameters of the socio-occupational structure of the core of the working class is a natural way to continue and complete that typology (see Table 3).

A methodological paper is no place for a detailed analysis of these parameters. However a simple comparison between them and the data obtained from the two separate classifications of jobs (by complexity and by mechanization of labor—see Tables 1 and 2) is persuasive evidence that a two-dimensional social typology of occupations is indeed a useful heuristic tool. This is not just a

Chart 1

Classification of Workers' Occupations of an Industrial Nature, by Level of Mechanization and Complexity of Work

Categories of occupations distinguished by generalized characteristics of mechanization / Categories of occupations distinguished by work complexity	Occupations with a preponderance of relatively simple work normally requiring no occupational training	Occupations with a preponderance of more complex work normally requiring training in vocational education institutions, in special courses, or at training centers	Occupations with a preponderance of highly complex work requiring lengthy training in vocational education institutions (including secondary specialized educational institutions)
Manual occupations not associated with flow-line work or with equipment maintenance or repair (occupations directly associated with premechanical-type work and nonmechanical work which is a technological appendage of industrial production)	Workers engaged in nonspecialized ancillary work, manual loading and unloading, and upkeep of production premises (loaders, ancillary workers, common laborers, janitors, etc.)	Workers engaged in specialized manual work (carpenters, plasterers, painters, joiners, tinsmiths, etc.)	

Mechanized and assembly-line occupations (occupations predominantly associated with work of the industrial assembly-line type)	Workers operating simple machinery and mechanical devices, employed in auxiliary work with machinery and mechanical devices and in extremely simple assembly-line work (metal cutters, punch operators, machine molders, packers, etc.)		Workers operating more complex machinery and mechanical devices, and also those employed in installation and assembly jobs in assembly-line production of more complex items (machine-tool operators, milling machinists, metal worker/assemblers, drivers, crane operators, etc.)
Occupations involving automated work and equipment maintenance and repair (occupations predominantly associated with work of a scientific-industrial type)	Workers operating semi-automatic and simple types of automatic equipment (automatic machine-tool operators, gas equipment operators, compressor operators, etc.)	Workers operating automated and highly mechanized equipment (computerized machine-tool operators, automated rolling mill operators, machine operators in the chemical industry, etc.)	Workers employed in maintenance, service, and repair of equipment, machinery, instruments, and apparatus (maintenance technicians, metalworker/repair technicians, automatic machine-tool service technicians, instrumentation technicians, etc.)

Table 3

Distribution of Workers Employed in Work of an Industrial Nature by Socio-occupational Groups, Distinguished by Complexity and Degree of Mechanization of Productive Activity (in %)

	Late 1950s	Late 1960s	Late 1970s
Workers directly employed in processing or reworking raw materials or finished articles, in construction or repair of buildings and other structures, in freight transport, etc.			
Total (millions)	36	45	55
(in %)	100	100	100
comprising:			
1. Employed in predominantly manual labor not associated with flow-line work, equipment maintenance or repair (predominantly premechanical-type work and nonmechanical type of work which is a technological appendage of industrial production)	52	38	35
—employed in relatively simple work not requiring occupational training prior to commencement of work activity (loaders, ancillary workers, common laborers, janitors, etc.)	36	25	23
—employed in more complex work requiring occupational training prior to commencement of work activity (painters, carpenters, tinsmiths, etc.)	16	13	12
2. Employed in mechanized and assembly-line work (work of the industrial-mechanical and assembly-line type)	38	49	52
—employed in relatively simple work not requiring occupational training prior to commencement of work activity (molders, packers, metal engravers, etc.)	4	4	4
—employed in complex work requiring occupational training prior to commencement of work activity (machine-tool operators, milling machine operators, metalworker/assemblers, drivers, crane operators, etc.)	34	45	48

Table 3 (continued)

	Late 1950s	Late 1960s	Late 1970s
3. Employed in automated work and in equipment maintenance and repair (work predominantly of the scientific-industrial type)	10	13	13
—employed in relatively simple work not requiring occupational training prior to commencement of work activity (compressor operators, gas equipment operators, automatic machine-tool operators, semi-automatic equipment operators, etc.)	3	3	3
—employed in complex work requiring occupational training prior to commencement of work activity (computerized machine-tool operators, rolling mill operators, steel workers, machine operators in the chemical industry, etc.)	1	1	1
—employed in highly complex work requiring lengthy occupational training prior to commencement of work activity (maintenance technicians, metalworker/repair technicians, machine-tool and automatic machinery service technicians, instrumentation technicians, etc.)	6	9	9

Note: this calculation includes all those engaged in work of an industrial nature, irrespective of the branch in which they are employed.

matter of summing the analytical potential of two separate one-dimensional distributions; rather, that potential is elevated to a higher plane, as it were. The excessively broad, diffuse categories that bring together jobs with some single point of similarity have been replaced as an object of analysis by occupational groups distinguished by the affinity of several leading characteristics. This almost always implies a commonality both in many aspects of position in the production process and in social and cultural traits, and means that such groups may be taken as basic elements in the socio-occupational structure.

The profile of groups such as these offers a far more concrete, clear, and profound view of the factors and contradictions of socio-occupational development than is provided by extremely broad occupational categories. It becomes clear that the increasing complexity of work and changes in technological type are in essence manifestations of a single complex process. During this process (provided that it takes place within the framework of a particular social system), the change in technological types of production is the crucial factor in socio-occupational change. A new type of production generates new occupations, imposes new demands on all those connected with it, alters their working and living conditions in some manner, and creates certain common social and cultural characteristics in them.

In a certain sense, changes in types of production increase the complexity of work. As a rule, the relative share of complex occupations is higher at each successive technological stage than it was in the preceding one. However, the occupations that typify the premechanical, industrial assembly-line, and scientific-industrial types of production encompass both relatively complex and relatively simple jobs, as is well illustrated by the socio-occupational structure of the working class's industrial core (see Table 3). The link between increasing complexity of work and technical/technological progress is therefore neither simple nor uniform in any way. Accordingly, the systematic resolution of emergent contradictions in this area cannot be a simple matter either. Moreover, the socio-occupational structure of the working class, which reflects changes in work complexity and type of production, convincingly demonstrates that strictly technical solutions—mechanization, automation, cybernetic procedures in production processes, and so on—are not in themselves sufficient to optimize society's occupational structure. No amount of technical development can, by itself, completely eliminate sociocultural distinctions between simple and complex occupations. Such development only alters the technical bases of those occupations. In this sense, socioeconomic and economic-political measures framed to develop socialist production relations, to improve all spheres of economic management, and to create better conditions for worker participation in management,[18] are just as important preconditions for the shaping of human potential in an intensive socialist economy as the maximum possible reduction in unskilled manual labor. Of course, there is also an intimate link between economic-political measures and the improvement of other facets of the socio-occupational structure. But that link deserves special examination.

Notes

1. *Materialy Plenuma Tsentral'nogo Komiteta KPSS 22 noiabria 1982 g.*, Moscow, 1982, p. 8.
2. See Iu. V. Andropov, *Shest'desiat let SSSR*, Moscow, 1982, p. 5.
3. In the 1960s and 1970s, these problems were addressed in the works of N. A. Aitov, N. I. Alekseev, A. A. Amvrosov, B. G. Antosenkov, Iu. V. Arutiunian, L. S. Bliakhman, B. L. Breev, E. K. Vasil'eva, T. I. Zaslavskaia, V. A. Kalmyk, Ia. B. Kvasha, E. V. Klopov, L. N. Kogan, G. P. Kozlova, V. V. Kolbanovskii, V. G. Komarov, V. V. Krevnevich, S. A. Kugel', Z. V. Kuprininov, Ia. P. Ladyzhinskii, N. I. Lapin, N. F. Naumova, V. S. Nemchenko, V. V. Nikitenko, V. I. Osipov, G. V. Osipov, V. A. Petrov, V. E. Poletaev, V. R. Polozov, I. M. Popova, A. I. Prigozhin, M. N. Rutkevich, R. V. Ryvkina, V. S. Semonov, S. L. Seniavskii, G. A. Slesarev, V. I. Staroverov, A. A. Sukhova, M. Kh. Titma, Z. I. Fainburg, F. R. Filippov, I. I. Changli, O. I. Shafranov, and O. I. Shkaratan.
4. The calculations for this table and those following were done by the authors and L. G. Perfil'eva, using: *Itogi Vsesoiuznoi perepisi naseleniia 1959 goda*, pp. 161–166; *Itogi Vsesoiuznoi perepisi naseleniia 1970 goda*, vol. VI, pp. 14–23; *Naselenie SSSR. Po dannym Vsesoiuznoi perepisi naseleniia 1979 g.*, pp. 19–20; *Vestnik statistiki*, 1980, no. 6, pp. 41–62; *ibid.* 1981, no. 1, pp. 63–67; *ibid.*, 1981, no. 2, pp. 63–78; *ibid.*, 1981, no. 4, p. 69; *ibid.*, 1981, no. 5, pp. 63–66; *Narodnoe khoziaistvo SSSR v 1972 g.*, pp. 518–521; *Narodnoe khoziaistvo SSSR. 1922-1982*, pp. 132–133, 145, 162, 321, 383, 399–402, 407; *Kommunisty i trudiaishchikhsia krupnykh gorodov v bor'be za sotsial'nyi i nauchno-tekhnicheskii progress*, Moscow, 1982, pp. 187–198, 214–222.
5. *Itogi Vsesoiuznoi perepisi naseleniia 1959 g. SSSR (Svodnyi tom)*, Moscow, 1962, p. 116.
6. *Itogi Vsesoiuznoi perepisi naseleniia 1970 g.*, Moscow, 1973, vol. 6, p. 610.
7. See the work of N. A. Aitov, V. V. Vodzinskaia, and V. N. Shubkin.
8. *Naselenie SSSR. Po dannym Vsesoiuznoi perepisi naseleniia 1979 g.*,

Moscow, 1980, p. 19.

9. *Materialy XXVI s"ezda KPSS*, pp. 57, 67.

10. *Ibid.*, pp. 57, 136, 141, 176.

11. See, for instance, K. Marx and F. Engels, *Sochinenie*, vol. 49, p. 89; V. I. Lenin, *Polnoe sobranie sochinenie*, vol. 3, p. 534.

12. Iu. A. Vasil'chuk, *Nauchno-tekhnicheskaia revoliutsiia i rabochii klass pri kapitalizme. Uglublenie protivorechii i problemy klassovoi bor'by*, Moscow, 1980, pp. 87-93.

13. At this juncture it is appropriate to recall Lenin's well-known dictum on the singularities of the factory or plant worker's social profile. He emphasized that workers associated with large-scale machine-based industry differ in their "structure of life," their "structure of family relations," and their "level of requirements" not only from representatives of the other laboring classes (the peasantry) but also from manufactory laborers, artisans, and so forth. (See V. I. Lenin, *Polnoe sobranie sochinenie*, vol. 3, p. 547.

14. *Materialy XXIV s"ezda KPSS*, Moscow, 1976, p. 39.

15. Strictly speaking, a certain number of collective farmers (workers in collective farm job-shops, collective farm construction workers, etc.) must be included among those doing physical and mental/physical work of an industrial nature. There are, however, relatively few people in such occupations.

16. This approach is made all the more feasible by the fact that occupational classification by level of mechanization has received detailed consideration in: Ia. B. Kvasha, *Statisticheskoe izuchenie mekhanizatsii truda*, Moscow, 1959; Z. I. Fainburg, G. P. Kozlova, "On the Question of Classifying Workers According to the Complexity of Their Work," in *Sotsial'nye issledovaniia*, issue 2, Moscow, 1968; O. I. Shafranova, *Professional'nyi sostav rabochikh promyshlennosti SSSR*, Moscow, 1972; and O. I. Shafranova, *Ratsional'noe ispol'zovanie trudovykh resursov—neotlozhnaia zadacha*, Moscow, 1980.

17. It is significant that our estimates are close to the results obtained by other methods by a group of Kiev sociologists and economists. Their calculations suggest that in 1973 12%-13% of industrial workers were employed in "scientific and technical revolution developed production" (the authors' coinage). (See *NTR i formirovanie dukhovnogo oblika sovetskogo rabochego*, Kiev, 1982, p. 113.)

18. See *Materialy Plenuma TsK KPSS 22 noiabria 1982 goda*, pp. 9, 23; *Materialy XXVI s"ezda KPSS*, pp. 49-66, 136-143, 197-202.

2. The Socio-occupational Structure of Contemporary Soviet Society

The Nature and Direction of Change*

L. A. GORDON and A. K. NAZIMOVA

As noted in the first part of this paper, our study attempts to use official statistical materials to highlight the basic directions and quantitative characteristics of development of the socio-occupational structure of mature socialist society—to examine, that is, the composition and changing relative importance of major occupational groups, membership in which affects not only the content of labor activity but also working people's entire social profile. Given the nature of available statistical materials, the most important of these groups may be determined by distinguishing occupations, first, according to the complexity and nature of the work performed and, second, according to their association with the technical/technological types of production that are prevalent in our country's economy (the early industrial, assembly-line industrial, and scientific-industrial types).

Soviet social science has produced a relatively sophisticated classification of occupations according to the nature and complexity of work performed. Thus there is no particular difficulty in applying this classification to actual statistical data (see Table 1 in the first part of this paper). It is more complicated to relate the generalized government statistics on occupations to particular technological types of production. Actually, the hard data currently available (not local surveys, but materials reflecting the

*Russian text © 1983 by "Progress" Publishers. "Sotsial′no-professional′-naia struktura sovremennogo sovetskogo obshchestva: kharakter i napravlenie peremen," *Rabochii klass i sovremennyi mir*, 1983, No. 3., pp. 59–72.

socio-occupational structure of society as a whole) permit us to establish an approximate linkage between any given production type and any given range of jobs only in industrial occupations, where the impact of scientific and technical progess is felt more directly and immediately. Changes in these occupations reflect the essential features of development of the socio-occupational structure of the working class (whose core is centered around these occupations) and, for that matter, society as a whole. They demonstrate the way in which changes in technological types affect the job composition of the economy's principal sectors, how an early industrial occupational structure gradually acquires a developed-industrial and, subsequently, a scientific-industrial character (see Tables 2 and 3 in our previous article).

But realignments in the composition of the core of the working class and in the industrial sector of the economy overall, important as they are, naturally do not reflect changes occurring throughout the socio-occupational structure in the course of the intensification of the socialist economy and its attainment of new thresholds of scientific and technical progress. To derive a fuller picture of these processes it is vital to ascertain the link between technological types of production and the development of the whole range of occupational positions (not only industrial occupations).

True enough, it has not yet been possible to establish such a direct link for all occupations (by identifying the jobs that relate to any given type of production, as was done in our analysis of industrial occupations). It is, however, possible to identify within the total occupational structure those groups of jobs and those socio-occupational divisions which are illustrative—albeit indirectly—of the general direction of occupational change generated by changes in technological types of production.

Technological types of production and dominant occupational groups

In determining the occupational groups that indirectly delineate the influence exerted by technological modes of production upon the socio-occupational structure of society, it is critically important to select categories (ranges) of occupations that correpond most closely to each of the modes of production. This is not to imply that this correspondence is absolute: occupations from the group in question are found outside the technical modality of which they are most typical, and, conversely, the occupational structure that is based upon the given modality can certainly accommodate occupations other than those from the most typical group. Nevertheless, the group of typical occupations reflects the most important, the most essential traits of the occupational structure of any given type of production. Borrowing a term from systems analysis, which is extremely appropriate in this instance, we can say that this occupational group constitutes a kind of structural dominant. In Marx's terms, it is "a unique ether which defines the specific gravity of everything contained in it."[1]

It is not difficult to see which occupations comprise the dominant element in the occupational structure of various types of production by addressing oneself to the logic behind the successive changes in these types, a matter that is examined in detail in the socioeconomic theory of Marxism-Leninism.

As we know, agriculture is the principal branch of the economy in the period of premechanical production (and to a lesser extent in the early industrial economic context as well). The preeminence of premechanical agriculture, in which elements of self-sufficiency and of the natural economy are always strongly in evidence, is responsible for the relative underdevelopment of the manufacturing sector and the specialized forms of service, and thus for the fairly limited and undifferentiated range of associated occupations. Accordingly, agricultural jobs are dominant in the occupational structure and encompass the vast majority of the population.

With the transition from premechanical to factory-industrial and assembly-line production, the economic and occupational structure becomes more complex. Agriculture, while remaining an intrinsic element of material production, ceases to play the decisive role in the economy. That role is assumed by various forms of industrial production, which gradually absorbs an increasing portion of the employed population. Jobs associated with the management and organization of production acquire an independent occupational status, and an increasing number of employed persons begin to specialize in providing scientific and design services to the production sphere.

The development of industrial production simultaneously requires the formation of a fairly complex productive-public service and sociocultural infrastructure. Universal primary schooling and mass-based social services are essential for the generation of a workforce capable of performing factory-industrial and assembly-line work.

In turn, the growth of education and general culture widens the range of jobs that must be created in order to raise social services and day-to-day material and living conditions to the requisite level. As a result, numerous and extremely complex jobs in education, health care, public services, residential construction, mass transit, and so forth, along with industrial jobs proper, become a necessary element of the occupational structure.

The occupational structure engendered by the industrial assembly-line technical/technological type of production—especially in the socialist context—thus becomes extremely complex and varied in nature. Therefore the leading occupations in this type of production come to assert their dominant role in increasingly complex forms. In particular, no group of jobs holds a clear majority position, as agricultural jobs typically did in the period of premechanical production. Nonetheless, industrial assembly-line production is obviously dominated by industrial-type jobs. First, when the economy reaches the assembly-line stage, more workers are engaged in industrial-type work than in any other kind of labor activity. Second, and this is most important—this group of occupations leaves its imprint upon the configuration of the entire occupational structure.

It is, we dare say, most difficult to identify the dominant group of occupations in the technological mode of production that replaces industrial assembly-line production. Since the scientific-industrial mode of production is currently in its formative phase, many of its traits and particularities have not yet fully emerged, or have not emerged in their classic forms. In particular, the occupations that are most typical of this mode of production as yet encompass a relatively small number of employed people—clearly fewer than its own developmental regularities dictate.

Nonetheless, independently of current or even future quantitative proportions, the tendencies of change in the system of division of labor engendered by today's scientific and technical revolution provide a starting point in the search for the dominant occupational groups that determine the occupational structure's general developmental perspectives.

As we know, the development of the scientific and technical revolution ''coincides with the development of science as an independent factor in the production process.''[2] Science may be said to permeate all spheres of social production, and determines its organization. The occupations associated with scientific research, experimental design, and the practical application of scientific achievement in the production sphere (including the ever-expanding mass-based worker occupations) are, naturally enough, beginning to play an enormous role within the employment structure.

Furthermore, the scientific nature of current production and its massive scope sharply increase the significance of information management and monitoring in the economy and in community life. This kind of activity has, of course, always existed in one form or another (including as an organic element of many types of work, primarily managerial and supervisory jobs). But previously it rarely functioned as a specialized occupation. In scientifically organized production the flow of information, its complexity and diversity, have grown to the point where handling information has become a discrete form of occupationally specialized activity. Both workers and employees hold jobs of this kind in production, much as they do in the scientific field.

In the final analysis, both of these groups of occupations—in science and scientific services, on the one hand, and in information management and monitoring on the other—form a single group of information-related jobs.

The rapid development of occupations in this group is unmistakably predicated upon the unfolding of the scientific and technical revolution and the establishment of scientific-industrial production. Accordingly, scientific and monitoring work (information-related work in general)—today and even more so in the future—can be seen as a dominant factor in the occupational structure which is gradually taking shape in the course of the scientific and technical revolution.

At the same time, changes in other jobs attest—by default, as it were—to the dominant nature of information-related occupations.

The sharp rise in production efficiency that is in prospect, under the impact of the scientific and technical revolution, presupposes a future reduction in employment in material production. Even more to the point, the nature of many occupations associated with industrial and agricultural labor is changing. Increasing importance now attaches to work in equipment installation, service and repair, as well as superintendence over complex machinery, apparatus, and technological processes. The organic link between the automation of production and qualitative changes in the activity of many maintenance, repair, and service technicians, operators, and so forth, allows us, in our analysis of the contemporary occupational structure, to regard them as a kind of supplement to the dominant group in scientific-industrial production.

The emergence of scientific-industrial production, in which information-related work is dominant within the occupational structure, also affects employment in the service sphere. From both a social and a production standpoint there is a need not only for primary schooling but for a sound and extended general education, which is actually an organic part of occupational training. Likewise, there is a growing need for, and possibility of, a sharp rise in material well-being, an improvement in living conditions, public health care, and cultural and public services. All this naturally sparks further growth in employment and occupational specialization in the service sphere. Undoubtedly the accelerated expansion of employment in occupations of this type that occurs during the scientific and technical revolution is the continuation of a process that began during prior phases of socioeconomic development. But it tends to extend the service sphere on a scale typical only of the scientific-industrial type of production.

In some respects the emergent occupational structure of scientific-industrial production is shaped approximately as much by changes in service sphere employment as by the dynamics of information-related work. It is not impossible that in the more distant future the work of "producing people"—i.e., service sphere occupations, in the broad sense of the term—will come to dominate the occupational structure in ensuing stages of the development of production.[3]

Socio-occupational groups distinguished by the specific material content of work

It goes without saying that the changes in dominant groups, as described above, represent merely a general theoretical schema. In concrete historical reality, changes such as these occur only over a very lengthy period of time. Occupations belonging to the most dissimilar technological types coexist within our country's economy. They also coexist within each of the dominant occupational groups (although, of course, the proportion of jobs intrinsic to any given type varies within each group).

It is nevertheless obvious that a change in the prevalence of dominant occupations provides a basis for assessing the developmental tendencies engendered within the socio-occupational structure by changes in types of production, if not on the scale of employment associated with a particular production type. Thus a classification of occupations according to their relation to dominant groups, impressionistic as it may be, is an important means of throwing light upon realignments of this kind.

From a certain standpoint the categories of occupations that are dominant in various technological types of production resemble the basic job groupings by economic branch. It might therefore seem that to single out the dominant groups, one need only inquire into the link between various occupations and any given branch of the national economy. However, in an analysis of occupational structure any such bald statement of equivalence leads to oversimplifications that are excessive even in relation to our readiness to work with approximations. We need only recall the huge number of "mixed" [skvoznye] occupations that are common in all branches of the economy.

It is more constructive therefore, to employ a rather more refined branch classification of jobs based upon material, item-specific conditions and the content of work performed in any occupation—the specific items and means of labor, the objects and other "tangible elements" of productive activity.[4] We note in passing that the division of occupations according to the item-specific content of the work typically involved has a social import of its own. Needless to say, workers develop many specific socio-cultural traits according to whether their work is associated with living things or inanimate objects, with information management or human services.

Researchers have already classified work by its material, item-specific content, although for purposes different from ours.[5] Another practical reason for using the material, item-specific content of work as a classificational criterion is its relative simplicity, which makes it easy to use in processing generalized official statistical data.

Bearing in mind the detail found in these statistics and the general goals of this paper (an analysis of occupational change at the level of society as a whole), we used the material, item-specific content of work performed as the distinguishing factor in drawing up the following occupational categories.

First, there are occupations of an agricultural nature, whose material, item-specific content is inseparable from living nature.

As Marx put it, work of this kind is predominantly accomplished "with the naturally occurring implements of production"[6] (ploughland, water, etc.). The link with biological processes is the decisive occupational characteristic here; it defines the rhythm of the work and its unique conditions. This approach does not mean that we consider all those who work in the "agricultural" branch of the economy as being engaged in work of an agricultural nature. The latter applies only to those whose activity is associated with the production of agricultural output (field hands, workers in livestock production, combine operators, agronomists, for instance—but not metalworker/repairmen, collective-farm and state-farm staff economists, etc.).

Second, there are occupations of an industrial nature whose content is associated with the working and processing of raw material and finished articles, constructing and repairing of buildings and other structures, freight transport, and so on. The object of labor in these occupations is raw material or a previously processed article. From a social standpoint it is extremely important that work in these occupations—more so than elsewhere—lends itself to mechanization and automation, to especially detailed subdivisions, and to scientific organization. The immediately social, collective nature of this work, and the high degree of concentration that is intrinsic to it are the most salient points here. The rhythm of work in these occupations is dictated by the machine or by the pace of the technological process, which demands a high degree of adaptability and self-discipline on the part of the workers concerned. This explains why workers in industrial occupations constitute the core of the working class. The category of industrial-type jobs does not, to be sure, wholly correspond to the totality of industrial-branch occupations. From the standpoint of material, item-specific content, jobs in this category are typically held by machine-tool operators, metalworkers, drivers, painters, and technologists, regardless of the branch in which they are employed, but this category does not include accountants, dispatchers, and so on, even those employed in industry, transport, and construction.

Third, there are the information-related occupations, where the main object of labor is information and symbol-systems. Scientific workers, designers, economists, and also laboratory technicians, computer operators, bookkeepers, and telegraph operators. From these examples alone it is evident that the information-related occupations cannot be wholly identified with any one economic branch, or even with a group of branches. Nevertheless the association with information-related work undoubtedly imbues the social profile of those who do this kind of work with certain common traits. All the occupations in this category (including the related mass-based worker occupations) entail a relatively large amount of mental work. The proportion of so-called "creative" jobs is larger here than in other kinds of activity. This circumstance inevitably affects attitudes toward work, people's interests, and the overall life-orientations and values of all those associated with information management, even of those whose activity is not directly creative. This influence is all the stronger because in current production people doing information-related work are increasingly concentrated in large specialized organizations. The growing convergence between people in the mass-based worker occupations and in the intellectual occupations is far more pronounced here than elsewhere.

Fourth, there are the occupations directly associated with training and education, with medical, recreational and cultural services, with municipal and trade services. The item-specific content of occupations of this kind—indeed, this type of work in general—is determined by the fact that its object is people, as consumers of goods and services. All distinctions apart, this is the common element in the work of doctors, teachers, retail clerks, hospital orderlies, nannies, barbers, and so forth. In a certain sense these occupations are related to such branches as health care, education, trade, and so on. However by no means are all those employed in the service sector connected with providing services to people. Thus loaders would not be included (even if they work in a store), nor would those working in a tailoring shop or factory laundry, except for those whose occupational position puts them into direct contact with the consumer (receptionist, registration clerk, etc.).

The direct link with servicing people and upbringing determines many of the socially significant characteristics of those employed in this occupational group. In addition to having had the requisite specialized training, it is especially important that these people be generally cultured, capable of dealing with people, communicative and versatile. It is no coincidence that in these groups of occupations there is a high proportion of intellectual work, and that the dividing line between intellectual and physical work is often all but indistinguishable. More and more of the work in providing services to people is being industrialized, though it is still a long way behind the industrial sector, agriculture, and information management in this respect. Some unique features, such as the relative scarcity of large collectives, and the individual quality of certain services (educator, masseur, doctor, coach, etc.) stem from this fact.

One other occupational/job category is characterized by the specific content of the work concerned. These occupations are associated with the supervision of people, with the organization of their production, social, and cultural activity. The object of labor here is human collectives and communities, both productive and geographic. This naturally confers distinctive traits upon the social profile of supervisory personnel. Obviously, the organizational occupations cannot be exclusively attached to any particular type of production. Furthermore, these occupations—as discussed in detail in our preceding paper—can be regarded as an element of the division of labor based upon complexity of work. Nevertheless, they must be placed in the range of groups distinguished by the material, item-specific content of the work concerned, since otherwise that range will not include all the jobs found in the national economy of the USSR, and will therefore be incomplete.

A dual classification of occupations by the material, item-specific content and complexity of work

The heuristic and substantive potential of an occupational classification according to the material, item-specific content of work increases if that classification is combined with a breakdown of jobs by the complexity and nature of work (for details on the principle behind that breakdown, see our previous article). Such a combination not only shows the movement of dominant groups but also makes it possible to encompass the totality of socio-occupational divisions typical of a developed socialist society (see Chart 1).

The system of socio-occupational groups represents an important cross-sectional aspect of social structure. Alongside other aspects of that structure (social divisions arising in the urbanization process, etc.), it offers some idea of the social groups that apparently will form elements of the classless social structure of socialist society.

But changes in the material, item-specific content of work, its nature and complexity reflect only some of the processes that have shaped the social structure of Soviet society in recent decades and will play a large role in the immediate future. It is especially important to remember that a description of changes in the relative importance of jobs yields genuinely valuable results only if movement in basic social relations and, above all, progressive developments in the social-class structure of society are simultaneously considered.

From this standpoint, it should be stressed that the distribution of the employed by occupational groups in accordance with the object of labor activity, the complexity of work and its link with technological types of production unambiguously and clearly matches the distribution of the USSR's employed population by classes and major social groups. Most collective farmers are engaged in agricultural-type work, and they account for approximately half of those employed in this occupational category. Workers constitute the bulk of those employed in simple or complex physical or mental/physical work of an industrial, information-management, and service type, and also account for a portion of those employed in agricultural-type work. People employed in simple or complex mental work, regardless of the material, item-specific content of their activity, belong to the intelligentsia or employees' categories. The network of material, item-specific, and skill-based divisions may be organically super-imposed upon the system of indices of social-class structure. It thus becomes a particular cross-section, a specific aspect of that structure.

We must, however, remember that with respect to the task we have set ourselves the most important thing is whether or not it is possible to superimpose this schema upon official statistical materials, and thus throw light upon the quantitative relationships among the job categories we have identified and their dynamics. Obviously, as in our analysis of the occupational structure of the core of the working class, here too we shall have to accept a high degree of approximation in assigning jobs to groups that are distinguished by the material, item-specific content and complexity of work. However, in the final analysis we can use these basic principles to classify—albeit in general terms and with occasional calls upon expert assessments—the official statistical data on the occupational affiliations of 85% to 90% of employed personnel (see Table 1).

The groups shown in the table combine occupations not by one trait, however important that trait may be, but by an aggregate of characteristics (material, item-specific content, complexity and nature of work), which determine common features in the position of employed personnel within the system of division of labor, and the consequent similarities in their social and cultural profile. Unlike a one-dimensional occupational distribution according to either of these traits (material, item-specific content or complexity of work), a dual type of distribution generates a kind of supplementary effect which permits a broader approach to examining socio-occupational realignments in the Soviet population over the past 40 years. Taken together with the data presented in earlier tables (see our previous article), this approach highlights in a more striking manner both the problems and contradictions of the dynamics of the socio-occupational structure and the connections between these dynamics and overall social development.

CHART 1 Classification of occupations and jobs by material, item-specific content and complexity of work performed

Occupational and job categories distinguished by complexity and nature of work / Occupational groups distinguished by material, item-specific content of work (object of labor activity)	Jobs and occupations with a preponderance of relatively-simple physical work not normally requiring occupational training	Jobs and occupations with a preponderance of more complex work normally requiring training in vocational education institutions, in special courses, etc.	
		Jobs and occupations traditionally classed as physical	Jobs and occupations traditionally classed as nonphysical (unskilled mental work)
Agricultural occupations and jobs where the basic object of labor is living nature (work directly associated with the production of agricultural output)	Nonspecialized personnel in crop husbandry, fodder supply, animal husbandry (dairy-maids, stable hands, cattle-yard workers on nonmechanized farms, etc.)	Machine operatives and workers in mechanized agricultural production (tractor drivers, combine operators, milking-machine operators, etc.)	Nonspecialized personnel in mental work connected with direct servicing of agricultural production (accounting clerks, etc.)
Industrial occupations and jobs where the basic object of labor is tangible, material items undergoing preliminary processing (work associated with processing and reworking of raw material and finished articles, construction of buildings and other structures, freight transportation and storage, etc.)	Ancillary and nonspecialized industrial-type personnel (common laborers, ancillary workers, janitors, stock and supply handlers, loaders, etc.)	Personnel in leading industrial, construction and transport occupations involving nonagricultural material production (machine-tool operators, metalworkers, maintenance technicians, installers, drivers, etc.)	Personnel in nonspecialized mental work employed in direct servicing of industry, transport, construction, and other branches of nonagricultural material production (timekeepers, expeditors, etc.)
Information-related occupations and jobs where information is the basic object of labor (work predominantly associated with information processing, information gathering, organization of information-related procedures)		Personnel in service jobs involving information processing and monitoring procedures (computer operators, laboratory technicians, inspectors, etc.)	Personnel engaged in simple information gathering and processing operations (draftsmen, book-keeping staff, etc.)
Service occupations and jobs where the basic object of labor is people, as consumers of goods and services (work directly associated with servicing and educating people)	Ancillary personnel in human services (nannies, hospital orderlies, cloakroom attendants, etc.)	Personnel in leading commercial and public service occupations (retail clerks, waiters, barbers, photographers, etc.)	Auxiliary personnel in services (polyclinic registrars, tailoring enterprise receiving clerks, etc.)

Jobs and occupations with a preponderance of complex and highly complex mental work requiring higher or secondary specialized education

Jobs and occupations not associated with direct supervision of people	Jobs and occupations associated with supervision of work collectives	Jobs and occupations associated with supervision of sociopolitical, territorial, and branch organizations and communities
Specialists directly engaged in the agrotechnical and zootechnical organization of agricultural production (agronomists, livestock experts, veterinarians, etc.)	Supervisors of agricultural enterprises and subdivisions thereof (state farm directors, collective farm chairmen, managers of specialized farms, etc.)	
Specialists employed in direct organization of the technical/technological process in industry, transport, construction, and other branches of nonagricultural material production (engineers, technicians-technologists, mechanics, etc.)	Supervisors of nonagricultural material prises in industry, production enterconstruction, transport, etc. (directors, deputy directors, shop superintendents, shift bosses, etc.)	
Specialists engaged in the generation, collection, storage, processing, and transmission of information, and the organization of information-related procedures (economists, scientific workers, etc.)	Supervisors of scientific research and design organizations and subdivisions thereof (directors of scientific research institutions, heads of laboratories, departments, sectors, etc.)	
Specialists directly engaged in provision of public and sociocultural services and education (kindergarten teachers, nurses, teachers, doctors, actors, etc.)	Supervisors of organizations engaged in provision of education and services (directors of schools, shops, enterprises, communal service agencies, chief physicians, higher educational institution rectors and their deputies, etc.)	Supervisors of state administrative bodies, of Party, Komsomol, trade union and other social organizations, and of their structural subdivisions (territorial and branch level)

Table 1   **Distribution of Employed Population by Principal Socio-Occupational Groups (estimate, in %)**

Socio-occupational groups	Late 1930s	Late 1950s	Late 1960s	Late 1970s
I. Employed in agricultural labor (directly associated with production of agricultural output)	52	38	23	18
—employed in predominantly physical labor, not requiring occupational training (work with horse-drawn implements, crop husbandry, animal husbandry, etc.)	47	33	19	13
—employed in predominantly physical labor requiring occupational training (machine operatives, land-reclamation workers, etc.)	2	3	3	4
—employed in nonphysical labor requiring occupational training (team-leaders, accounting clerks, etc.)	2	1	negligible	negligible
—employed in predominantly mental labor requiring secondary specialized or higher education (agronomists, livestock experts, veterinarians, etc.)	1	1	1	1
II. Employed in industrial-type work (directly associated with the working and processing of raw materials and finished articles, the construction and repair of buildings and other structures, goods transport, etc.)	33	42	48	51
—employed in predominantly physical labor not requiring occupational training (loaders, common laborers, workers attending extremely simple machines and mechanical devices, etc.)	16	17	14	13
—employed in predominantly physical labor normally requiring occupational training (machine-tool operators, installers, machinery operators, repair technicians, drivers, construction hands, workers in complex manual work, etc.)	15	23	29	31

Table 1 (continued)

Socio-occupational groups	Late 1930s	Late 1950s	Late 1960s	Late 1970s
—employed in nonphysical labor requiring specialized occupational training (purchasing agents, expeditors, timekeepers, etc.)	negligible	negligible	1	1
—employed in predominantly mental labor requiring secondary specialized or higher education (industrial engineers, mechanical engineers, flight mechanics, etc.)	1	2	4	6
III. Employed in labor predominantly associated with information processing, information gathering and organization of information-related procedures	6	7	10	12
—employed in predominantly physical labor requiring specialized occupational training (computer operators, radio operators, telegraph operators, quality control inspectors, laboratory technicians, etc.)	negligible	1	2	3
—employed in nonphysical labor requiring specialized occupational training (draftsmen, dispatchers, bookkeeping staff, etc.)	5	3	4	4
—employed in predominantly mental labor requiring secondary specialized or higher education (design engineers, economists, scientific workers, etc.)	1	3	4	5
IV. Employed in labor directly associated with provision of services and education	7	9	14	14
—employed in predominantly physical labor not requiring specialized occupational training (kindergarten nannies, hospital orderlies, cloakroom attendants)	1	2	2	2

Table 1 (continued)

Distribution of Employed Population by Principal Socio-Occupational Groups (estimate, in %)

Socio-occupational groups	Late 1930s	Late 1950s	Late 1960s	Late 1970s
—employed in physical and nonphysical service work requiring specialized occupational training (retail clerks, waiters, barbers, etc.)	2	2	4	4
—employed in predominantly mental labor requiring secondary specialized or higher education (teachers, doctors, lawyers, artists, etc.)	4	5	8	8
V. Employed in labor associated with the supervision of collectives and organizations, and of people's production, social or cultural activity	2	4	5	5
Total (all those employed in above occupational classifications), %	100	100	100	100
millions	69	91	102	122
Other employed people (including those in occupations which cannot be unequivocally assigned to any of the groups listed above) millions	10	8	13	13
Total employed millions	79	99	115	135
Share of those employed in the classified occupations as percent of total employed	87	92	89	90

Calculations and estimates derived from data published in: *Itogi Vsesoiuznoi perepisi naseleniia 1959 g. SSSR. Svodnyi tom*, Moscow, 1962, pp. 161–166; *Itogi Vsesoiuznoi perepisi naseleniia 1970 g.*, vol. VI, Moscow, 1973, pp. 14–23; *Naselenie SSSR. Po dannym Vsesoiuznoi perepisi naseleniia 1979 g.*, Moscow, 1980, pp. 19–20; *Vestnik statistiki*, 1980, no. 6, pp. 41–62; *ibid.*, 1981, no. 1, pp. 63–67; *ibid.* 1981, no. 2, pp. 63–78; *ibid.*, 1981, no. 4, p. 69; *ibid.*, 1981, no. 5, pp. 63–66; *Narodnoe khoziaistvo SSSR v 1972 g.*, Moscow, 1973, pp. 518–521; *Narodnoe khoziaistvo SSSR 1922–1982. Iubileinyi statezhegodnik*, Moscow, 1982, pp. 132–133, 145, 162, 315–317, 321–322, 383, 399–402, 407; *Kommunisty i trudiashchiesia krupnykh gorodov v bor'be za sotsial'nyi i nauchno-tekhnicheskii progress*, Moscow, 1982, pp. 187–198; L. A. Gordon, A. K. Nazimova, L. G. Perfil'eva, "Technical-Technological Changes and the Development of the Occupational Structure: Some Approaches to the Sociological Analyses of Employment Statistics," in *Sotsial'noe i kulturnoe razvitie rabochego klassa v sotsialisticheskom obshchestve (Metodicheskie i metodologicheskie voprosy)*, part I, Moscow, 1982. *i kulturnoe razvitie rabochego klassa v sotsialisticheskom obshchestve (Metodicheskie i metodologicheskie voprosy)*, part I, Moscow, 1982.

Changes in socio-occupational structure and some problems of socio-occupational development

Generally speaking, problems of socio-occupational develop-ment that are in some way connected with changes in the general occupational structure warrant separate study. However, we shall examine here some of those problems which bear most urgently upon the intensification of the economy and the acceleration of social progress. In particular, the data presented in the table clearly show that the past four decades have witnessed a change in the relative importance of occupational groups distinguished ac-cording to the material, item-specific content and complexity of work performed, which is itself a reflection of the dynamic nature of the dominant elements of the socio-occupational structure. This helps us to understand many of the changes in the social and economic situation engendered by a succession of technological types of production, by society's transition to the industrial and scientific-industrial types of production.

An analysis of the actual proportions within the occupational structure shows that the 1950s to 1970s were a decisive watershed in the evolution of an occupational structure of a developed indus-trial type.

In terms of the character of production and the structure of national income, of course, the USSR became an industrial power as far back as the 1930s. However, in terms of the composition of its population, its immediate working and living conditions, and the overall sociocultural situation, the transforming effects of industrialization were felt only in a few key branches of the economy during that period. As is clear from the table, most people were employed in jobs of a preindustrial and early indus-trial (primarily agricultural) nature at that time. Moreover, even in the late 1950s there were about as many employed people in occupations of that kind as there were in industrial occupations—over one-third of the employed in each case. And no less than half of the industrial core of the working class was employed in jobs of a premechanical and early industrial nature during those years.

Another way of looking at the occupational structure—the distribution of jobs according to level of complexity of work—points up the distinctive nature of industrializing realignments right into the late 1950s and early 1960s. By the end of the 1950s almost two-thirds of working people were employed in occupations involving relatively simple work that did not require specialized occupational training prior to the commencement of labor activity. Even among those employed in industrial-type work some two-fifths were in occupations of that kind.

The turning point that marked the transition from an early industrial to a developed employment structure came in the 1960s and 1970s. By the beginning of the present decade the dominant group in the occupational structure comprised jobs that were directly associated with the working and processing of raw materials and finished articles, the construction and repair of buildings and other structures, freight transport, and so on. And the dominant position within this group was held by occupations involving physical and mental/physical work that required a sound general education and specialized occupational training prior to the commencement of labor activity, and by workers' occupations associated with industrial-mechanical and assembly-line work.

The absolute and relative growth of employment in industrial-type occupations during the 1960s and the 1970s was naturally accompanied by a scarcely less rapid absolute and relative expansion in the number of those employed in sectors associated with services and education. Actually, at this time the sociocultural profile and mode of life not just of individual categories of working people but of virtually the entire population took on traits that emerged under the influence of developed industrial production. Until the 1960s and 1970s such traits had directly determined the work, daily life, and culture of only part of the Soviet people. For the first time in its history, our country became industrialized with respect to the composition of its population.

No less significant, though, are the changes prompted by the fact that the current phase of transition to a developed industrial economy coincides with the beginning of another process—namely, the transition to scientific-industrial production.

Naturally enough, as long as the scientific and technical revolution is only transforming particular branches of the economy, scientific-industrial traits will not show up very clearly in the occupational structure. Employment in information-related occupations—which in principle constitute the dominant group within the occupational structure of the scientific-industrial type—today lags far behind employment in industrial occupations. Similarly, among workers in industrial occupations the proportion of those employed in automated work and in equipment maintenance and service is much below the proportion in machine-based assembly-line work. Nonetheless the mass-based occupations associated with the production of information are already numerically comparable with jobs in the service sphere and agricultural-type jobs (12%, 14%, and 18% respectively at the end of the 1970s).

Even more important, the rate of growth in the number of people associated with information-related work is now outpacing that of all other major occupational groups. This becomes particularly evident if the principal occupational categories are ranked by indicators of numerical growth (the percentage increase in number employed over the relevant period, as given in parentheses):

1960s	1970s
1. Industrial occupations (109%)	1. Information-related occupations (30%)
2. Education and services (64%)	2. Industrial occupations (23%)
3. Information-related occupations (58%)	3. Education and services (18%)

It is also highly symptomatic that within the occupational groups in information-related work the most rapid growth is seen in those jobs which involve skilled mental work and especially mental/physical work associated with contemporary information-processing technology (which increased by 36% and 51% respectively between 1970 and 1979).

It is true that these figures—like the data on changes in the occupational structure of the population as a whole (see Table 1)—make it clear that the 1970s witnessed a considerable slowing down in the development of the occupational structure. Thus, during the 1960s the relative share of jobs whose item-specific content most clearly manifested the influence of the scientific and technical revolution increased by about 50%. In approximate terms the proportion of people in information-related work rose during that decade from 7% to 10%; in services and education, from 9% to 14%; and in industry, from 42% to 48%. Within the latter category the relative share of people associated with assembly-line industrial work and scientific-industrial work rose from one-half to two-thirds. Over the same period the extent of the simplest kinds of agricultural work shrank from 33% to 18%.

Change was far slower in the 1970s. Employment in information-related work rose only from 10% to 12% during this decade. The share of employment in services and education remained virtually unchanged, while employment in industry rose from 48% to 51% (and the internal structure of industrial occupations was almost static). The simplest forms of agricultural work declined from 19% to 13%.

The distinct slowing of progressive occupational changes is part of a broader pattern which has caused a slackening of economic growth rates during the most recent Five-Year Plan.[7] In this sense the relatively slow movement in the socio-occupational structure in the 1970s constitutes a complex problem that warrants close attention and special study. However, no matter how important this phenomenon may be in itself, it does not alter the general direction and substance of changes in the occupational composition of the population. The general emergence of scientific-industrial production and the occupational structure corresponding to it are as instrumental in determining the nature of contemporary development as industrial production and the industrial job structure.

Obviously, a clear-cut and unambiguous mapping of changes generated by the transition from early industrial production to developed industrial production, on the one hand, and from developed industrial to scientific-industrial production, on the other, is only possible in theoretical terms. In socioeconomic reality, on the surface of community life, these transitions appear as a single flow in which the two sets of changes are interconnected, interwoven, literally blended. Nevertheless the conception of the dyadic nature of this process is not arbitrary. The complexity it exhibits is a reflection of the complex nature of reality—the fact that our society's occupational structure presently accommodates occupations of the scientific-industrial type (the embodiment of its future), occupations of the assembly-line type (which are characteristic of today's prevailing forms of employment), and early industrial or even preindustrial types of occupations (a sort of enclave of times past, of social labor's bygone days). Mass-based occupational groups, encompassing tens of millions of people, are attached to each of these three types. As can be seen from the data presented above the scope of these occupational categories is measurable within the same order of magnitude, so to speak. The complex nature of the occupational structure—one of the consequences of the intensive development of Soviet society, and an arena of interaction between quantitatively comparable groups of people doing scientific-industrial, developed industrial, and preindustrial work—is responsible for the specific character of the problems whose solution is pivotal for further economic and social progress. The substance of such problems is largely determined by the fact that the principal occupational groups within the employed population differ considerably in terms of their sociocultural profile, needs, and interests. In other words society is simultaneously confronted with challenges that seem to relate to different stages of socioeconomic development. Understandably, their solution requires dissimilar methods.

The November 1982 plenary session of the CPSU Central Committee stressed that it is essential to create the economic and organizational conditions that will "stimulate high-quality, productive labor, initiative, and an enterprising attitude."[8] To achieve this goal during the establishment of scientific-industrial production and the mass development of associated occupations objectively requires the kind of restructuring of the mechanism of economic and social management in which the once-prevalent methods of directive-type and peremptory administration and planning are gradually supplanted by a variety of forms of predominantly indirect, systematic regulation, where the economic and social units possess extensive authority and opportunities for self-organization. It is only natural that the CPSU Central Committee is today posing the task of solving the issue of extending the independence of associations, enterprises, and collective and state farms.[9]

Of course, many facets of work activity in scientific-industrial production are actually prescribed, more unambiguously than ever before, by technological requirements. On the whole, however, if scientific-industrial production is to function efficiently, if those employed in this area are to work at capacity, and finally, if the workforce is to be adequately reproduced, "there must be the further development of socialist democracy in the very widest sense of the term–that is, the increasingly active participation of the working masses in the management of state and community affairs."[10]

Obviously, the absence of self-directed activity and initiative on the part of the people runs fundamentally counter to the ethos of socialism, since success in the construction of the new society can only be achieved, as Lenin put it, "through the independent historical creativity of the majority of the populace, and primarily of the majority of working people."[11] However, it is precisely at the stage of mature socialism and the scientific and technical revolution that the need for self-organization is felt more acutely than ever before.

The emergence of scientific-industrial production is one of the factors that makes the development of democracy in our country particularly urgent at present.

Changes in the sociocultural profile of working people are of decisive significance in this connection. The typically high level of education generates a system of interests and values, prominent among which are the need for self-realization, self-directed activity, and self-organization in all aspects of social activity. It is highly significant that growing numbers of working people are increasingly oriented to participating in management, primarily in the management of their own work collectives.

The need to strengthen the elements of self-organization among working people and their collectives is dictated also by certain peculiarities of scientific-industrial production, where economic effectiveness hinges not upon external control but upon a high degree of work motivation and activism among the mass of working people.

It is clear that motivation of this kind will become widespread only if, aside from all else, working people and their collectives are extensively involved in self-directed activity, if their "feeling of being masters of the enterprise" is universally developed and if, in addition, conditions are created whereby each worker feels that he is "not only a master of his factory but a representative of his country."[12] The transformation of organizational and managerial relations, with a view to broadening the self-directed activity and the rights and responsibilities of enterprises and associations, is very obviously the next step.[13]

However, the objective conditions of development in the various elements of the occupational structure are such that the need for broader self-reliance and self-organization is more pressing in some areas than others.

In particular, it is very much to the point that in those units of the economy where preindustrial and early industrial production are especially widespread, there is a concentration of large groups of people engaged in simple work that for the most part does not require any up-to-the-minute occupational training. Here are concentrated virtually all remaining working people in society with a low level of education. Understandably enough, their sociocultural requirements differ markedly from those of the majority of working people. Even an influx of well-educated young people has relatively little effect upon the structure of requirements among workers engaged in preindustrial labor. Preindustrial production frequently preserves and reproduces individuals of a certain sociocultural type, who feel no need for a management system strongly rooted in the self-directed activity and self-reliance of labor collectives.

Paradoxical as it may seem, it is a fact that the simple, undifferentiated content of work in preindustrial production, and especially in agriculture, lends itself well to the development of elements of self-organization. We note, however, that in the preindustrial economy the need for self-reliance is chiefly felt within the primary production units, while on the macroeconomic level, this kind of economy is prone to a high degree of centralization.

The relationship between the restructuring of the economic mechanism and the objective conditions prevailing in industrial and assembly-line industrial production (which at the moment contains the most common occupations) is equally complex. But individual factors influence the situation in an entirely different way in this case. This is the area of concentration of workers with a relatively advanced, predominantly urban culture. Under socialism, moreover, their cultural development is higher in some respects than is required by strictly production needs. Their need for self-expression is as intrinsic to their sociocultural profile as that observed among people employed in scientific-industrial work. Accordingly, the culture of these workers is an essential factor in the development of the democratic principle in economic matters and throughout public life.

Still, the conditions of production and content of work in the majority of occupations in industrial production are not so complex that manifold and all-inclusive self-organization (which is intrinsic to scientific-industrial production) is a *sine qua non* of work efficiency here. At this level of development of the productive forces, the contradiction between the organizational and technological structure of production and the existing management relations—which go hand-in-hand with centralized planning, the strict regulation of activity at all levels, and organization by managerial fiat—is less accentuated than in scientific-industrial production.

In reality, apart from purely technological considerations, the role of sociopolitical and sociocultural factors is, of course, enormous. In socialist society, strict regulation and the administrative directive are always combined, to some degree, with the living creativity of the people and the unregulated initiative of working people. However, in certain historical circumstances, centralized planning and management-by-directive have given a powerful impetus to development in industrial-type production. In the process of socialist industrialization of the USSR methods such as these accelerated the transition from preindustrial and early industrial production to industrial assembly-line production. The effectiveness of management-by-directive methods naturally led to a highly centralized structure of the entire system of economic institutions and agencies, and led to the formation of an economic mindset that could well be dubbed "administrative-centralist" and whose inherent inertia is still felt to this day.

Since large groups of workers associated with diverse technical/technological types of production coexist within the socio-occupational structure, the present stage is characterized by an extremely intricate mix of heterogeneous socioeconomic requirements. The conditions of scientific-industrial production require thoroughgoing changes in the longstanding relationship between centralism and the democratic principle. Since scientific-industrial production is the leading technical/technological modality in the contemporary Soviet economy, this requirement must be our chief guideline in optimizing the socioeconomic mechanism of mature socialist society. It is an essential precondition for the intensification of social production. This is precisely how party documents have stated the issue in recent years.

A high cultural level is not, in the strict sense, the exclusive preserve of scientific-industrial personnel; it is characteristic of all industrial personnel. The optimization of social and economic relations is, therefore, mandated by the cultural development of the majority of working people. Nevertheless in evaluating the current state of social requirements, we must allow for the fact that the technology and organization of assembly-line industrial production can be combined, in principle, with various forms of management-by-directive. In the not too distant past, these were judged to be the only viable managerial forms.

On the other hand, the existence of vestiges of preindustrial production implies that there are in society some rather large groups of working people whose social and cultural needs are less well-developed but whose labor frequently (especially in the case of agriculture) will not yield the intended results unless there is a high level of self-organization.

To sum up the current situation, alongside the factors creating a need for restructuring the economic mechanism as society's leading socioeconomic requirement, there persist certain objective conditions which still lend support to the management-by-directive style. This, clearly, is one of the reasons why the restructuring of the economic mechanism and the optimization of the system of economic management called for in the November 1982 plenary session of the CPSU Central Committee is proceeding so slowly. Moreover, the very existence within the economy of certain units whose efficiency can supposedly be raised through the improvement of traditional methods causes a certain amount of foot-dragging in restructuring planning methods and the management system, and a sluggish approach to restructuring the economic mechanism,[14] and is responsible for all-too-frequent attempts to limit such changes to isolated areas and levels of the economy and to individual aspects of the economic mechanism.

Such half-way solutions are often ineffective. Conservative economic thought can then cite the subsequent difficulties and failures in their contentions against any kind of innovation. Quite to the contrary, an examination of these difficulties in the broader socioeconomic and political context points to the conclusion underlined in party documents—that it is essential to continue and extend decisively the policy directed toward the comprehensive improvement of the economic system, to bring it into full conformity with mature socialist relations, with the requirements of the contemporary worker and the needs of a developed industrial economy whose functional context is the scientific and technical revolution and the intensification of production.

Notes

1. K. Marx, F. Engels, *Sochinenie*, Vol. 46, part I, p. 43.
2. *Ibid.*, Vol. 47, p. 553.
3. *Sotsial'no-politicheskie problemy NTR i ideologicheskaia bor'ba*, Kiev, 1978, pp. 357–360.
4. See Marx, Engels, *Sochinenie*, vol. 26, part II, pp. 144, 576.
5. See *Chelovek i professiia*, Edited by E. A. Klimov et al., Issue 1, Leningrad, 1975, p. 13; Issue 2, Leningrad, p. 5.
6. Marx, Engels, *Sochinenie*, vol. 3, p. 65.
7. See *Pravda*, 24 February 1982; *Kommunist*, 1982, no. 3, p. 26.
8. *Materialy Plenuma TsK KPSS 22 noiabria 1982 goda*, Moscow, 1982, p. 9.
9. *Ibid.*
10. *Ibid.*, p. 23.
11. V. I. Lenin, *Polnoe sobranie sochinenii*, Vol. 35, p. 357.
12. *Ibid.*, Vol. 36, p. 369.
13. *Materialy XXVI s"ezda KPSS*, p. 54; *Materialy Plenuma TsK KPSS 22 noiabria 1982 goda*, p. 9.
14. See *Materialy Plenuma TsK KPSS 22 noiabria 1982 goda*, p. 8.

Part II

Social Stratification: Theoretical Issues and Empirical Studies

3. On the Question of Social Differentiation in Developed Socialist Society*

M. Kh. TITMA

Research into the problems of the social structure of developed socialist society has advanced significantly over the past decade. These studies can now be regarded as having reached a qualitatively new stage, characterized by emphasis upon the specific features of the chosen approach, be it philosophical, historical, sociological, or whatever else. It is very important that in elaborating this many-sided problem no single scientific discipline should be taken as universally valid and that the essence of controversial issues should not be distorted by pseudoscientific ratiocination.

In this paper we shall seek to validate some of the principles and goals of research on social structure.

One of the basic structure-generating elements of society, as long as social heterogeneity still exists, is the process of social differentiation. However, the overwhelming bulk of current research on the social structure of Soviet society—especially its social-class structure—is devoted to studying ways of achieving full social homogeneity. In this connection it is taken as axiomatic that overcoming the socioeconomic division of labor is the foun-

*Russian text © 1980 by "Nauka" Publishers. "K voprosu o sotsial'noi differentisatsii v razvitom sotsialisticheskom obshchestve," *Sotsiologicheskie issledovaniia*, 1980, No. 3, pp. 35–43.

dation for movement in that direction. But there is little real hope that even simple physical work will completely disappear in the foreseeable future. There is even less justification for regarding mental work as socially homogeneous. Nor should the developmental dialectic between the implements of production and the personality of the productive agent be overlooked. As the production process grows more complex, man himself changes: work that once seemed creative is no longer perceived as such. This is a ubiquitous phenomenon. For instance, the majority of jobs associated with calculation (cashier, accountant, even computer-related work) are now becoming a matter of simple routine for the developed personality. All the more probable that these processes will continue in the future. Therefore excessive haste in resolving the issue of overcoming the socioeconomic division of labor seems to us unwarranted. In other words, the social nature of the division of labor is predicated upon the developmental level of society as a whole. Variants of labor activity which are socially homogeneous in certain circumstances are heterogeneous in others.

The above is of critical significance to a study of the social structure and especially to sociological research in this field, a process undertaken to gain *concrete knowledge about society*. The sociologist is required to produce more than a simple assertion that our society is moving toward social homogeneity. He must also reveal how changes in the social structure are reflected in the life of society as a whole and its institutions. Neither science nor actual practice have any use for the sociologist's assurance that we are on the right track; what they need is knowledge of the course that actual processes are taking, so as to use this knowledge in raising the scientific level of management. If we want to achieve a genuinely scientific basis for an effective social policy, we must direct our attention to smaller elements of the social structure than social groups and classes.[1]

As we see it, to assert that the intelligentsia contains no social strata, and that no new strata can appear within the intelligentsia under socialism, while at the same time consigning everyone engaged in mental work to the intelligentsia,[2] cannot be regarded as a constructive approach to the problems of the development of social structure in socialist society. Essentially, this view limits research to the pronouncement of truisms about the need for convergence between classes and social groups and about the erosion of social distinctions between them. In reality, though, the scientific management of the development of social structure requires concrete knowledge.

Moreover, it must be noted that many bourgeois scholars have been led to pronounce the power of integrating factors in the development of social structure to be so absolute that the working class is allegedly "vanishing" and blending with the intelligentsia.[3] It is undoubtedly true that employment in predominantly mental work characterizes some sections of the working class. But mental work itself has undergone substantial differentiation: many of its operations have been standardized to the point that, for a person with secondary education, mental work seems no more socially advanced than simple physical work. In this context the division of labor differs in nature at various stages in society's socioeconomic history. Thus, during the scientific and technical revolution those doing mental labor come to form two relatively independent social groups—employees and specialists—whose social position differs substantially. As M. N. Rutkevich and V. S. Semenov have convincingly shown, these groups are distinguished by their level of education, skill, and so forth, and not only by the content of their work. The social differences between these groups are no less than those between specialists and the working class.

In brief, one may safely predict that, as the relative importance of mental work in social production grows, both occupational and social differentiation within the intelligentsia will steadily increase and more elements of mental work will appear in the occupational activity of the worker.

We come now to the problem of *identifying strata within the social-class structure*. This involves a level of analysis conducted at a lower level of abstraction than that applied in the study of classes and social groups. It is erroneous to suppose that the boundaries between them are hard and fast: only at a high level of abstraction can a social structure be so configured. A more concrete examination shows that the structure is segmented and that within its classes and social groups it is not difficult to discern qualitatively different strata, each occupying its own specific social position. Taken together, they form a discrete cross-section of the social structure which is of great interest to the management and planning system.

Thus, the erosion of social differences has led to the formation of new borderline strata—for instance, worker-intellectuals. (We shall not concern ourselves here with the validity of any particular term.) In principle, we cannot deny the possibility that new strata or complements may arise. The critical issue is whether or not a given social group has acquired sufficient specific features to qualify as a stratum.[4]

The identification of elements of the social structure is unquestionably one of the basic problems of research in this field because it is firmly tied in with the exact placement of social subjects, and this is essential to an effective social policy.

At the root of distinctions between strata, complements, and groups lies their specific social position. It determines the specific interests which the individuals in the group have and which identify that group as a social subject. The affinity of interests of social subjects is determined by the general principle which serves to identify them—namely, the nature of the division of labor, which also creates similarities in the degree of social activity of the individuals in the group. Thus changes in the social character of the division of labor affect the degree of differentiation in the social structure (making it more homogeneous), and have an impact upon both the social interests and the level of activity of social subjects. Uncovering the interconnections between the various components of social structure will enable us to grasp more fully its essence as a developing integral whole.

For some time it has been customary to examine the country's social structure at the following levels: mental and physical work, town and countryside, classes, and social and national groups; social strata and complements; social-branch and socio-occupational structures. Usually these are identified as self-contained elements; the interaction between them is seldom addressed. To present the social structure as an integral whole and to show the interconnections among its various levels while demonstrating their unique features strikes us as one of the more promising approaches to the study of social structure.

We take as an example the distinctions between town and countryside. The concentration of branches of production, which reflects one of the fundamental trends of social progress in urban areas, determines the high level of development of the urban infrastructure. But differences within it, which are contingent upon the nature and volume of production, are more substantial than those between the countryside and small towns.[5] In other words, the social stratification of cities runs deeper than the differences between town and countryside. It is primarily defined by the nature of industrial and intellectual production, which is concentrated in large cities. Statistical data show that in the country's major large cities, and also in regional social and economic centers, social development is proceeding far more rapidly than in small and middle-sized cities. Consequently, the distinctions between these two types of cities are growing.

Up to now, however, sociological studies of the singular features of small, middle-sized, large, and very large cities have not produced a description that encompasses all cross-sections of the social structure, nor have they offered any scientifically validated recommendations on the management of migration. The high level of migration is evidence that some social subjects—villages and small towns—are incapable of interesting their residents in the conduct of local affairs. Their social activity takes the form of heightened migratory activity.[6] This crucial social problem can only be solved if it is realized that the behavior of people is conditioned by their specific social position, and, hence, by their social interests.

In this regard, we would like to underline the significance of research recently conducted by N. A. Aitov, T. I. Zaslavskaia, V. I. Staroverov, and O. I. Shkaratan, which demonstrates the close connection between social-class infrastructure and residential infrastructure. The profile of the working class and the intelligentsia are so heavily dependent upon the type of city in question that in large cities some worker strata are more socially developed than portions of the intelligentsia residing in small towns. These distinctions are most clearly seen in studying new recruits to the various strata in large cities. These recruits are, as a rule, migrants from less developed areas. This process can result in some substantial social anomalies—one example being that workers from large cities are trained as recruits for cadres in less developed residential infrastructures.

Research into *social mobility* (intra- and intergenerational) and migratory trends are among the important directions in the study of social structure. There have been some signal successes in this area since the appearance of the book by M. N. Rutkevich and F. R. Filippov, *Social Mobility* [Sotsial'nye peremeshcheniia] (Moscow, 1970).[7] A number of problems—methodological problems in particular—remain unsolved, however. Some scholars have devoted most of their attention to the gradual surmounting of both interclass and intraclass differences. This, they believe, will guarantee society's steady advance toward total social homogeneity. Anyone who so much as suggests the idea of a contrary social direction in migration and mobility is liable to be accused, by this viewpoint's champions, of "fabricating" social differentiation within classes and social groups, while supposedly there exist in reality only occupational-skill strata.

Yet it strikes us as similarly one-sided to identify only social differences which arise in the process of reproduction of any given social structure. This approach has an overly narrow theoretical basis and may point only to the problematic aspects of mobility, which, let it be said, are obvious enough as it is.

In formulating social policy it is vital to know exactly how to regulate mobility flows in the required directions. A qualitative description of social subjects is of paramount significance here.

General statistical data can provide only the outlines of migratory movement. For instance, between the population censuses of 1959 and 1970, almost six million rural residents moved from the countryside to the city. Clearly, the general migratory trend was a flow of population from less developed to more developed structures. It is, however, vital to supplement that bare fact with a systematic picture of mobility paths. If the social characteristics of some principal subjects in this process are brought to light, it will be possible to find more effective ways of solving problems that arise in this area.

Another fact: when a certain category of working people is assigned to jobs that necessarily entail simple, low-skilled, physical work, this circumstance makes for a low level of social activity among people (they become most prone to absenteeism, violations of labor discipline, etc.).[8] In the context of developed socialism, the strata of working people engaged in simple physical work are gradually disappearing. At the same time, the work they do is still absolutely vital to society. A partial solution to this problem is to offer various kinds of extra perquisites. This, however, does not guarantee the desired level of social activity because the social interests of these strata, determined as they are by the position of the people concerned, remain undeveloped. The complete elimination of these strata is bound up with the development of new forms of the division of labor.[9]

The process of reducing social differences is sometimes equated exclusively with a realignment in the division of labor—that is, with the disappearance of its less socially developed forms. In our opinion, another promising direction in the development of the social structure would lie in overcoming the lifetime attachment of individuals to the socially less developed forms of work, which would in itself serve to eliminate the social strata in question. Our confidence in the correctness of this approach stems from the law of work rotation, which was first formulated by Marx and Engels in *The German Ideology*.[10] In the 1960s, scholars interpreted this law from a strictly economic perspective, wherein work rotation occurred with no change in social standing. Even today this view surfaces now and again.

It should be stressed that work rotation represents not a mere succession of different kinds of labor but the development of the individual's occupational aptitudes. By broadening the prospects for advancement, at work and in society, it can be expected to become a powerful catalyst of social progress. The essential point is that the more or less protracted attachment of an individual to any given kind of low-content work must be supplanted by a graduated system of advancement which must, moreover, be so arranged that the bulk of young people would first be assigned to the simpler and relatively less developed varieties of work and would subsequently move on to more substantive kinds of work best suited to their emergent inclinations and aptitudes. To achieve this, it is vital to chart with care the basic types of work careers, and to carefully adjust the mechanism of advancement in the world of work.

As things presently stand this advancement is normally a haphazard process, since the very system of job assignment already predetermines for most members of society a stable position within the national economy. If a system of basic, clearly defined types of work careers is instituted, the situation will change radically: there will be assignment not to a concrete form of work but to a type of work career. This implies growth of the individual in such areas as nature of work, skill, occupational title, compensation, and so forth. The individual is thus objectively placed in a situation which obliges him to marshall all his energies and abilities. In the final analysis, it becomes possible to harmoniously combine the individual's personal aspirations and the requirements of society.

This route could lead to the gradual ''atrophy'' of strata and complements of working people engaged in the least developed varieties of work, which will, undoubtedly, constitute a step forward in the erosion of social differences. And, without question, a study of the above mentioned problems has a considerable bearing on the elaboration of mechanisms for achieving social homogeneity.

Empirical studies of intragenerational mobility have an important role to play in the development of optimal forms of social mobility. An analysis of the age-structure of the principal occupational groups shows that there is a very substantial amount of intragenerational social mobility, which can be used to heighten the social activity of the population at large.[11] Special studies are needed to establish the direction, intensity, and especially the causes of intragenerational mobility. These studies should establish not only the appropriate material and moral stimuli but also the intervening link between them—social stimuli.

In the study of social structure, increasing attention is being devoted to research into the *individual's community activity*. As we know, society realizes its interests by the attachment of its members to a particular position within the social structure. The latter, for its part, determines the specific ways in which the interests of society are expressed in personal interests. Social differences serve to differentiate social interest. Normally, the activity of social subjects is greater when the direction of that activity is connected with the realization of their interests. That activity can thus be purposefully utilized to accelerate social progress.

In developed socialist society, where social differentiation still exists, the interests of social subjects do not always coincide. This does not mean (as it does under capitalism) that there are fundamental differences, much less antagonisms, between those interests. Nevertheless, in designing social policy it is necessary to examine the social structure of Soviet society with a view to modifying the interests of certain social groups. Community of interests is frequently stressed in discussions of this matter. This is, in general, perfectly legitimate, but we must not completely ignore the specific aspects of those interests, for this would reduce the effectiveness of social policy.

Each element of the social structure contributes to the reproduction of social relations in accordance with group interests, which are predicated upon the group's position in the social structure. The aggregate social interest is differentiated in the given social and territorial community in accordance with its socioeconomic infrastructure. It is materialized as a "local" interest, which public opinion usually views in a negative light, as a circumscribed set of concerns that run counter to the common interest. In reality, though, it reflects the given subject's potential and prospects in the country's social and economic development; only after this does it reflect specific aspects of social differences at this level of social structure (large, middle-sized, or small city, village, etc.). Thus, the specific features of social interest are embodied in the specific features of the reproduction of social structure. The interest here is directed toward preserving or changing the subject's social position.

The social subject's interests are expressed through requirements. Quite frequently, the particularities of the interconnection between social interest and the requirements of society are mechanically transferred to the concrete elements of social structure. But social requirements act on the interests of social subjects in mediated form. As previously noted, they are determined by the location of the subject in the system of division of labor and by the social position which corresponds to it. Requirements are significantly individualized as they are assimilated by various social subjects, a process significantly connected with the direction of interests as a whole.

The activity of social subjects is greatest when their specific interests are being realized: their activity is expressed in a change in the profile of a given element of the social structure (level of education, skill, political organization, group consciousness, etc.). This feature is usually overlooked in descriptions of the role of various social groups in the reproduction of social structure, and is only analyzed in studies of social mobility.

Heavy migratory flows and intragenerational social mobility both attest to the existence of substantial differences in the interests of many social subjects. To a smaller degree, the specific tenor of interests is manifested in the kind of intergenerational mobility which expresses in mediated form the direction of interests of the previous generation. In this sense, the "atrophy" of some of the less developed complements within the collective farm peasantry and the working class is an indicative sign: groups such as these have no interest in reproducing themselves although society requires the attachment of some of its members to work of this sort.

Individual differences in social interests present great difficulties when it comes to utilizing them in any well-planned way. It is an especially complex matter to locate the point beyond which interest evaporates, so that the individual's social activity slackens off, and it becomes necessary to arouse interest in a different direction. Thus, in intragenerational and intergenerational mobility it is possible to pinpoint empirically for all strata the particular conditions which, once achieved, bring about a substantial fall in the social activity of individuals (for instance, the basic flow of people from countryside to town is channeled through the vocational and technical training schools into the ranks of the working class, and the attainment of this standing, as a rule, marks the limit of the given generation's aspirations).

Equally undesirable is the formation of stimuli in the individual personality that incite it to vigorous activity in directions which are alien to the norms of socialist morality, and the inadequate development of interests in clearly promising directions. The limited interests of people engaged in simple physical work to a large extent predispose them to a high incidence of drunkenness, hooliganism, and other antisocial manifestations.[12] Further, the desire to acquire, say, a car can at times be accompanied by a striving to satisfy that requirement via unearned income. Solving the problem of appropriate measures to regulate the direction taken by the interests of each social subject is the basis for implementing an effective social policy.

It is particularly important now not only to study the different social interests, but also the process by which subjects become aware of their interests and the formation of stable orientations directed to realizing people's own interests. An analysis of the nexus *"social subject—social position—interest (requirement)— its recognition and selection—activity"* throws light on the causal link between socioeconomic conditions and the conscious activity of social subjects. Models of this sort can and should be constructed on the basis of empirical research findings.

In studying the factors making for social differentiation, it is important from a methodological standpoint to distinguish the degree to which regularities associated with various levels of the community influence the shaping and reproduction of the social structure. The theoretical basis for such an analysis is Lenin's definition of classes. Lenin established what are usually called class-generating indicators. They are the basis for the identification of the principal elements of social structure. With the movement of society toward social homogeneity, the description of these elements requires an analysis of the socially typical in the occupational, cultural, and political particularities of life-activity and, ultimately, in the whole mode of life of different groups in Soviet society.

Primary among these traits are the subjective-objective indicators of a given group or stratum which occupies a certain position in the social structure. Indices such as gender, age, skill, education, and so forth are, on the one hand, important in examining the population of a given area, branch, class, social group, complement, or stratum. On the other hand, these characteristics contribute to social differentiation under socialism. Although they are often confused with class-generating indicators (education is a case in point here), this is incorrect, since they characterize neither actual social relations nor the position actually occupied in the division of labor but primarily the individuals comprising a group.

The same objective socioeconomic position of individuals may entail diverse social consequences—consequences which can at times be much greater than the differences in objective social position. In this sense superstructural characteristics are among the factors which determine the social subjects' current stage of development and are an expression of differences among them.

At the same time there are still many unresolved questions in the study of class-generating indicators. It is commonly recognized that collective farm-cooperative property serves to differentiate between classes, that it makes for differences between the collective farm peasantry and the rural contingent of the working class. At the theoretical level there are no disagreements on this issue. But at the practical level it is exceedingly important to establish the extent to which the specific social identity and activity of these groups is determined by the form of property and the extent to which it is determined by the level of development of agricultural labor in collective farms and state farms.

The problem of the link between the personal property and social position of certain population groups has not been sufficiently investigated. Normally, the possession of a private household plot, a kitchen garden, a house, or summer home is seen merely as a means of satisfying certain requirements of their owners. But this is also a mode of redistributing the social product (we have in mind the income from goods produced for the market, from housing rental, and so on). At times the emergence of private property interests and the activity corresponding to those interests are explained in strictly subjective terms, while in reality phenomena of this sort are determined by a group of factors—in particular, the commodity-money relations that exist under socialism. Hence the need for the sociological study of the role which individual property plays in shaping the interests of any given population group.

The significance of the social organization of labor in social differentiation is often reduced to the influence it exerts upon the character of labor. However, empirical research has confirmed the extremely important role that worker organization plays in the social development of the various worker groups (as already noted in the classics of Marxism-Leninism in their descriptions of the working class). Even workers in a given specialty employed in a large enterprise are very different (in terms of both objective and subjective characteristics) from those employed in a small enterprise.

In his analysis of production relations Marx dwelt on the nature of individual activity. Soviet researchers pay particular attention to the individual's participation in management. There is, though, another important question to consider—namely, the relation between social interest and the interests of concrete social subjects. If the organization of labor presupposes the integral character of human activity and the clear identification of its social import and goals, then the objective social interest will be reflected most fully in the interest of the given subject.

Among the class-generating indicators, an important place is accorded to the means by which the subject receives a share of social wealth, and the extent of that share. Studies of social structure frequently reduce this aspect to the incomes of the population and sometimes even to wages and salaries. As a result, the singular features of social interests and the sources of activity among various social groups are interpreted too narrowly. In reality, social interest is determined not only by the amount of income but also by its actual content and by the manner in which it is obtained. The share of the social product at the disposal of one or another group of social subjects is no longer limited to wages: job sharing, other ways of utilizing knowledge and work habits, income from personal property, and so forth substantially modify the real income levels of various population groups. Moreover, payments from social consumption funds, whose size depends largely upon a person's social position, also exert a great influence upon real income. The social interest generated by the size of a person's share in social wealth and by the means of acquiring that share is an important factor in raising the level of individual social activity. However, the realization of that social interest should neither increase requirements excessively (this invariably leads to a search for extra—and possibly unearned—income), on the one hand, nor, on the other, give a surfeit of satisfaction (which has a dampening effect upon the social activity of the given category of working people).

Summing up the above, it must be noted that the socially differentiating role of class-generating indicators, as well as other factors which influence changes in social structure await additional in-depth investigation. The position of those scholars who attempt to reduce the complex web of problems arising from a study of the social structure of developed socialism merely to uncovering the current level of social homogeneity is without foundation. Actual social practice and documents recently endorsed by the Party direct sociologists toward a profound and comprehensive analysis of reality, so that what has been learned about actual social processes occurring during Communist construction can be put to effective use.

Notes

1. See M. N. Rutkevich, *Tendentsii razvitiia sotsial'noi struktury sovetskogo obshchestva*, Moscow, 1975.
2. See Ts. A. Stepanian, "The Soviet Intelligentsia and the Principal Paths of its Formation," *Voprosy filosofii*, 1979, no. 1, pp. 50, 52–55.
3. See *Osobennosti vosproizvodstva rabochego klassa razvitykh kapitalisticheskikh stran*, Moscow, 1978, pp. 63–73, 95–105, 117–125.
4. See A. M. Geliuta, V. I. Staroverov, *Sotsial'nyi oblik rabochego-intelligenta*, Moscow, 1977.
5. See B. S. Khorev, *Problemy gorodov*, Moscow, 1975; N. A. Aitov, *Sotsial'noe razvitie gorodov: sushchnost' i perspektivy*, Moscow, 1979; M. I. Mezhevich, *Gorod i sotsial'noe razvitie*, Leningrad, 1979; *Gorod: metodologicheskie problemy kompleksnogo sotsial'nogo i ekonomicheskogo planirovaniia*, Moscow, 1975.
6. See, among others, *Migratsiia sel'skogo naseleniia*, Moscow, 1970; N. A. Aitov, *Tekhnicheskii progress i dvizhenie rabochikh kadrov*, Moscow, 1972; V. I. Staroverov, *Sotsial'no-demograficheskie problemy derevni*, Moscow, 1975; B. S. Khorev, V. N. Chapek, *Problemy izucheniia migratsii naseleniia*, Moscow, 1978; *Sotsial'nye faktory i osobennosti migratsii naseleniia SSSR*, Moscow, 1978.
7. See, among others, *Vysshaia shkola kak faktor izmeneniia sotsial'noi struktury razvitogo sotsialisticheskogo obshchestva*, Moscow, 1978.
8. See N. A. Aitov, *Tekhnicheskii progress i dvizhenie rabochikh kadrov*, Moscow, 1972; *Sotsial'noe razvitie rabochego klassa. Sotsiologicheskie ocherki*, Moscow, 1977.
9. Such a division of labor between various age-cohorts is evolving even now. (See E. K. Vasil'eva, *Sotsial'no-ekonomicheskaia struktura naseleniia SSSR. Statistiko-demograficheskii analiz*, Moscow, 1978.)
10. K. Marx, F. Engels, *Sochineni*, vol. 3, pp. 30–32.
11. Population census data illustrates the existence of sharp distinctions in the age-structure of various occupational specialities. (See *Itogi Vsesoiuznoi*

perepisi naseleniia 1970 goda, vol. VI, Moscow, 1973.)

12. See V. N. Kudriavtsev, *Prichiny pravonarushenii*, Moscow, 1976, pp. 8–41, 130–182.

13. For this purpose, much can be gained from comparing statistical data on social production and social structure. See, for instance, F. Kharvat, *Sotsial'naia struktura sotsialisticheskogo obshchestva i ee razvitie v Chekhoslovakii: sravnitel'nyi analiz, vosproizvodstvo, perspektivy*, Prague, 1978.

4. Social Strata in the Class Structure of Socialist Society*

O. I. SHKARATAN and V. O. RUKAVISHNIKOV

Theoretical principles of the study

The class-based approach is the critical principle in the Marxist analysis of social life. Class relations are the dominant element in social structure. Classes, in turn, have their own intraclass structure, whose fundamental element is the social stratum. Strata may be identified by means of criteria that reflect the objective, dialectical interconnection between strata and class characteristics. In this process class indicators serve as the general and stratum indicators as the particular. These propositions are accepted by virtually all sociologists whose work has appeared in print or who have spoken at any of the three All-Union conferences on the social structure of Soviet society.

However, in moving to a more concrete analysis—beginning with the search for criteria of differentiation—researchers' views begin to diverge. In particular, some focus their attention on the urban/rural division of the working class, others on divisions in spheres of activity (agriculture, industry, services). In our view, important as it may be to distinguish the specific qualities of urban and rural workers or of workers engaged in differing

*Russian text © 1977 by "Nauka" Publishers. "Sotsial'nye sloi v klassovoi strukture sotsialisticheskogo obshchestva," *Sotsiologicheskie issledovaniia*, 1977, No. 2, pp. 62–73.

spheres of activity, these are not leading indicators in the system of social division of labor. Moreover, it must be remembered that the development of the working class and collective farm peasantry in the USSR is based upon a single (socialist) type of property. From this we deduce the need for a unified set of criteria to distinguish the basic intraclass elements.

Our point of departure in analyzing social differences in our society is the principle that they are connected not only with the existence of two forms of socialist property but also with a certain socioeconomic heterogeneity of labor, i.e., with its division into mental versus physical work, executive-type versus executor-type work, skilled versus unskilled work. This division, in our opinion, is of decisive importance in shaping the internal structure of classes in developed socialist society.

At this juncture there arises a need for a set of auxiliary categories that would enable us to identify actual social strata, distinguished primarily by the kind of work performed. In the literature on this subject the concepts of skill and complexity, content and character of work are normally enlisted for this purpose. The empirical indicators used are: occupational grouping (by complexity and skill-level); the distribution (of workers) by wage grades; division according to the duration of general education and occupational training. In all cases, the empirical data show that there are substantial distinctions in the behavioral and motivational characteristics of the ''strata'' thus identified. This bestows upon the chosen criteria a certain legitimacy which is, in principle, not unwarranted. By virtue of the interconnections among the diverse aspects of labor activity and labor relations, it is possible in all these cases to bring empiricial evidence to bear in depicting some real manifestations of the socioeconomic heterogeneity of labor. It therefore becomes necessary to determine which of the above categories (which are borrowed from the conceptual apparatus of economics) are of grestest value in the sociological analysis of social strata.

The concept of "skill" is given a twofold meaning by economists. In the first sense ''we refer to the totality of knowledge and habits corresponding to a certain level of work complexity characterized by objective indicators; in the second, to the degree to which a worker is prepared for the performance of the work, which, depending upon the extent to which the necessary knowledge and habits are assimilated, can deviate from the average requirements."[1] Apparently, this concept, which can be more strictly interpreted in the empirical sense as occupational skill, and more loosely as differences in wage grades, cannot serve as a point of departure in determining intraclass differences.

The concept of "work complexity," which is closely connected with the preceding concept, is useful for making the point that there are skilled and unskilled types of work which are differently valued by society and therefore yield differing monetary rewards. This concept, in our view, is also an inadequate basis for elaborating criteria of social strata. At the same time, though, both concepts are vital in describing strata that have already been identified.

A characteristic tendency in the development of mature socialism is the movement from partial to complete social homogeneity, from work as a necessity, the sole source of subsistence, to work as a requirement of the comprehensively developed personality. In this connection it is necessary to identify, first of all, the essential traits of the still remaining differences in the world of work, on the one hand, and the integrative processes found therein, on the other. The concept that reflects these traits could serve as the criterion which we are seeking to identify social strata. That concept, in our opinion, is the "character of work." When this concept is applied in the study of the social structure it has a wider meaning than in the sociology of work, where it is predominantly linked with the particular features of the branch division of labor.[2] In this case, though, the category of "character of work" is part of the conceptual complex "social division of labor"—"socioeconomic heterogeneity of labor"—"social-class structure of society." This is not the first time that the character of work and social structure have been studied in tandem in the Soviet literature.[3] However, since the content of the "character of work'' concept is variously interpreted, the connections between the aforementioned categories have not been unambiguously established.

The "character of work" concept, in our view, expresses the essential socioeconomic characteristics of work in general and the socioeconomic "genres" of work in particular. It serves to reveal the content of work and the social conditions in which it is performed, and also the connection between the content of concrete kinds of work, the assessment of their social significance and the extent to which a person's creative capacities are developed in the given kind of work.

We come now to the task of providing an empirical interpretation of this complex theoretical phenomenon. In previous studies we took occupation as the basic empirical indicator of character of work (and hence as our means of tackling the task of identifying strata). There were solid grounds for this decision.

As we know, the "surface" manifestation of socioeconomic diversity in work is the specialization of members of society in discrete kinds of work (occupational multiplicity, that is). The occupational division of labor is realized in a historically determined system of social relations. This is precisely what Lenin had in mind when he declared that employment statistics "can and should be used for an *approximate* determination of the way in which the population of Russia is divided into *basic* categories according to *class* position—that is, according to its position in the social system of production."[4] Lenin's observation is also applicable to research into social strata that presupposes a natural connection between certain groups of occupations and social strata.

The basic procedure for constructing a typology of strata in our earlier studies was the grouping of occupations. However, occupations *per se* directly reflect only the technical (functional) division of labor, not its economic heterogeneity. It is no accident that the use of occupation as an empirical indicator of social differentiation in sociological research has always required invoking additional indicators.

We have now concluded that it is inappropriate to directly use occupation as the sole indicator in describing the character of work. An occupational designation contains, in "coded" form, countless characteristics of the concrete work involved; it indicates the totality ("syndrome") of qualities, habits, abilities, and knowledge which the occupational activity demands of a worker. Therefore, in our empirical research, we sought to unravel this "syndrome" into its constituent elements, as it were, so as to make an informed assessment of such components of the character of work as: the degree of variety in the functions performed, the extent of self-organization, and the relative importance of executor-type and executive-type functions (bearing in mind the branch and the organizational specifics of the enterprise concerned). Job responsibilities and skills were also considered along with occupation.

It is possible to partially operationalize the "character of work" concept by structuring its basic components.

The first component is work content. This term is normally of help in pointing up the division of functions among job positions in the productive process (management of people, management of technological processes, performance of particular shop-floor operations). This category too, however, has varying degrees of applicability in sociological research on problems of work and in the study of social structure. In the latter case, the main focus is upon the socioeconomic (not the technical/organizational) facet of work content. The point is that each concrete kind of work has its own intrinsic technical/organizational content. As for the interrelation between the individual's work and the work of society, it is basically the same for all members of the given social group.

The empirical construct of "work content" is variously interpreted in the literature. In many cases, it is used so as to include the factors and results of work with a certain kind of content, but the exact content of work is not made sufficiently operational. For instance, level of mechanization—which is often taken as an indicator—is a factor of work with a particular content. On the other hand, many researchers turn to the workers themselves for information on the richness of content of the work they do. Then scales are drawn up showing "comparable measures" of the content of the work done by various worker groups. But it is obvious that there exist no hard-and-fast standards of comparison for the phenomena under investigation and that in comparing self-assessments, therefore, we are comparing elements that have been measured by different yardsticks.

It would appear that, in studying the content of labor, the unit of observation, the element which logically deserves consideration when measuring certain characteristics of work content, should be job position. This is the vehicle for those functions which invest work with a particular content. For various reasons, workers can make differing uses of the "resources" of a job position. This, however, depends upon the concrete individual. In our view, the characteristics of work content in a given job position should be measured not through self-assessments but by expert evaluations based upon specially designed scales of indicators that may be used to describe that content. As one possible approach, we shall examine below in more detail the partially operationalized concept of "work content" that was applied in our empirical research investigation.

Work of diverse content divorced from the context of the socioeconomic conditions under which it is performed is a source of formation of the units of social structure. Socioeconomic conditions are, as it happens, the second basic component of the character of work; they determine the division of society into major social units. In the broad sense, these latter comprise the entire system of socioeconomic relations in society. We shall examine some of the traits of these relations, in pursuit of our task of identifying strata. First of all, we consider the circumstance that under socialism all working people are simultaneously the co-owners of the country's means of production. Thus, property in the means of production is an integrating—not a differentiating—factor.

Second, it is vital to take account of the social attachment of categories of people to work with diverse content—which is another way of saying that various groups of people perform various functions. The degree of social attachment is not a strata-differentiating indicator: it simply depicts the general historical conditions of existence of strata.

Third, we consider the socioeconomic assessment of employed personnel as functional units in job positions, performing work with a particular content (not the assessment of the worker as an individual). This is a strata-differentiating indicator. Since they are engaged in economically heterogeneous work and participate to varying degrees in the satisfaction of society's requirements, workers are differentially assessed by society, as a result of which they either remain in the given kind of work or are encouraged to move on to another. Socioeconomic assessment is always concretely historical in nature; that is, it considers the scarcity of various benefits at society's disposal (wages, housing accommodation, etc.). In other words, the distribution of material and spiritual benefits is an economic mechanism for socially attaching people to work with diverse content.[5]

Thus, having undertaken to operationalize the character of work, we conclude that this is not wholly possible. But traits of the character of work which are embodied in the characteristics and functions of job positions (the socioeconomic content of work) and in the socioeconomic assessment of those who typically do work of a particular content, are accessible to indirect measurement.

**Methodology of measurement of
differences in the character of work**

In our study the content of work was structured as follows: 1) according to the relative importance of executor-type and executive-type functions; 2) according to the degree of variety of functions and mental pressure, the possibilities for innovation (lack of stereotyping, creativity, heuristic potential) in decision-making; 3) according to the degree of independence in regulating the sequence of work operations and the actual time of the job (degree of self-organization at work); and, 4) according to the amount of general education and occupational training required (complexity of work). As a rule, these characteristics of work content are not parameters, details that may be derived directly from the standard items in a job description. They are secondary characteristics derived from primary characteristics that are directly measurable.

We employed the following scales for the structural components of work content identified above, graded in rising order of intensity:

1. The scale for the indicator of "relative importance of executor-type and executive-type functions" had eight gradations: 1) executor; 2) leader of a small labor collective whose immediate subordinates have an average educational level up to the ninth grade; . . . 8) leader of a self-contained organization whose immediate subordinates have, on average, some kind of higher education.

2. The scale for the indicator of "degree of variety of functions, lack of stereotyping, creativity, heuristic potential" had five gradations (from "completely routine work" to "virtual absence of routine work"). Experts' assessments were used to assign a concrete job position to the appropriate gradation on the scale based on the following empirical indicators: occupation, job responsibilities, subsection (of enterprise or organization), and branch.

3. The scale for the indicator of "degree of self-organization at work (degree of independence in regulating the sequence of work operations, actual time of the job)" had three gradations, from "under detailed supervision" to "receives general instructions." Concrete job positions were assigned to the relevant gradations by experts on the basis of the same indicators as in the previous scale.

4. The scale for the indicator of "economic assessment of work complexity in the job position" was based upon the scale for the indicator of "educational level at the time of the survey." As we know, the economic assessment of work complexity in a job

position can be derived indirectly, by measuring outlays on the training of workers capable of performing work at the given level of complexity—that is, by measuring the required level of education and occupational training. In the interbranch and interzonal comparisons included in our task, it proved impossible to establish the comparability of length of occupational training. We therefore assessed work complexity in the job position by evaluating the necessary (requisite) level of education. We assumed a general correspondence between requisite and actual levels of worker education at the present time. This enabled us to use adjusted parameters of actual educational level as an indicator of work complexity for representatives of a given occupational group.

The second component of character of work, the socioeconomic conditions under which labor activity proceeds, was partially operationalized in accordance with one of its basic constituents, namely the assessment of the socioeconomic significance of work with a particular content (which we have chosen to call the "socioeconomic assessment of the worker").

The indicator for "socioeconomic assessment of the worker" was scaled by combining two indices: a) wages; and, b) qualitative and quantitative characteristics of housing. This eight-fold scale ranged from: 1) wages up to 100 rubles; a room in a communal apartment with living space of up to nine square meters per family member, or several rooms (which could be a separate apartment) with living space of up to seven square meters per family member; to 8) wages of more than 250 rubles; a separate apartment (two rooms or more) or a separate house with living space of more than nine square meters per family member.

Given that government statistics do not provide the necessary combinations of social data, we solved our problem by using local material collected during a special survey. In 1974 and 1975, we conducted a follow-up survey among the working population of three cities in the Tatar ASSR—Kazan', Al'met'evsk, and Menzelinsk.[6] The initial study had been conducted in 1967 as part of the research program of the USSR Academy of Sciences Institute of Ethnography. Our reasons for choosing Tataria and those three cities are already on record.[7]

We present below the results obtained by processing the data gathered in Kazan' (total sample: 3,600 persons). An analysis of the empirical data collected during the survey revealed the following very close links: degree of self-organization at work and variety of functions (T [Chuprov's coefficient] = 0.619), economic assessment and variety of functions (T = 0.434), economic assessment and self-organization (T = 0.438).

Their close mutual connections notwithstanding, the components of work content correlate far less strongly with socioeconomic assessment of the worker (the relationship between the latter and the degree of self-organization at work is T = 0.167, the degree of variety of functions—T = 0.175, the economic assessment of job position—T = 0.186, the relative importance of executor-type and executive-type functions—T = 0.157), which to some extent confirms our earlier suggestion that the character of work does, in fact, comprise two components.

By combining the distribution of individuals into groups according to the diverse content of their work with their distribution according to socioeconomic assessments, we end up with a totality of individuals distinguished by the charactrer of work performed. However, in actual practice it is inconvenient to work with this criterion, determined, as it is in the multidimensional space of its constituent elements. It therefore seemed natural to reduce it to some maximally appropriate, measurable, "index-type" variable that would enable us to produce a unidimensional, integral assessment of the character of work for every individual. This index would have to be highly "elastic," so that objects which differ substantially according to the given criterion (a plant director and a low skilled worker, for instance) could be accommodated at opposite ends of the resultant scale.

We shall designate the above-named structural components of work content as S_1, S_2, S_3, and S_4, with S_5 as the mean socioeconomic assessment of work with a given content.[8] We thus obtain a value, $I = S_1 S_2 S_3 S_4 S_5$, which can be called the Index of the

Character of Work (ICW).

Let us examine some of our results. For ease of analysis and computerized data processing, each of the approximately 1,000 occupations (or job titles) in the sample were initially assigned to one of 92 consolidated groups which were homogeneous in terms of functional work content.[9] The indices of character of work were calculated for these groups. (The results of these calculations are given in Table 1 and plotted on the figure.)

It is apparent from these calculations that our proposed ICW, though simple in construction, provides us with a sufficiently reliable division of the different items and an unambiguous interpretation of results. It is possible that, in applying our index formula, the same value of the index might be assigned to individuals with varying combinations of scores (gradations of particular components)—which is to say that an identical value of the index can be generated by differing sets of factors. In such situations, generally speaking, it is technically possible to draw erroneous conclusions in interpreting the results. In our case, however, there is a strong statistical relationship between the ICW and its components: the index and its constituent elements change in tandem, index construction allows for the interaction of factors, and the scales vary in length.[10] All of this virtually eliminates the possibility of persons being grouped together on the basis of an aggregate index if the assigned values for individual components are antithetical for whatever reason.

A typology of social strata

Since the underlying element in distinguishing strata is differentiation in the character for work, in the final analysis we can accept the fact that all individuals performing work of a particular nature belong to a given concrete stratum. In stricter and more precise terms we may formulate the following definition: a stratum is a social community that emerges and exists as the result of the social positioning of economically divided labor, when differences in the character of work create differences in requirements,

Table 1

Distribution of Occupational Groups in the Urban Population of Kazan' According to the Index of Character of Work

No.	Structural components of character of work Designation and number of occupational group (arranged in a consolidated 92-group tabulation)	Degree of variety of functions S_1	Degree of self-organiza-tion, S_2	Executor-executive, S_3	Average economic assessment of work complexity, S_4	Average socio-economic assessment S_5	Value of index of character of work
1.	Hospital orderly (24)	1	1	1.0	5.91	1.7	10.047
2.	Building custodian (23)	1	1	1.05	5.95	1.9	11.871
3.	Watchman (22)	1	1	1.05	5.75	2.2	13.284
4.	Unskilled and low skilled agricultural worker (15)	2	1	1	5.83	1.3	15.158
5.	Loader (19)	1	1	1.1	6.88	3	22.704
6.	Teletype operator (47)	1	1	1.1	9.96	2.2	23.232
7.	Sewing machine operator (25)	1	1	1.3	8.55	2.5	27.788
8.	Packer, laboratory technician without education (21)	1	1	1.2	9.20	2.6	28.704
9.	Ladle operator (18)	1	1	1.1	7.30	3.8	30.514
10.	Weaver (27)	1	1	1.3	7.65	3.3	32.824
11.	Linen store manager (56)	2	1	1.3	7.67	2.1	41.878
12.	Punch machine operator (26)	1	1	1.3	8.14	4.1	43.386
13.	Rigger (17)	2	1	6.83†	3.7†	3.7	43.712
14.	Barber (48)	2	2	1.0	7.43	1.5	44.580

15.	Cook (50)	2	1	1.5	8.91	1.8	48.114
16.	Draftsman (53)	2	1	1.2	9.70	2.1	48.888
17.	Electroplater (36)	2	1	1.1	7.81	3.6	56.232
18.	Installer (32)	1	1	1.5	10.07	4.2	63.441
19.	Retail sales clerk (30)	2	1	1.5	9.24	2.3	63.756
20.	Motor maintenance technician (33)	2	1	1.05	8.14	3.8	64.957
21.	Photolab technician (28)	2	1	1.1	10.09	3.0	66.594
22.	Quality checker (29)	2	1	1.3	9.96	2.6	67.330
23.	Carpenter, painter (52)	2	1	1.2	7.97	3.5	66.948
24.	Laboratory technician at scientific research institute (52)	2	1	1.4	11.07	2.0	66.024
25.	Operator (31)	2	1	1.3	8.55	3.1	68.913
26.	Timekeeper (55)	2	1	1.4	10.50	2.6	76.440
27.	Machine-tool operator (38)	2	1	1.1	8.64	4.1	77.933
28.	Bookkeeper/cashier (54)	2	1	1.6	10.06	2.7	86.918
29.	Furnace operator (44)	3	1	1.0	8.67	3.3	85.833
30.	Metalsmith (40)	2	1	1.5	6.67	4.6	92.046
31.	Excavator operator (34)	2	1	1.5	6.83	4.6	94.254
32.	Arc welder (39)	2	1	1.2	8.26	5.4	107.050
33.	Truck driver (35)	3	1	1.1	8.78	3.9	112.999
34.	Electrician (41)	3	1	1.3	9.29	3.6	130.422
35.	Metalworker/mechanic (42)	3	1	1.3	8.73	4.1	139.593
36.	Metalworker/installer (43)	3	1	1.3	9.11	4.3	152.755
37.	Accountant (77)	3	1	1.6	11.38	2.9	158.41
38.	Pharmaceutical dispenser (63)	3	1	1.8	12.44	2.4	162.518
39.	Streetcar or taxi driver (49)	3	2	1.0	9.20	3.7	204.240
40.	Projectionist (51)	2	2	1.7	8.89	3.5	211.582
41.	Actor (72)	5	1	1.1	12.27	3.6	242.946

Table 1

Distribution of Occupational Groups in the Urban Population of Kazan' According to the Index of Character of Work

No.	Structural components of character of work Designation and number of occupational group (arranged in a consolidated 92-group tabulation)	Degree of variety of functions S(1)	Degree of self-organiza-tion, S(2)	Executor-executive, S(3)	Average economic assessment of work complexity, S(4)	Average socio-economic assessment S(5)	Values of index of character of work
42.	Inventory manager (58)	3	2	2.3	8.52	2.2	258.667
43.	Kindergarten teacher (61)	3	2	1.4	12.55	2.6	274.092
44.	Nurse (64)	4	2	1.5	12.52	2.2	330.528
45.	Maintenance technician (45)	4	2	1.1	9.44	4.0	332.288
46.	Cutter (46)	4	2	1.5	9.89	3.6	427.248
47.	Production training instructor (62)	4	2	1.5	12.60	3.4	514.08
48.	Technician (78)	4	2	1.6	12.29	3.3	519.130
49.	Technicum teacher (62)	4	2	1.2	14.64	4.1	576.230
50.	Chief of security (59)	3	2	3.0	10.59	3.2	609.984
51.	Librarian (68)	3	2	1.9	13.84	3.9	615.326
52.	Retail store manager (65)	4	3	1.9	10.75	2.8	686.280
53.	Railway technician (79)	4	2	2.0	13.13	3.2	672.266
54.	Forestry worker (60)	4	2	2.0	11.33	4.2	765.408
55.	Postmaster (66)	4	3	2.0	12.25	3.0	882.00
56.	Engineer-economist (81)	4	2	2.1	13.93	3.9	912.694

57.	Head nurse (67)	4	2	3.2	14.20	2.7	981.504
58.	Section chief (80)	4	2	2.7	11.73	4.2	1,064.140
59.	Doctor (71)	4	2	2.3	14.58	4.2	1,126.74
60.	Instructor at higher educational institution; scientific research institute junior supervisory staff (70)	4	2	1.8	15.44	5.2	1,133.91
61.	Design engineer (83)	4	2	2.4	14.48	4.0	1,112.064
62.	Engineer-technologist (82)	4	2	2.6	13.95	4.1	1,189.656
63.	Militia officer (9)	4	2	2.1	13.80	5.5	1,275.120
64.	Army officer (7)	4	2	3.0	13.84	4.4	1,461.504
65.	Journalist (73)	5	3	2.0	14.21	5.3	2,259.390
66.	School principal (75)	5	3	3.2	13.91	4.1	2,737.488
67.	Party executive (89)	5	2	4.0	14.50	5.0	2,900.000
68.	Chief engineer (84)	5	2	3.9	14.38	5.2	2,916.264
69.	Shop superintendent (86)	4	3	4.1	13.67	4.6	3,093.794
70.	Head of planning section (85)	5	3	3.1	13.33	5.2	3,223.194
71.	Chief physician (76)	5	3	3.7	13.56	4.8	3,612.384
72.	Section head of district food products trade organization (74)	5	3	3.5	14.0	5.0	3,675.00
73.	Department head or laboratory superintendent (90)	5	3	3.7	16.22	4.4	3,960.924
74.	Director of scientific research institute (88)	5	3	3.8	15.20	5.9	5,111.76
75.	Director or chief engineer of industrial enterprise (87)	5	3	4.8	14.51	5.5	5,745.960

†These figures seem incorrect and are presumably misprints in the Russian text. —M.Y.

Scale of Index of Character of Work

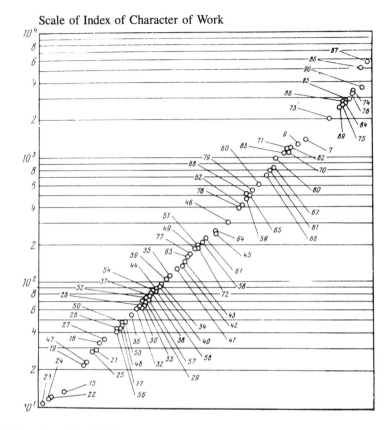

The scale of the ICW is presented in logarithmic values. The numbers in the figure correspond to the numbers assigned to groups in the 92-item tabulation (see Table 1). The dispersion of individual values of the ICW around a group mean is not shown, in the interests of visual clarity.

in the means of satisfying them, and in the structure of nonwork activity.

Social strata combine people who perform work that is similar in content and in socioeconomic assessment, and thus share similar levels of education, skill, income level, working and living conditions, and social ties. These human aggregates are attached to economically distinct types of work (labor activity) and therefore contribute unequally to economic and cultural growth, develop their capacities to diverse degrees, and typically exhibit varying levels of social and political activity.

From all the above it follows that a classification of individuals who vary according to the character of the work they perform may be used as the basis for constructing a typology of social strata. In our study such a classification was the natural result of our analysis of the empirical distribution of individuals according to the Index of Character of Work.

Once again we call the reader's attention to Table 1 and the figure. It is easy to see that the entire set of values of the ICW is naturally divided into subsets which differ according to the character of the work performed. We may observe a rather strict ordering of the social units under consideration according to the ICW. A substantial difference between the intelligentsia and workers is apparent. Similarly, we view as important the fact that the social stratum of employees, which a whole set of factors justify distinguishing as a separate stratum, turned out to be divided into two parts according to the ICW—employees without specialized training (nonspecialist employees), similar in social and economic position to skilled workers, and employees with secondary specialized education, similar to the group of highly skilled workers whose work combines mental and physical functions.

We present below a version of the typology of social strata in the population of a Soviet city, based upon a classification of individuals constructed from the proposed index. In deriving this typology we considered, of course, not only differences in the value of the index but also other circumstances determining both the singular features of the mode of life of strata as well as the convenience of applying the given typology when working with official statistical materials (Table 2).

We should stress once again that the calculated ICW values must not be applied beyond the local unit under study, without further verification. There is undoubtedly only one ''checklist'' of social strata, but the particular stratum affiliation of specific occupations can vary in some instances depending upon the local social situation.

On the basis of our results, the following strata may be identified in the Soviet urban population:

Table 2

Stability of Occupational Position and Social Stratum Affiliation in an Urban Population (Kazan', 1974)

Social stratum affiliation in previous job (former occupation and job responsibility)	All respondents, absolute percentage		no change in occupation and social affiliation	change in occupation, but same social affiliation	change in occupation and social affiliation	workers in low skilled physical work	workers in skilled, predominantly physical work	workers in highly skilled work combining physical and mental functions	employees in low skilled work not requiring specialized education	employees in skilled mental work requiring higher education*	employees in skilled mental work requiring higher education	employees in highly skilled mental executor-type or managerial work	other
						percentage of total							
Collective farmers and agricultural workers	73	100	2.5	—	97.5	40.0	40.0	9.5	4.0	6.0	1.25	1.25	2.5
Workers in low skilled physical work	486	100	22.3	28.8	48.9	24.6	0.8	8.4	9.8	3.8	1.6	—	

Workers in skilled, predominantly physical work	1,303	100	39.7	28.0	32.3	8.5	2.4	3.0	10.9	5.1	1.5	0.9
Workers in highly skilled work combining physical and mental functions	41	100	9.6	2.4	88.0	7.3	51.6	4.8	9.6	12.2	2.4	—
Employees in low skilled mental work not requiring specialized secondary or higher education	351	100	32.2	17.1	50.7	11.4	10.0	0.5	18.9	9.7	0.2	—
Employees in skilled mental work not requiring secondary or specialized education	567	100	38.2	18.5	43.3	2.9	5.4	0.2		24.0	5.3	5.7
Employees in skilled mental work requiring higher education	421	100	54.3	18.5	27.2	0.2	0.9	—	7.9		17.0	0.7
Employees in highly skilled mental executor-type work requiring higher education and supplementary training	136	100	38.3	38.3	23.4	1.4	0.7	0.7	5.1	15.3	—	—
Others	133	100	—	—	—	—	—	—	—	—	—	—
Total	3,516	100	35.3	26.9	37.6	5.8	6.6	1.1	3.4	8.0	3.7	0.7

*This column heading, which is duplicated by the one that follows, may have been intended to read: "employees in skilled mental work not requiring secondary or specialized education." —M.Y.

A. Workers
1. Workers in minimally skilled and low skilled physical work;
2. Workers in skilled, predominantly physical work;
3. Workers in highly skilled work that combines mental and physical functions.

B. Employees and specialists

4. Personnel in low-skilled mental work for which higher or secondary specialized education is not required (nonspecialist employees);
5. Personnel in skilled mental work for which secondary specialized education is required;
6. Personnel in skilled mental work for which higher education is required;
7. Personnel in highly skilled mental work for which higher education and supplementary training is required (scientific workers with academic degrees, high-caliber artistic intelligentsia, etc.)
8. Personnel in highly skilled managerial work.

We are thus able to distinguish: a) social strata; b) aggregates of people performing work of a similar nature; c) the social standing (social position, social status) of specific individuals in socialist society.

On the matter of gauging the social standing of individuals, in our view it must be said that an individual's social standing is determined not by the character of the work he performs per se, but by the extent (degree) of his socially developed preparedness to perform work of a particular content (education, skills). This must include the realization of the socially developed preparedness for work, which is embodied in the individual's contribution to the creation of material and spiritual goods and is individually assessed by society (for example, not the statistically average wage for work of a given content but the individual rate of pay)—

in other words, the individual socioeconomic assessment.[11] Moreover, a person's participation in management and his prestige (being chosen to join a self-management body, work-loads, commendations)—his social assessment, that is—is strictly individualized in the conditions under which social institutions operate in socialist society.

A social stratum is not just an arithmetic sum of individuals who perform similar functions and possess similar characteristics. Still less is it a sum of individuals who enjoy a similar social status (social standing). A stratum, as a scientific abstraction and an actual social unit, is a bearer of systemic qualities which cannot be reduced to the characteristics of individuals. These traits of a stratum come into view when the entire course of actual sociohistorical development and the functioning of a particular society are analyzed. These traits reveal a stratum's place in the system of intra- and interclass relations, its functions in the economy and in political life, its developmental trends, its past and its future.

We note in conclusion that in this sense our approach is diametrically antithetical to the theoretical constructs of Western sociology, which normally equate an individual's social position, his membership in a particular stratum (and class) and the characteristics of that stratum (or class).[12]

Notes

1. Ia. I. Gomberg, *Kvalifitsirovannyi trud i metody ego izmereniia*, Moscow, 1972, p. 91.
2. See, for instance, I. I. Changli, *Trud*, Moscow, 1973; V. Ia. Suslov, *Sotsiologiia truda*, Leningrad, 1971.
3. See, for instance, *Sotsial'naia struktura razvitogo sotsialisticheskogo obshchestva v SSSR*, eds.-in-chief M. N. Rutkevich, F. R. Filippov, Moscow, 1976; V. I. Osipov, *Sotsial'noe razvitie rabochego klassa v usloviiakh nauchno-tekhnicheskoi revoliutsii*, Saratov, 1975; *Rabochii klass i tekhnicheskii progress*, ed. G. V. Osipov et al., Moscow, 1965.
4. V. I. Lenin, *Polnoe sobranie sochinenie*, vol. 3, p. 502.
5. Marx was making an important point when he noted that under Communism differences in activity, in work, would not entail any privileges in terms of ownership and consumption.

6. The 1974–1975 study was conducted by the sector of social development of cities and regions of the USSR Academy of Sciences, Institute of Sociological Research (project director: O. I. Shkaratan, D. Hist. Sc., section head) in conjunction with the statistics department of the N. A. Voznesenskii Finance and Economics Institute of Leningrad (head of faculty: E. K. Vasil'-eva, D. Econ. Sc.). The study of the social differentiation of the urban population, while important, was not the sole research task. The following worked together to formulate the methodological materials for the research tasks: O. I. Shkaratan, E. K. Vasil'eva, M. V. Borshchevskii, V. O. Rukavishnikov, A. N. Alekseev, O. B. Bozhkov, G. V. Burkovskii, A. A. Veikher, V. D. Glukhov, E. Kh. Kunin, V. A. Petrov, T. Z. Protasenko, S. M. Rozet, I. V. Riabikova, and Iu. A. Shchegolev. The design of the sample (according to respondent's place of residence) was prepared by E. K. Vasil'eva and I. I. Eliseeva. The survey was supervised by O. B. Bozhkov, M. V. Borshchevskii, and I. V. Riabikova. The design of the information processing program was supervised by V. O. Rukavishnikov.

7. O. I. Shkaratan, "Problems of Social Structure of the Soviet City," *Filosofskie nauki*, 1970, no. 5; *Sotsial'noe i natsional'noe. Opyt etnosotsiologicheskogo issledovaniia*, Moscow, 1973.

8. It is essential to average the socioeconomic assessment of the worker in view of individual fluctuations in the values of a given parameter, which are caused by many factors, primary among which is the influence of the worker's personality. We examine the assessment of workers merely as functional units in a job position, performing work of a particular content. We do not examine society's aggregate socioeconomic assessment of its individual members.

9. The occupational grouping was done by V. A. Petrov and Iu. A. Shchegolev, staff members of the N. A. Voznesenkii Finance and Economics Institute of Leningrad.

10. The unevenness of our scales is essentially equivalent to the weighting of relevant components when scales of equal length are used.

11. The point is that the mathematical concept of a stratum as a "diffuse set" seems to approximate reality when a concrete individual's affiliation to a given stratum can only be established with a greater or lesser degree of probability. When the ICW is calculated, assigning individual indicator values to each person, there is a definite dispersion of the values of the ICW around the mean that typifies a given occupational group. This dispersion is caused by individual differences in the socioeconomic assessment of workers (wages, housing), and the potential divergence between the complexity of the work performed and a person's actual education. The ICW cannot, therefore, be used as an index of personal social status.

12. In Western research on social structure there is a glaringly obvious and sizable rift between fact and theory, which is typical of contemporary bourgeois sociology. On the empirical plane, researchers are content to simply record social inequality, using for descriptive purposes such indicators as the socioeconomic status of a given occupation, and individuals' education and income, for instance—taking, that is, a phenomenological approach to the problem of

social stratification. Yet when describing large social units and explaining the phenomenon of stratification, they violate the principle of correspondence of levels of generalization. This is the natural consequence of the positivist (more precisely Parsonian) concept of the correlation between the social, economic, occupational, and institutional structures of society, which explains a person's individual position in society in terms of his individual conduct. The "social" is dissolved in the "individual."

5. Changes in the Social Profile of Urban Residents*

O. I. Shkaratan

Among the most crucial tasks in the phase of developed socialism are the transformation of the social structure and the management of the process of establishing social homogeneity. At the territorial level, naturally enough, these planning and administrative tasks are formulated with due regard, first, for the social functions of the territorial communities (and specifically to guarantee optimum conditions for the sociodemographic reproduction of the entire population) and, second, for the specific conditions of the particular area and city.

The precondition for a valid solution of this set of problems consists in establishing the degree of integration and differentiation of the population, thus revealing existing strata and substrata, uncovering their developmental tendencies and the factors promoting the process of convergence, gauging the extent of differences in social parameters of urban communities that vary in functional characteristics and other indices of development for the given milieu, and studying territorial peculiarities in requirements and consumption, and other factors, modes and mechanisms of reproduction of the social structure. Once the problem is put this way, the need for a solid conception of the reproduction

*Russian text © 1982 by "Nauka" Publishers. "Peremeny v sotsial'nom oblike gorozhan," Akademiia nauk SSSR, Institut sotsiologicheskikh issledovanii, *Sovetskaia sotsiologiia*, Vol. II, Moscow, 1982, pp. 39–52.

of social structure in a territorial community becomes obvious. In turn, the elaboration of such a conception requires repeated studies of the population.

By replicating a study, whose results are given below, we can demonstrate that the same social-class groups and social strata are to be found in all territorial communities, although their proportions vary substantially in cities and urban conurbations of different types. These differences influence social relations.

Another important point is that territorial communities are the arena of consumption (nonproduction) activity, which encompasses all inhabitants, including those not participating in social production. It is vital, therefore, that, in addition to the dominant grouping by location within the system of social production, urban residents be grouped separately, according to the position they hold in consumption activity. We were able to identify nine groups in a typology based on the nature of nonproduction activity. These groups did not correspond to social strata distinguished according to the character of work. At the same time we established the existence of a predominant "range" of types of nonproduction activity for each social stratum.[1]

We also obtained certain results bearing on the problem of reproduction of social structure in urban territorial communities. In this chapter we shall discuss only those conclusions that point to the dynamic of the Soviet urban resident's social profile.

1. Reasons for choice of research subject

In the course of our study of social structure and the reproduction of the urban population of the USSR, we were faced with the task of choosing the particular research subject.

A typological selection that took account of the regional diversity in the conditions under which social population groups function and develop would have committed us to examining a large number of subjects. Our team could never have contrived to do full justice to all those subjects. It was therefore decided to restrict our examination of regional idiosyncracies to the limited government statistics we already had at hand.

Given our intention of selecting a research subject that would enable us to conduct an in-depth study of social indices, we started from the position that the average statistical indices of the subject should reflect present levels of economic and cultural development across the USSR. Strictly speaking, material gathered from such a subject is representative only of that subject. Yet, in view of the common features of basic socioeconomic and day-to-day cultural processes in the USSR, and the absence of qualitative differences in socioeconomic relations among regions of the country, one can accept the position that in basic respects these data depict a situation that is characteristic of the country as a whole.

After analyzing the statistical indices, we settled on the Tatar ASSR as our research subject. This republic qualified by meeting our basic research criteria. Its socioeconomic conditions are reasonably close to the countrywide norm; the population is multinational; the level of development may be rated as average relative to other areas of the USSR.

Tataria had long been part of the all-Russia market, so that capitalism was at an average level of development there by the time of the socialist revolution. After the revolution, in the course of socialist construction, it outstripped the other autonomous republics of the Volga region in attaining indices of socioeconomic and cultural development that were close to those of indigenous Russian regions.

Today, Tataria is an industrial-agrarian republic with a rather well-developed industry and agriculture. The republic resembles the rest of the Soviet Union not only in basic socioeconomic indices but also in sociodemographic indices. The censuses of 1959, 1970, and 1979 reveal a tendency for further convergence between these indices in Tataria and the average in the USSR as a whole. In 1959 the republican profile was rather more agrarian than the national average. The percentage of people engaged in mental work, the proportion of workers and employees, and also the percentage of those with higher or secondary education were somewhat below the national average. However, in none of these cases was the lag substantial. The 1979 census found that the Tatar ASSR was drawing ever closer to the All-Union norm in many indices. For instance, in the USSR as a whole, 62% of the population was urban, and in the Tatar ASSR, 63%.

Tataria is a highly developed and yet typical area, which reflects to a significant extent the social structure and social processes in the country as a whole. The basic classes and social strata of the population are quite well represented there.

With its large-scale industry, its scientific research institutes, higher educational institutions and cultural establishments, the Tatar ASSR offers its inhabitants broad opportunities for all kinds of activity, as well as for social mobility.

Ethnic processes are highly pronounced in Tataria, which was particularly important for our research objectives, considering the multinational nature of the Soviet state. Although the ethnic composition of the republic's population is extremely varied, the representatives of two ethnic groups—the Turkic and the Slavic—predominate.

We were thus able to examine the interaction of two economically and culturally developed Soviet nations (Russians and Tatars) which have lived side by side for a long time but still have significantly diverse cultural traditions and mores. The study was conducted in the heart of the Tatar settlement. The social composition of the Russian population in the towns of Tataria corresponds to population composition indices in indigenous Russian regions.

To proceed with the research it was necessary to select concrete venues, relying on a theoretical typology of cities. This typology was based upon indices of city size and branch structure, and upon occupational and national population composition. The choice finally came to rest upon Kazan', Al'met'evsk, and Menzelinsk.

Kazan' is the center of a centripetal conurbation. It is a large city with a multibranch economy, in which all the basic social groups of the population are represented, and a city with a high level of social mobility. In 1970 62.3% of the country's urban population lived in such cities. Kazan' may be compared with large cities such as Perm', Cheliabinsk, and Novosibirsk, not only in number of inhabitants but also in other sociodemographic indices.

Al'met'evsk is a middle-sized, rapidly developing industrial city, whose principal industry is oil. Occupational mobility is relatively intensive. Interbranch mobility, especially in the sphere of material production, is limited. In number of inhabitants and employment structure, Al'met'evsk may be compared with cities in the RSFSR such as Balashov (Saratov region), Kuznetsk (Penza region), Troitsk (Cheliabinsk region), and Bataisk (Rostov region). In 1970, 18% of the country's urban residents lived in cities like these.

Menzelinsk is a smallish town, with underdeveloped, predominantly local industry which contains only isolated elements of the social structure of the country's urban population. The opportunities for social mobility are extremely limited. This is an old town, founded in 1645, which is not now part of any conurbation. Menzelinsk can be compared with old, rather small towns in the RSFSR such as Iaransk (Kirov region), Nazyvaevsk (Omsk region), and Pochep (Briansk region). In 1970, 14.8% of the country's population lived in such towns.

The immediate subject of study in these three Tatar ASSR cities was the permanently resident adult working population. This concretization of our research subject precluded any analysis of the specific social characteristics of young people who had left their jobs to take up full-time study, and also people of working age who were not engaged in social production.

The first stage of the research, a sample survey of the population in these three cities, was conducted in 1967,[2] and the followup was done in 1974–1975.[3]

As we know, there are various ways to sample a population that is engaged in social production: selection and questioning by place of work; selection by place of work; questioning by place of residence; selection and questioning by place of residence (door-to-door survey).

In 1974–1975, we chose the latter method, since it enabled us to shed light on the socio-occupational structure of the urban population as a whole and made it possible to study the entire system of intraurban social ties, the pattern of reproduction of various population groups, and the level and structure of consumption.

Passport office records and voter lists were used as the most practicable way of constructing the sample. In Kazan' and Al'-met'evsk we utilized a three-tier sampling model, divided into districts. In Menzelinsk, a town of compact dimensions, respondents were mechanically selected from voter lists. The sample comprised 856 working people. A final sample of 3600 permanently resident working adults was selected in Kazan', while in Al'met'evsk there were 1895 subjects, bunched around 100 control points.

2. Interpretation of data and conclusions

The relative number of representatives from a given social-class group or stratum in the total working population of Kazan', Al'-met'evsk, and Menzelinsk varied because of the distinctive branch structure of the economy in each city. Thus, the percentage of people employed in industry in Kazan' and Al'met'evsk in 1974 was almost identical, and significantly higher than in Menzelinsk. A larger share of the population of Al'met'evsk was employed in the construction industry than was the case in Kazan' or Menzelinsk. Kazan', though, had a far higher proportion of people employed in highly skilled mental work, and a noticeably smaller percentage of unskilled and low–skilled workers.

As might have been expected, the proportion of people engaged in the more skilled kinds of work rose considerably in all three cities between 1967 and 1975.

Tables 1, 2, and 3 present the principal social-production characteristics of the employed and their dynamics from 1967 to 1975.

Table 1

Educational Levels of Urban Residents

Social stratum	City*	Education at commencement of labor activity, years		Education at time of survey, years	
		1967	1975	1967	1975
Workers:					
in unskilled and low skilled	K	6.6	6.42	7.0	6.8
physical work	A	5.6	6.2	6.1	6.3
	M	5.6	5.33	5.8	6.0
in skilled, predominantly	K	7.4	8.1	7.9	8.6
physical work	A	7.0	7.8	7.5	8.1
	M	6.8	7.2	7.4	7.3
in highly skilled work	K	8.2	9.5	10.4	10.9
combining mental and	A	9.6	10.0	11.6	11.4
physical functions	M	11.3	8.5	12.8	9.1
Employees and specialists:					
in low skilled mental work	K	8.8	9.6	9.2	10.2
(nonspecialist employees)	A	9.1	9.4	9.4	10.0
	M	8.9	9.5	9.1	9.8
in skilled (mental) work	K	12.5	11.9	14.0	13.4
requiring secondary specialized	A	11.6	11.8	13.2	13.1
or higher education	M	12.5	11.8	13.5	12.7
in highly skilled mental work	K	12.1	13.4	14.3	15.0
requiring higher education and	A	13.4	11.8	14.5	13.8
supplementary training (personnel with academic degrees, high-caliber artistic intelligentsia)	M	—	—	—	—
in highly skilled managerial	K	11.1	11.7	12.9	14.5
work	A	11.0	11.5	12.9	13.6
	M	11.7	10.6	12.2	12.9

* K = Kazan'; A = Al'met'evsk; M = Menzelinsk

The data demonstrate a stability of cadres in the economy of these cities: a preponderance of people with relatively prolonged work experience, both overall experience and by occupation. The next, equally obvious, conclusion is that working people's level of educational training rises considerably in the course of their labor activity. Typically, those who make the transition to the intelligentsia exhibit greater increases in education than those who remain workers (Table 1). For instance, the average level of education of persons in highly skilled managerial work was 14.5 years of schooling at the time of the survey and 11.7 years at the beginning of their work activity. This means that a significant portion of these managerial cadres had been promoted from the ranks of workers—i.e., increases in educational attainment lead in most cases to a change in social position.

As was to be expected, the social-production parameters of highly skilled workers, worker-intellectuals, are particularly high.

As for wages, this indicator reveals little differentiation between strata, but, as our data show (Table 2), there is considerable differentiation within strata on grounds of pay. This means that today payment for work is, to a decisive extent, merely an indicator of the labor contribution of the individual and is far less indicative of the significance that society attaches to work of varying content.

These tables, along with other material, demonstrate that the social strata we have identified here do actually exist. They also permit us to makes judgments about the "zones" (aspects of social life) where the processes of convergence are strongest and those where integrating processes are lagging somewhat.

It is interesting to observe changes in the indices of the identified social strata from 1967 to 1975. In Kazan', for example, there was a rise in the average educational level of skilled and highly skilled workers (by an average of 0.8 years of schooling), while the educational level of people doing unskilled physical work slipped a little (from 7.0 to 6.8 years of schooling). The educational level of highly skilled managerial personnel rose to 14.5 years of schooling, compared to 12.9 years in 1967.

This jump in the average educational level of managerial cadres is explained by a substantial decrease in the number of uncredentialed specialists with practical experience in these positions (7.1% of the 1975 respondents had been educated only through grades 10–11, compared to 27.9% in 1967) and an increase in the percentage of specialists with higher education (65.0% in 1975 compared to 44.1% in 1967).

Table 2

Average Wages of Urban Residents

| | | | | | Percentage of minimum** | |
Social stratum	City*	1967	1975	1975 as % of 1967	1967	1975
Workers:						
in unskilled and low skilled	K	73.8	93.8	127.10	100	100
physical work	A	62.9	82.8	131.63	100	100
	M	57.9	77.5	133.85	100	100
in skilled,	K	99.5	139.4	140.10	134.82	148.61
predominantly	K	105.7	141.3	133.88	167.25	170.10
physical work	K	87.3	113.4	129.95	150.77	146.38
in highly skilled work	K	97.9	142.4	145.45	132.65	151.81
combining mental and	A	115.6	175.0	151.38	183.78	211.35
physical functions	M	—	—	—	—	—
Employees and specialists:						
in low skilled	K	75.7	99.6	131.57	102.57	106.18
mental work	A	77.4	98.6	127.39	123.05	119.08
(nonspecialist employees)	M	67.1	85.3	127.12	115.89	110.06
in skilled mental work re-	K	111.0	129.7	116.84	150.41	138.27
quiring secondary	A	111.7	128,6	115.13	177.58	155.31
specialized or higher	M	106.6	117.1	109.85	184.11	151.09
education						
in highly skilled mental work	K	159.9	166.0	106.41	212.60	176.97
requiring higher education	A	146.3	153.0	105.19	232.59	185.87
and supplementary training	M	—	—	—	—	—
(personnel with academic						
degrees, high-caliber artistic						
intelligentsia)						
in highly skilled	K	164.3	204.9	124.71	222.63	218.44
managerial work	A	178.3	203.4	114.07	283.46	245.65
	K	141.8	169.4	119.46	244.90	218.58

* K = Kazan'; A = Al'met'evsk; M = Menzelinsk
** The wages of unskilled and low skilled workers are taken as the minimum.

The data attest to a sharp rise in the educational level of
workers. It is symptomatic that in Kazan' the average educational
level at the commencement of labor activity rose in all the designated strata, except among people doing unskilled physical work.
(In 1975, it was at no less than an eight-grade level for all groups,
which was a substantial improvement over 1967.) The most striking rise was in the average educational level ''at the starting

Table 3

Differences in Levels of Living (Kazan')*

Index	Social stratum	1967	1975
Wage, rubles	Average for whole sample	99.3	130.8
	Personnel in highly skilled managerial work	164.3	204.9
	Workers in unskilled physical work	73.8	93.8
	Workers in skilled work	99.5	139.4
	Personnel in skilled mental work	111.0	129.7
Size of living space per family member, sq. m.	Average for whole sample	6.0	7.3
	Personnel in highly skilled managerial work	7.8	9.2
	Workers in skilled work	5.9	6.7
	Personnel in skilled mental work	6.9	7.8
Income per family member, rubles	Average for whole sample	59.3	77.5
	Personnel in highly skilled managerial work	74.1	101.2
	Workers in unskilled physical work	50.0	68.0
	Workers in skilled work	58.4	78.3
	Personnel in skilled mental work	66.4	90.0

* Maximum and minimum values shown for each index

block'' for workers in highly skilled work combining mental and physical functions—9.5 grades in 1975, compared to 8.2 in 1967. It should be noted that in 1975 the education level for all the designated social strata was higher than the average educational level ''at the starting block''—for the same respondents. This is evidence that people are advancing their education without interrupting their labor activity.

Let us compare wage indices in 1967 and 1975. Wages were much higher in 1975 for all social strata. In the cities of Tataria the general relationship between maximum and minimum wages of the social strata was only slightly over 2:1 and remained almost

Table 4

Social Activity of Urban Residents

Social stratum	City*	Proportion involved in rationalization and invention, %		Proportion of CPSU members, %	
		1967	1975	1967	1975
Workers:					
in unskilled and low skilled	K	3.0	4.8	3.7	4.5
physical work	A	4.8	3.3	3.8	1.2
	M	2.5	3.4	3.8	2.2
in skilled, predominantly	K	14.5	26.5	9.5	7.9
physical work	A	17.2	24.3	9.6	7.4
	M	15.7	13.8	11.4	5.8
in highly skilled work	K	36.6	29.5	20.0	15.9
combining mental and	A	32.4	83.3	35.1	41.6
physical functions	M	—	—	—	—
Employees and specialists:					
in low skilled mental	K	4.9	9.2	7.3	8.8
work (nonspecialist	A	4.8	5.9	8.1	7.2
employees)	M	3.6	4.8	7.8	7.1
in skilled mental work	K	21.9	22.4	18.9	20.0
requiring secondary special-	A	15.2	20.7	24.2	13.8
ized or higher education	M	9.6	11.4	29.6	21.2
in highly skilled mental work	K	43.5	43.4	25.9	14.8
requiring higher education and	A	54.5	35.7	54.5	21.4
supplementary training (personnel	M	—	—	—	—
with academic degrees, high-caliber					
artistic intelligentsia)					
in highly skilled	K	61.1	43.6	61.3	60.7
managerial work	A	50.0	49.2	55.1	48.3
	M	9.1	29.6	54.5	66.7

'*K = Kazan '; A = Al 'met 'evsk; M = Menzelinsk

unchanged in the seven years between the two surveys.

Table 3 presents some information on living standards of strata showing the minimum and maximum values of relevant parameters, and also of the mass strata of skilled workers and skilled personnel doing mental work.

Table 4 traces changes in social activity among urban residents in the period under consideration. The data bespeak a rise in creative activity among representatives of all social strata and a reduction in differences in the level of that activity.

Stability in social and occupational position is an important social-production characteristic of the population. To study the degree of stability among the social categories of the urban population, the questionnaire used in the 1974–1975 interviews inquired about the respondent's previous occupation and job responsibilities, as well as his current situation. The information we received enabled us to examine the direction of occupational and social mobility, and the extent to which changes in occupational and social position are connected.

It was found that among the Kazan' residents questioned, 38.3% had changed neither their occupation nor, by the same token, their social position over the course of their labor activity; 29.6% had changed their occupation and job responsibilities, but, according to the classification we had adopted, had remained within the same social stratum. For 37.6% of the respondents a change of occupational position and job responsibilities had led to a change in social position.

Analysis shows that, of the Kazan' residents questioned who had begun their labor activity as collective farmers or agricultural workers, 40% initially became unskilled workers, and 40% skilled workers. In 22.3% of the cases unskilled workers retained their previous occupation and social position, and in 22.8% of the cases changed occupations while remaining in the same social stratum, i.e., somewhat more than 50% of unskilled workers are stable in their social status. The majority of those who changed their social position became skilled workers (24.6%) or employees without specialized education (8.4%). A certain portion of unskilled workers—people whose social standing is fluid—are simultaneously studying in secondary or higher educational institutions. The data confirm this: of previously unskilled workers, 9.8% have taken on job responsibilities which require specialized education, and 3.8% are in positions requiring higher education.

As for skilled workers—the status of some 68% of them is stable. About 40% of these are also occupationally stable; 17.5% of erstwhile skilled workers become specialists whose job responsibilities require specialized secondary or higher education. This is a natural and extremely healthy tendency which betokens, on the one hand, high stability of the skilled worker cadre core, and, on the other, an overwhelming propensity to become specialists when social mobility does occur.

In only one respect did our findings surprise us at first sight. Highly skilled workers (worker-intellectuals) were found to be exceedingly unstable in both social and occupational position: 88% of them changed occupations—51.6% took up skilled physical work, 7.3% became unskilled workers, and 23.5% became specialists with secondary specialized or higher education. Instability of this kind calls for further analysis. However, the findings given above on changes in education and other indices of workers in this category furnish sufficient grounds for suggesting that people originally chosen for these job positions did not have the requisite potential and were obliged to return to their previous occupations. This confirms an opinion already voiced in the press: that the process of shaping a worker-intellectual stratum is only just beginning, as the occupational groups appropriate to that stratum make their appearance among employed personnel.

As for occupational and social mobility among the intelligentsia, the important thing here is that stability of social position is accompanied by a high level of occupational mobility associated with interoccupational movement. A change of occupation by persons with higher education doing mental work is often accompanied by an upward shift in social position. Of the 27.2% whose social position changed, 17.0% moved into the stratum of personnel in highly skilled work and supervisors of large work collectives. The social position of those doing highly skilled mental work was the most stable of all, and a significant portion of those who changed their social position transferred into the stratum of personnel with higher education doing mental work.

A comparison of changes in the level of cultural consumption produced interesting results. In order to yield a description of cultural activity, the questionnaire listed 30 indices covering the principal ways in which urban residents occupy their time outside working hours.

An analysis of the interconnections between types of cultural activity and social position among the inhabitants of Kazan' allowed us to identify the following as the most informative indices:[4]

1. Reading materials in one's specialty (T = 0.185)
2. Personal collection of books (T = 0.169)
3. Reading works of fiction (T = 0.110)
4. Cinema-going (T = 0.107)
5. Theater-going (T = 0.106).

We shall divide our findings in three ways in order to compare the indices of cultural activity in the various types of cities. First of all, we shall seek to establish the disparity in consumption among the cities as a whole, then between the social strata within each city, and finally between identical social strata in different cities.

For almost all kinds of cultural activity the advantages of living in a large city are obvious. Certain exceptions—a higher rate of cinema attendance in Menzelinsk, for instance—stem from the fact that since a small town has significantly fewer informational channels, those which do exist carry a heavier load.

For a more detailed analysis, we shall limit our examination of cultural activity to such indices as the reading of fiction and theatergoing. For these parameters, too, a large city has its advantages over middle-sized and small cities. People read fiction and go to the theater an average of 1.1 times more in Kazan' than in Al'met'evsk and Menzelinsk (1.3 times more in 1967).

To describe the cultural activity of social strata we shall take the two most numerous groups: a) skilled workers; and b) skilled personnel in mental work which requires specialized secondary or higher education. Table 5 enables us to observe the differences in cultural consumption between the designated social strata within each city.

From Table 5 it can clearly be seen that the gap between social strata is wider the larger the city (Kazan': 1.3–1.6; Menzelinsk: 1.1–1.3). Things have changed since 1967, when the larger the city the narrower was the gap between strata.

We may note, therefore, that the large city has apparently been

Table 5

Intensity of Various Forms of Cultural Activity*

		1967		1975	
Index	City**	Skilled workers	Skilled intelligentsia	Skilled workers	Skilled intelligentsia
Reading works	K	1	1.3	1	1.3
of fiction	A	1	1.5	1	1.2
	M	1	0.9	1	1.1
Theater-going	K	1	1.3	1	1.6
	A	1	2.0	1	1.2
	M	1	1.4	1	1.3

*Numbers given in the table refer to number of times one group surpasses the other in intensity of involvement in the particular kind of cultural activity
** K = Kazan'; A = Al'met'evsk; M = Menzelinsk

the scene of an increase in interstratum differentiation of the population in the cultural sphere, while in middle-sized and small cities, on the other hand, the process of convergence of strata has been strengthened.

Examining the cultural activity of identical social strata in various cities, we note that the gap between cities is approximately the same for both indices (1.1 times, on average). In 1967, there was a more significant gap between cities. For instance, the skilled workers of Al'met'evsk and Menzelinsk visited the theater about 1.6 times more frequently than their counterparts in Kazan', while representatives of Kazan"s skilled intelligentsia surpassed their counterparts in Al'met'evsk and Menzelinsk by 2.3 to 3.7 times for the same index.

Thus, characteristics of social strata in cities of differing types revealed a clear tendency toward convergence in the years between the two surveys.

These are some of the findings concerning changes in the social profile of residents of three typical Soviet cities over a relatively short period of time.

Notes

1. See O. I. Shkaratan, G. V. Eremicheva, G. V. Kanygin, I. V. Riabikova, "The Character of Non-Work Activity and Social Differentiation of Urban Residents," *Sotsiologicheskie issledovaniia*, 1979, no. 4.

2. The research was conducted by the USSR Academy of Sciences' Institute of Ethnography (supervisor: O. I. Shkaratan). See *Sotsial'noe i natsional'-noe: Opyt etnologicheskikh issledovanii po materialam Tatarskoi ASSR*, Moscow, 1973; O. I. Shkaratan, *Problemy sotsial'noi struktury rabochego klassa SSSR*, Moscow, 1970; I. P. Trufanov, *Problemy byta gorodskogo naseleniia SSSR*, Leningrad, 1973.

3. The survey was conducted by the Section of Social Development of Cities and Villages, USSR Academy of Sciences, Institute of Sociological Research (supervisor: O. I. Shkaratan) with assistance from the Statistics Department of the N. A. Voznesenskii Finance and Economics Institute of Leningrad (supervisor: E. K. Vasil'eva). The survey materials have never been published in monograph form.

4. T = Chuprov's coefficient.

6. The Interconnection between Work and Consumption

A Provisional Typological Analysis*

A. A. OVSIANNIKOV

The analysis of the problem of work activity is confined, as a rule, to an examination of the sphere of production. The discussion usually covers improvements in rates of pay, raising the occupational and skill levels of workers, relations within the collective, and so forth. The shaping of economic wants and interests that encourage participation in social production and, hence, the measure of consumption resulting from work efforts, more often than not remain outside of the researchers' field of vision. But the successful stimulation of work activity requires the study of the mechanism of interaction between work and consumption activity.

Economic interests and work incentives are characterized primarily by the current state and developmental level of the consumption sphere. It makes no sense to speak of stimulating work activity without due observation of the relationship between the measure of work and the measure of consumption. [1]

The public's main sources of monetary income are work in social production, payments from the social consumption fund,

*Russian text © 1984 by "Nauka" Publishers. "Vzaimosviaz' truda i potrebleniia: opyt tipologicheskogo analiza," *Sotsiologicheskie issledovaniia*, 1984, No. 1, pp. 84–87.

and the sale of produce from personal household plots. The relative shares of these components differ significantly for representatives of the various social groups. There is economic justification for the kind of differentiation between families within the consumption sphere which is based on differences in the quantity and quality of work performed by employed members of these families.

Hence we conclude that to stimulate work activity it is necessary to adopt a differentiated approach which will establish a correspondence between categories of workers with differing conditions and character of work, on the one hand, and the consumption groups to which their families belong, on the other. By comparing the results of people's work activity and the behavior of their families in the consumption sphere, it is possible to uncover the system of requirements and interests that is specific to each group, and, consequently, to strengthen incentives for work activity.

This approach is also advisable because it is necessary to "pin the problem down," to define its precise boundaries and its concrete social location. What we have in mind is obtaining information on the working and living conditions not of the population as a whole but of particular types within the population which differ in the nature of their activity in the spheres of production and consumption. Obviously, the degree of imbalance in the measure of labor and consumption among representatives of the various groups varies, and the measures taken will be most effective if they are directed first and foremost toward those groups where that imbalance is most palpable.

According to data from experimental research conducted as part of a project devoted to the study of the mode of life [3, 4], the basic cause of the differentiation of the population in the consumption sphere (in 42.7% of the cases) is work activity, evaluated by means of factor and component analysis according to the conditions and results of the work performed by employed family members.

Table 1

Some Indices of Family Material Welfare

Consumption type*	Age of Family, in years	Per capita income, in rubles	Family load**	Proportion of families with per capita income of more than 90 rubles, in %	Living space, square meters per person	Amount of property, in thousands of rubles
I	40.9	46.6	1.10	3.3	14.3†	2.3
II	13.5	65.5	1.17	12.3	7.9	3.6
III	7.9	62.5	1.96	5.9	6.1	2.2
IV	15.5	65.2	1.86	12.5	8.3	4.6
V	16.9	74.3	1.28	26.3	8.4	5.2
VI	15.2	77.3	1.40	25.8	8.7	6.0
VII	20.0	74.9	1.35	40.9	8.3	9.3
VIII	23.8	83.5	1.41	61.5	8.8	8.0
Average for sample	17.9	63.5	1.54	19.8	8.3	5.0

*Type I basically comprises retirees; Type II, families of unskilled workers; Type III, families of mixed social composition which are, as a rule, young; Type IV, skilled workers; Type V, nonspecialist employees; Type VI, employees in middle-level management; Type VII, education and healthcare personnel; and Type VIII, employees holding leading positions.

** Family load is calculated by dividing the total number of family members by the number of working family members.

† This figure seems incorrect and is presumably a misprint in the Russian text.—M.Y.

Table 2

Nature of Labor Activity Performed by Working Family Members

Consumption type	Social position of family members, in %					Participation in work organization, in %			Proportion of family members with secondary specialized or higher education, in %
	Employees and engineering-technical personnel	Education and healthcare personnel	Workers		Retirees and dependents	Supervisors	Executives	Executors	
			Skilled workers	Unskilled workers					
I	3.6	—	8.1	5.1	83.2	—	7.1	92.9	1.2
II	2.7	0.9	14.4	40.1	41.9	—	2.3	97.7	—
III	5.0	2.8	26.5	17.3	48.4	0.7	7.7	91.6	13.6
IV	3.3	1.6	40.6	13.6	40.9	0.5	12.0	87.5	12.4
V	15.2	4.1	20.1	14.9	45.7	4.6	21.6	73.8	22.8
VI	21.3	1.6	28.5	9.9	38.7	6.1	53.9	40.0	32.8
VII	11.4	13.8	16.9	6.7	51.2	9.1	20.4	71.5	33.1
VIII	35.8	7.3	19.5	5.9	31.5	25.2	16.2	58.5	34.4
Average for sample	8.7	3.3	24.5	16.8	46.7	3.7	15.9	80.4	14.9

The data in the tables point to a close link between the nature of work activity and the level of material well-being. Housing conditions and the structure and volume of family consumption are higher and better in those groups whose representatives have been engaged in more complex, higher quality work over a period of many years. And yet one cannot help but notice that in our sample the families of employees engaged in trade, everyday services, and organs of administration, who typically perform executor-type work and whose pay and income level in general are relatively low, still own a fairly significant amount of property in value terms (double the average indicator).

One final point: a rise in per capita income above the 90-ruble level, as a result of pay raises, bonuses, and so forth, does not affect the structure and volume of consumption. This is most applicable to families belonging to consumption types VII and VIII, but also applies to types V and VI. Working people in families whose monetary income is above this threshold will evidently be more responsive to such inducements to work activity as expenses-paid trips, coupons for the acquisition of scarce goods, and moral approbation. A rise in per capita income is instrumental in stimulating work activity among other types of families.

While the conclusions presented here are based upon experimental data, the factors we have noted show that a differentiated approach to the study of ways and means of stimulating work activity enables us not only to describe this phenomenon, but also to frame concrete recommendations. Of course, the potential of a typological approach in this field will not be fully realized until wider empirical research is done. Such was the gist of decisions taken at the June 1983 plenary session of the CPSU Central Committee, where it was stressed that "such questions as the optimization of distributive relations . . . are especially pressing. . . ." [2] Only work, and the results of that work, should determine working people's material welfare.

Bibliography

1. V. I. Lenin, [On Trade Unions, the Current Moment and the Mistakes of Comrade Trotsky], *Polnoe sobranie sochinenie, vol. 42, p. 212.*

2. *Materialy Plenuma Tsentral'nogo Komiteta KPSS. 14–15 iuniia 1983 g.*, Moscow, Politizdat, 1983, p. 70.

3. N. M. Rimashevskaia, A. A. Ovsiannikov, [The Consumption Behavior of the Population: Theory and Results of Modeling], *Ekonomika i matematicheskie metody*, issue 6, 1981.

4. A. A. Ovsiannikov, [The Differentiation of Consumption Behavior], *Sotsiologicheskie issledovaniia*, 1982, No. 3.

5. *Tipologiia potrebleniia*, Moscow, Nauka, 1978.

7. The Statics and Dynamics of Occupational Prestige

From the Findings of the Comparative International Research Project "The Life-Paths of Young People in Socialist Society"*

T. A. BABUSHKINA and V. N. SHUBKIN

During the period when the research project entitled "The Life-Paths of Young People in Socialist Society" [*Zhiznennye puti molodezhi v sotsialisticheskom obshchestve*] was being prepared and conducted, a series of theoretical and empirical studies were carried out in the USSR, including a pilot survey ("Starting Out" [*Nachalo puti*]) that was conducted among young workers and students who some years previously, before leaving secondary school, had filled out our "School-leaver Questionnaire" [*Anketa vypusknikov*].[1] In addition, materials from questionnaires administered annually to young people for over a decade were processed. (This paper uses findings from the 1963 and 1973 surveys.) In 1978, young workers and employees in Kostroma, from 16 to 30 years of age, were also asked to complete a questionnaire in a special mass survey which was simultaneously launched in the Hungarian People's Republic, the German

*Russian text © 1980 by "Rabochii klass i sovremennyi mir," "Progress" Publishers. "Prestizh professii v statike i dinamike (po materialam sravnitel'nogo mezhdunarodnogo issledovaniia 'Zhiznennye puti molodezhi v sotsialisticheskom obshchestve')," *Rabochii klass i sovremennyi mir*, 1980, No 5, pp. 54–63.

Democratic Republic, the Polish People's Republic, the People's Republic of Bulgaria, and the Czechoslovak Soviet Socialist Republic.[2]

We feel that some of the results of these studies are interesting on their own merits. This is particularly true of the problem of occupational prestige—the attitude of young men and women to jobs involving physical or mental work, specific variations in these assessments in different parts of the country, and the changing nature of these assessments.

Great theoretical and practical significance attaches to the study of prestige, of the attractiveness of various occupations as perceived by differing social and demographic groups. However, empirical sociological research into occupational prestige was only begun here relatively recently.

Evaluations of occupational prestige used by sociologists are subjective assessments which reflect the given individual's attitude toward various occupations. But this does not mean that they are random. "Even misty formations in people's brains are necessary products, a kind of vapor emanating from their material life process which can be empirically established and which is linked with material preconditions."[3]

The evaluation of occupational prestige carries, as it were, the stamp of past and present conceptions which a given group has developed on the basis of its interaction with other groups. Naturally, these evaluations are not merely the results of personal experience. They are a kind of amalgam of personal and past experience—that is, a form of social information which a person inherits, to a certain extent, from previous generations.

A person develops an attitude toward various occupations even before coming into contact with representatives of those occupations. Thanks precisely to that "inherited information" which a person acquires during the process of his socialization (through family, school, friends, the mass media), he has already had some orientation to evaluating given jobs, given routes to take, even before he is faced with the need to choose an occupation. The stability of this "inherited information" creates a certain stability and repetitiveness in the occupational and behavioral evaluations of members of the same social strata.

Moreover, human knowledge about social life, the experience which a particular class or social stratum possesses, is not invariably universal in nature. Knowledge reflects the objective position which the given class or stratum occupies in the social structure, and its relations with representatives of other social strata. Evaluations, therefore, have stratum-specific nuances. Attitudes toward an occupation, as an indicator of social links that are based on the social division of labor, are no exception in this regard. These evaluations differ among different strata. They are determined by the accumulated experience of a given class, stratum, or group, and by their specific interests. And this brings about a unique metamorphosis, wherein a structure which is by its very nature unordered comes to be regarded as hierarchical. This is because different social aggregates view the social structure through the prism of differing value systems. Thus the notion of "superiority" and "inferiority" comes to be applied to various elements of the social structure.

Occupational prestige results from a complex interaction of personal experience and information acquired in the socialization process. At the same time it exercises considerable influence upon our understanding of our own capacities and our occupational position. As Marx wrote: "Misapprehension with respect to our capacities for a certain occupation is an error which avenges itself and, even it if encounters no censure from the outside world, still causes us torments more fearsome than those which the outside world is able to occasion."[4]

As things presently stand, the significance of these problems grows sharply as the transition to universal secondary education nears completion. What actually happens to the school graduates? What occupations do they choose as they join the ranks of the working class? Which vacancies are filled as a result, and which still remain open? The efficiency of social production and the tempo of our social development depend to an enormous extent upon our being able to resolve these problems.

To solve practical management problems, it is very important to bear in mind that occupational prestige varies over time as well as with location.

For instance, the occupational prestige scale differs in different countries, in different areas of the same country, in town and countryside.

And these differences change, each in its own way, over time. Thus, for example, the scientific and technical revolution, urbanization, and the development of the mass media substantially affect the assessment of occupational prestige among urban and rural youth. This may be illustrated as follows. Let us imagine the process of change in occupational prestige among urban and rural youth over three years, on a chart whose horizontal axis contains the 80 occupations under consideration (ranging from specialties in physical work to the mental occupations) and whose vertical axis shows occupational prestige on a scale of one to ten. A change in occupational prestige will be reflected in a changed position of the graph.

In the course of our research we established the existence of a particular kind of "scissors effect"—in the assessment of manual and mental occupations among urban and rural youth. Rural youth, that is, assessed predominantly manual occupations more highly, while urban youth gave higher ratings to occupations involving mental work. Since the same items were surveyed repeatedly over a number of years, it was possible to track the movement of these "scissors." The chart shows clearly that they are closing, but in a highly distinctive manner. That is, the evaluations of urban youth have remained essentially unchanged, while the evaluations of rural youth are increasingly approximating them. This can be interpreted as a process in which rural evaluations are drawing closer to urban evaluations, as a result of which the above-mentioned orientation toward mental work is becoming increasingly prevalent.

Thus, the "scissors" of urban-rural evaluations are visibly closing, and the countryside is deferring to the town. The rural stereotype is unstable. It is taking its cue from the urban stereotype, which acts as a kind of standard. The latter is more balanced, firm, and conservative, thanks to its universality. A large degree of isolation (an underdeveloped road network, and fewer television sets, radios, newspapers, magazines, and books per person in the countryside than in the town) is responsible for the large fluctuations in rural evaluations. Conversely, urbanization and the ubiquitous mass media generate evaluations that are more universal, on the one hand, and highly stable, on the other. It must also be mentioned that comparable tendencies are typical in some of the other socialist countries.

On the subject of occupational prestige as assessed by young people in various countries, one notes—despite national idiosyncracies, dissimilarities in educational systems and occupational training, in the demographic situation, and so forth—similar tendencies in all the countries of the socialist community.

Using three countries—Bulgaria, Hungary, and the USSR—as an example (Tables 1 and 2), let us observe how young people (in particular the two polar groups of unskilled workers and specialists with higher education) evaluate certain manual and mental specialties.

As can be seen from these tables, unskilled workers rate occupations in manual work more highly than do specialists. The average scores for these occupations (out of a maximum of 10) among young unskilled workers in Bulgaria, Hungary, and the USSR were 4.12, 5.21, and 4.79 respectively.

Specialists with higher education rated specialties in mental work as more attractive. The average scores were quite high: 5.90 in Bulgaria, 6.52 in Hungary, and 7.52 in the USSR. The occupation of engineer was generally assessed most highly by young people in these countries, though doctor topped the list in the USSR.

All this seems quite logical. But here we must also draw the reader's attention to another point—namely, the high prestige accorded to occupations involving mental work by those doing manual work, in particular by unskilled workers. A unique process of convergence of evaluations is occurring, as the prestige of

Table 1

Evaluation of Selected Manual Occupations by Unskilled Workers and Specialists with Higher Education, Bulgaria, Hungary, and the USSR

Occupation	People's Republic of Bulgaria		Hungarian People's Republic		USSR	
	unskilled workers	specialists with higher education	unskilled workers	specialists with higher education	unskilled workers	specialists with higher education
Metallurgist	3.44	3.57	5.27	4.36	6.26	5.90
Carpenter	4.31	2.72	5.27	5.77	3.78	4.07
Turner	4.34	3.66	5.39	5.28	4.40	4.21
Tractor driver	4.19	2.68	4.82	3.38	4.93	3.61
Weaver	4.40	2.43	5.29	3.23	4.59	3.64

mental specialties rises in the eyes of ordinary workers. If in this context we employ the "scissors" concept again, we may say that the blades are closing—that evaluations of occupational prestige among the representatives of the various social strata are converging. This is an interesting and complex phenomenon which is predicated upon many factors, primarily upon such factors as the constant rise in educational levels and the development of the educational system, intensive economic development, including the mechanization and automation of production processes, and so on.

To get a clearer picture of the special features of occupational prestige, let us examine it in developmental terms, as a dynamic. In order to do this we shall present data for the USSR, and compare the occupational evaluations of secondary school graduates in the 1970s with those of graduates of the same schools ten years earlier.[5]

Evaluations are generally trending upward. Significantly, this affects the majority of workers' occupations and the mass-based jobs which do not require higher education. Thus the boys and

Table 2

Evaluation of Selected Mental Occupations by Unskilled Workers and Specialists with Higher Education, Bulgaria, Hungary, and the USSR

Occupation	People's Republic of Bulgaria		Hungarian People's Republic		USSR	
	unskilled workers	specialists with higher education	unskilled workers	specialists with higher education	unskilled workers	specialists with higher education
Doctor	6.80	5.91	6.91	5.71	7.99	8.12
Writer	5.47	4.94	6.19	5.47	7.17	7.57
Research physicist	5.26	5.80	5.62	6.98	6.71	7.33
Research chemist	5.25	4.95	5.64	6.16	6.37	6.81
Engineer	6.45	7.90	6.77	8.29	6.65	7.79

girls of Novosibirsk unanimously increased their ratings of the attractiveness of agricultural work and transport and service jobs, the construction trades (boys), and worker specialties in light industry and the food industry (girls) (see Table 3). The notable thing about young people's higher evaluations of jobs in health care, education, and culture is that there was a more signficant rise for the occupations of nurse, cultural-educational worker, and librarian than for the occupations of doctor, writer, and journalist. Typically, also, the prestige of research social scientists and biologists rose and that of physicists and mathematicians fell.

A rise in the prestige of humanities-based occupations among young people in the early 1970s can also be discerned at the level of everyday consciousness. Here, however, the rise is often exaggerated, since judgments are made solely on the basis of heightened competition for admission to the relevant higher educational institutions and to particular departments, without comparing the relative magnitudes of enrollment in technical and engineering institutes with those of the humanities faculties and specialties. Competition for the latter can easily be inflated by the slightest swing in their direction. Data on the dynamics of occupational prestige are a considerably more meaningful and reliable index. Young people, for example, find an array of engineering specialties highly attractive.

There was negligible change in the attractiveness of machine-building and metalworking occupations. The attractiveness of sales and bookkeeping occupations and of many occupations in material production rose, but remained low.

In analyzing the occupational plans of graduates of secondary schools in Novosibirsk region rural localities, it must be noted that here they evaluate the prestige of many occupations in a substantially different manner (Table 4). Rural schoolchildren rate occupations requiring higher education (especially scientific occupations) considerably lower, and occupations involving manual work considerably higher, than do their urban counterparts. Among occupations requiring higher education, engineering occupations were clearly preferred to scientific ones.

Rural girls rated the occupation of secondary school teacher at the very top of the prestige ladder, ranking it second out of 71—or first, if one discounts the occupation of pilot, an occupation in which there are virtually no women. By the 1970s rural girls had significantly downgraded the prestige of teaching, though they still rated it incomparably higher than did rural boys, urban boys, and even urban girls. This implies a large percentage of female rural school graduates in the student body of pedagogical higher educational institutions, and on the teaching staff of schools in the future.

Unfortunately the prestige of agricultural occupations—except that of machine operative and jobs requiring higher education—is low in the countryside. This circumstance is one of the reasons behind rural youth's strong urge to move to the city and the excessive exodus of young people from the countryside in many areas of the country. In the countryside, as in the city, the lowest prestige rating is given to occupations in the service sphere, which makes it difficult to improve standards of work in this field.

Table 3

Evaluation of Occupations by Secondary School Graduates In Novosibirsk*

Occupation	1963		1973	
	Rank	Points	Rank	Points
		Boys		
Research physicist	1	8.4	7	7.4
Pilot	3	8.0	1	8.1
Engineer-geologist	7	7.1	3	7.5
Research-geologist	11	6.7	5	7.5
Doctor	16	6.3	22	6.4
Higher educational institution instructor	19	6.0	29	5.8
Miner	25	5.6	28	6.2
Driver	27	5.5	19	6.7
Construction worker-installer	31	5.1	33	5.5
Electrician	33	5.0	36	5.2
Secondary school teacher	39	4.5	38	5.0
Tractor driver combine operator	48	3.7	46	4.6
Elementary school teacher	51	3.5	49	4.4
Field hand	63	2.7	59	3.6
Public food service staff	67	2.6	58	3.6
Clerical worker	69	2.1	71	2.0
Retail clerk	71	2.0	63	3.2

The occupational prestige scale is a fairly sensitive instrument, able to record changes in public consciousness. Changes revealed in successive surveys can stem from changes in social life, from the results of work on career guidance done in schools, or from the rising percentage of youngsters now completing the tenth grade.

The introduction of compulsory secondary education changed the social composition of secondary school graduating classes.

Table 3 (continued)

Occupation	1963		1973	
	Rank	Points	Rank	Points
		Girls		
Research physician	1	8.3	3	8.1
Pilot	3	8.2	1	8.5
Doctor	6	7.9	2	8.3
Higher educational institution instructor	10	7.5	6	7.7
Research geologist	12	7.3	4	8.0
Secondary school teacher	23	6.5	14	7.3
Elementary school teacher	31	5.3	25	6.6
Nurse, medical orderly, midwife	40	4.8	28	6.4
Field hand	61	3.3	50	4.5
Livestock hand	62	3.1	57	3.9
Retail clerk	69	2.6	51	4.4
Clerical worker	71	2.3	71	2.9
Bookkeeper	68	3.0	54	4.3
Typographer	61	3.6	49	4.5
Machine-tool operator-metalworker	48	4.5	66	3.0
Arc welder	52	4.3	63	3.5
Electrician	47	4.5	61	3.5

During the survey the boys and girls were asked to evaluate the prestige of 71 occupations on a 10-point scale, giving 10 points to the most attractive occupation and one point to the least attractive, with intermediate occupations being scored accordingly. By way of example this table presents only the specialities that are most common and representative for the given group of young people.

Among those completing the tenth grade in the 1970s there was a better balance of children of intellectuals, workers, and collective farmers than there had been in the 1960s. This also influenced changes in occupational prestige. Along with a rise in the attractiveness of mental specialties, evaluations of many occupations involving manual work also rose—a spin-off, to a certain extent,

Table 4*

Evaluation of Occupations by Rural Secondary School Graduates In Novosibirsk Region

	1963		1973	
Occupation	Rank	Points	Rank	Points
		Boys		
Research physicist	8	6.9	12	6.6
Pilot	1	8.0	1	8.0
Engineer-geologist	5	7.3	3	7.3
Research geologist	14	6.4	10	6.6
Doctor	35	5.3	25	5.8
Higher educational institution instructor	29	5.6	22	5.8
Miner	24	6.0	18	6.0
Driver	21	6.0	2	7.8
Construction worker-installer	28	5.6	26	5.8
Electrician	19	6.1	28	5.6
Secondary school teacher	39	4.9	32	5.4
Tractor driver combine operator	17	6.2	8	6.7
Elementary school teacher	51	4.2	40	4.7
Field hand	48	4.4	36	5.1
Public food service staff	62	3.0	64	3.1
Clerical worker	70	2.3	71	2.3
Retail clerk	71	2.3	60	3.3

of the orientation exhibited by the children of collective farmers and workers toward occupations involving manual work, especially those associated with machinery, mechanical devices, and so forth.

After leaving school young people embark on a new phase of their lives, in which they come into direct contact with the actual institutions of society—industrial and agricultural enterprises, construction projects, various organizations, vocational education institutions. This is a period of intensive social maturation, a

Table 4* (continued)

Occupation	1963		1973	
	Rank	Points	Rank	Points
		Girls		
Research physician	4	7.2	5	7.1
Pilot	1	7.9	1	8.8
Doctor	5	7.2	3	7.8
Higher educational institution instructor	6	7.1	7	7.0
Research geologist	15	6.4	4	7.6
Secondary school teacher	2	7.3	11	6.9
Elementary school teacher	9	6.7	9	7.0
Nurse, medical orderly, midwife	26	5.8	8	7.0
Field hand	46	4.5	52	4.7
Livestock hand	50	4.4	53	4.6
Retail clerk	65	3.4	39	5.4
Clerical worker	71	2.3	59	3.9
Bookkeeper	68	3.0	54	4.3
Typographer	61	3.6	71	2.1
Machine-tool operator-metalworker	48	4.5	66	3.4
Arc welder	52	4.3	63	3.5
Electrician	47	4.5	61	3.8

*For ease of comparison, the occupations are here arranged in the same order as in Table 3.

time to revise the stereotypes, to verify notions appropriated from others and to replace them with other ideas based upon personal experience. Is there a connection between social maturation and a change of attitude toward various occupations? If there is, then how does the perception of occupational prestige change as a person grows up and acquires personal experience (between the ages of seventeen and twenty-five, for instance)?

We shall compare evaluations of occupational prestige given by seventeen-year-old boys and girls with those given by the same people at age twenty-five.

If the occupational evaluations of seventeen-year-olds are ranked—from most to least prestigious—the resultant curve is characterized by a very sharp differentiation of evaluations. Eight years later the curve plotted for the same respondents straightens out, as extreme positions are abandoned. Evaluations of the most prestigious occupations, which are primarily associated with science (mathematics, physics, chemistry, and so on) have fallen, while evaluations of the least prestigious occupations (waiter, cook, retail clerk) have risen. Though the gap between the groups of occupations at either end of the scale is, of course, still wide, it has narrowed substantially. This graphically illustrates the abandonment of extremes in the judgments of youth, and marks the transition from a black-and-white view of the world to a "polychrome" vision.

But this is a change in conceptions that affects young people as a whole. Independent life commits boys and girls to a multiplicity of social roles, and this brings an individualized tenor to each person's social experience. One of the most powerful differentiating factors during this period is gender.

Female school graduates evaluate most occupations more highly than do their male age-mates. This phenomenon shows up consistently in surveys conducted in various parts of the country. The explanations of this phenomenon have included suggestions that girls have more idealized conceptions of occupations, of the world of work, and so forth.

After a direct encounter with the realities of work activity male-female occupational evaluations tend to move in differing directions: female evaluations on the whole fall somewhat, but not indiscriminately. Thus in the female estimation the attractiveness of workers' occupations in industry and transport—men's jobs in the the sphere of material production, generally speaking—declines rather markedly. But the evaluations of occupations which employ women for the most part—service sector jobs (except for waiting on tables), deskwork, humanities-based, medical, and pedagogical jobs—remain fairly stable. Some of them even gain in prestige.

Males, unlike their female age-mates, raise their occupational evaluations as they mature. They find it easier to part company with the extreme judgments of earlier days and are more generous in conferring extra points upon the majority of occupations. Only jobs in the service sphere, the minimally skilled office jobs, and some mass-based ''female'' occupations (weaver, dairymaid) remain unattractive to them. Significantly enough, the most marked evaluational upgrading occurs with regard to occupations in the sphere of material production—especially ordinary workers' jobs. A number of factors could be operative here: a change in value-systems, a more realistic view of the occupational scene (always a more distinctively masculine trait, which is now strengthened by the appearance of a wife and children), and so on.

The two sexes gradually evolve a more adequate perception of their own occupational and social roles. An indicator of this may be seen in the age-related changes in evaluations of occupational prestige among men compared to women. At the age of 22, women rate 31 occupations out of 40 more highly than men; 23 out of 40, at the age of 24; 13 out of 40 at the age of 26; and by 28 years of age, only eight.

Thus, the distinction between traditionally ''female'' and traditionally ''male'' jobs becomes more salient with age. It is likely that this kind of dynamic of occupational prestige reflects the woman's awareness of her occupational roles and opportunities, on the one hand, and, on the other, a growing perception of her social role in the wider perspective—of her position as a woman, both in the family and in society.

All this shows that in the course of an independent working life a young person's view of the occupational world becomes enriched, more concrete, and more realistic.

A natural question to ask is: how are attitudes toward the various occupations influenced by a person's own job?

Direct work experience provides the fullest understanding of any job. Everyone knows his own line of work better than any other, and usually values it more. It is, therefore, understandable that a person will assess his own occupation more highly than

Table 5

Comparative Evaluations of Occupational Prestige* (mean scores)

Occupation	Evaluation by those in the given occupation	Evaluation by the whole group of young people
Turner	7.0	4.0
Metalworker	7.1	4.3
Seamstress	7.1	4.6
Secondary school teacher	8.2	6.5
Doctor	9.8	8.0

*Data for the USSR only.

others (Table 5). Another point is that people oftener than not choose an occupation which they rate above other occupations and evaluate more highly than other people do, and that those who are disappointed by their current occupation frequently leave it. Finally, it should not be forgotten that a person simply gets used to his occupation.

An analysis of the data provided by sociological research on occupational prestige invites the conclusion that at the present time it is imperative to raise substantially the prestige of agricultural occupations, many industrial occupations, and the vast majority of occupations in the service sphere.

In the final analysis, young people are distributed among economic branches and jobs in the way that best suits society. Thus far, however, this is achieved at a considerable cost. Insufficient career guidance and an inadequate acquaintance with the work world cause many people to choose occupations that do not tally with their personal qualities, which affects labor productivity, job satisfaction, personnel turnover, and so forth—it is very costly, that is, in economic and social terms. Efficient utilization of the potential generated by rationalizing the process through which young people embark upon their working lives can serve as a substantial reserve of economic and social development.

Bearing the above-mentioned theoretical and methodological issues in mind, we pass now to the evaluations of occupational prestige recorded during the comparative international research project entitled "Life Directions of Young People in Socialist Society" (see Table 6).

To analyze these data, we began by determining the "mixed" [*sksvoznye*], i.e., comparable, occupations. Then the average occupational evaluations were calculated, based on the points awarded in each country.

If we provisionally split the occupational prestige structure into three groups (low-prestige occupations: 2 to 5 points; medium-prestige occupations: 5 to 7 points; young people's most popular occupations: 7 points and up), we can see that the evaluations given by boys and girls in Bulgaria, Hungary, and the USSR (Table 6) have a lot in common. The occupations of doctor and engineer are among those which enjoy the highest prestige. The high social prestige of these jobs is evidenced by the fact that they were rated highly by virtually all categories of young workers and employees in all these countries.

Young people's least favorite occupations were weaver, tractor driver, retail clerk, and waiter (Bulgaria, USSR), and construction worker and bookkeeper (Hungary, USSR). Basically, specialties involving manual work and jobs in the service sphere were low in prestige. And this raises a very serious problem. It is no secret that present-day economic development requires not only highly educated and highly skilled personnel but also semi-skilled and even low-skilled workers. Society's requirements for a limited number of cosmonauts and artists are being comfortably filled, but there is a significantly greater need for workers with the most varied specialties and skills. Hence it is vital that the upbringing which young people receive teaches them to make a sober and realistic appraisal of society's personnel requirements as well as of their own capabilities, without suppressing their creative occupational aspirations.

It is, therefore, very important to conduct systematic research into such youth-related problems as occupational choice, changes

Table 6

Mean Occupational Prestige Scores Given by Young People in Bulgaria (B), Hungary (H), and the USSR (U)

Socio-occupational group / Occupation	Unskilled workers			Semi-skilled workers			Highly skilled workers			Employees without specialized training			Employees with specialized training			Employees with higher education		
	B	H	U	B	H	U	B	H	U	B	H	U	B	H	U	B	H	U
Agronomist	5.06	5.27	5.26	4.32	5.61	5.30	3.80	4.96	5.03	4.29	5.61	4.90	4.28	5.14	5.04	3.48	5.50	4.71
Artist	6.12	6.83	7.23	5.83	6.14	6.98	5.31	5.54	6.79	6.25	6.42	6.86	5.71	4.96	6.86	4.61	4.60	6.16
Bookkeeper	4.46	4.46	4.09	3.61	4.36	4.31	3.05	3.50	3.70	3.81	4.75	4.03	4.02	3.22	4.11	2.44	2.55	3.02
Doctor	6.80	5.40	7.99	6.24	6.76	8.28	5.81	5.46	7.83	6.47	8.74	8.32	6.41	6.01	7.90	5.90	5.56	8.12
Scientific worker in chemistry	5.24	5.67	6.37	4.97	6.31	6.50	4.39	6.05	6.44	5.42	6.79	7.48	2.93	6.36	6.52	4.94	6.17	6.81
Journalist	5.41	5.37	6.52	5.79	5.04	6.20	5.21	5.08	6.50	6.26	7.90	7.45	5.71	5.73	7.35	5.56	4.90	7.44
Engineer	6.45	6.76	6.65	6.25	6.30	6.74	6.32	6.36	6.86	6.44	4.90	6.89	6.74	5.91	7.39	7.89	5.00	7.79
Stonemason construction worker	3.09	5.23	4.28	3.10	4.95	5.50	3.10	4.43	4.89	2.84	4.26	4.57	2.73	3.83	4.69	2.57	3.92	3.78

Metallurgist	3.43	5.16	6.26	3.87	4.86	6.32	3.77	4.72	6.35	3.92	5.81	7.45	3.39	4.86	6.22	3.27	4.36	5.90
Sailor	5.38	5.92	6.45	5.30	5.34	6.71	5.06	5.27	6.54	5.18	5.03	4.22	6.20	4.55	4.76	6.08	4.36	5.90
Writer	5.47	7.17	6.71	5.25	6.30	7.36	4.68	5.68	7.14	5.20	6.48	8.34	4.87	5.69	7.13	4.93	5.47	7.58
Retail clerk	3.96	5.54	5.09	3.64	5.37	5.14	3.45	4.21	4.54	3.48	4.97	3.58	3.50	3.67	4.37	2.50	3.21	3.68
Turner	4.34	5.41	4.48	4.50	5.46	5.45	4.79	5.67	5.16	3.65	5.07	4.21	3.74	4.87	4.69	3.65	5.28	4.21
Weaver	4.39	5.26	4.59	3.24	4.67	5.10	2.97	4.09	4.74	3.10	3.94	4.67	2.63	3.25	4.03	2.43	3.23	3.64
Tractor driver	4.19	4.78	4.93	3.58	4.49	5.64	3.22	3.85	5.09	3.20	3.57	4.87	3.13	3.49	4.54	2.67	3.38	3.64
Secondary school teacher	6.49	6.56	6.72	6.28	6.76	6.99	6.11	6.14	6.53	6.77	6.46	7.18	6.87	6.70	6.09	6.75	7.12	5.72
Scientific worker in physics	5.25	6.34	6.71	5.13	6.19	6.71	4.93	6.30	6.79	5.13	5.45	7.50	5.24	6.24	6.93	5.79	6.98	7.33
Waiter	3.70	6.21	3.65	3.43	5.54	3.92	3.14	4.74	3.39	3.19	5.06	2.78	2.82	3.77	3.31	2.37	2.87	2.66

in occupational prestige, and the occupational self-determination of young men and women. This is vital, primarily to enable us not only to detect changes in young people's occupational preferences in a timely manner but also to factor those changes into the processes of social planning and management.

Analyzing the occupational prestige rankings, one notices, first and foremost, a high correlation between occupational evaluations in the USSR, Bulgaria, and Hungary. In certain instances the rank order virtually coincides and often it is identical.

The materials gathered in the course of this comparative international research project attest to the fact that young people in all these countries rate occupations involving mental work more highly than those involving manual work. The scientific and technical revolution and its related phenomena are elevating everywhere—and especially among young people—the prestige of occupations in science, occupations associated with the newest technology, and so forth. Thus in Hungary and Bulgaria the occupations of engineer, scientific worker in the field of physics, and so on, are highly rated. In the USSR young people gave the highest rating to the occupation of doctor.

Data obtained in the course of this research enable us to conclude that for all the peculiarities noted above in evaluations of manual jobs, the lowest prestige attaches not to these specialties but to service occupations. And though there are pronounced differences between the countries in this respect (for example, the occupations of waiter and retail clerk are evaluated more highly in Hungary than elsewhere), raising the prestige of these occupations among young people is an important international task.

It is not surprising that the occupation of sailor is rated lower in Hungary than in the other countries. However, the rating of secondary school teacher in the USSR—placed fourth by females and eleventh by males—can hardly be considered normal. Nor can the low prestige accorded to the profession of metallurgist and tractor driver in Hungary, and of agronomist in Bulgaria and the USSR. Obviously, these data need supplementary verification and investigation. If, however, they are confirmed as correct,

Table 7

Occupational Prestige Ranking by Young People in Bulgaria, Hungary and the USSR

	USSR		Hungarian People's Republic		Republic of Bulgaria	
	male	female	male	female	male	female
Doctor	1	1	5	2	3	2
Engineer	2	6	1	3	1	3
Writer	3	2	3	6	9	8
Sailor	4	9	9	12	5	9
Scientific worker in physics	5	5	2	4	7	6
Metallurgist	6	10	12	17	11	14
Artist	7	3	8	7	6	4
Journalist	8	8	10	9	4	5
Scientific worker in chemistry	9	7	6	5	10	7
Turner	10	16	7	13	8	13
Secondary school teacher	11	4	4	1	2	1
Tractor driver	12	14	16	19	14	17
Stonemason	13	15	13	18	16	19
Painter	14	18	11	15	13	16
Agronomist	15	11	14	8	12	10
Weaver	16	13	18	14	18	15
Retail clerk	17	12	17	10	17	12
Bookkeeper	18	17	19	16	19	11
Waiter	19	19	15	11	15	18

then this will definitely indicate a need for a variety of special measures to raise the prestige of certain occupations in various countries of the socialist community.

In conclusion, let us examine the summary table (Table 7), which combines male and female prestige rankings.[6]

In the national surveys of occupational prestige it was established empirically that women, as a rule, give higher assessments than do men. As the survey findings showed, this is the case not only in the USSR, but also in Bulgaria, Hungary, and apparently in the other European socialist countries as well. The only exceptions were the expressly masculine occupations (metallurgist, carpenter, metalworker).

As can be seen from the data presented in Table 7, females in all three countries, as a rule, assess such occupations as teacher, doctor, and writer more highly than do males. Jobs in the scientific field are also differentiated: females give a higher rating to the occupation of scientific worker in chemistry, for instance, while males favor physics.

It is especially important to stress that females assess more highly those service sphere occupations which males view as least prestigious of all (retail clerk, bookkeeper, waiter). Here again, our international research corroborated the results of research into occupational prestige in individual countries. It seems to us that these results, too, could and should be taken into account when new measures are drawn up to further the economic integration of the countries of the socialist community.

There has as yet been no reasonably comparable empirical research into the dynamics of occupational prestige in the countries of the socialist community. However, indirect data give us grounds to suppose that economic integration, the growth of cultural ties, tourism, and so on, are fostering the convergence of occupational prestige evaluations by working youth in the socialist countries. And this process is reflected in the results presented above, in the close correlation between occupational prestige rankings in various countries. It would, however, be naive to assume that differences associated with idiosyncracies in the development of productive forces, with cultural-historical traditions, could vanish in a matter of decades. And, indeed, it is hardly desirable to strive for the eradication of all differences in this way. There is more to be said, perhaps, for simply determining to overcome those differences in occupational prestige which reflect the obsolete, constraining features of the social division of labor. On the contrary, just as it would hardly make sense to strive for a complete levelling in male–female evaluations of occupational prestige, so too it is apparently not always necessary to aim for the elimination of all distinctions in the evaluation of occupational prestige in different countries. The preservation of specific traits that have been acquired in the course of cultural-historical development—including idiosyncratic evaluations of occupational prestige—will serve to enrich the entire socialist community as a whole, in the course of economic integration.

At the same time, one cannot help but see that at the present moment a situation is shaping up wherein it will be possible to influence occupational prestige from several different angles—by means of the mass media, on the one hand, and, on the other, by transforming the very structure of the social division of labor, by systematically eliminating unprestigious jobs in the course of economic integration. This is very important if the actual structure of work is to be brought into greater conformity with the occupational aspirations of young people in the countries of the socialist community.

An important role in this belongs to career guidance for young people, an area in which the countries of the socialist community have had extensive and varied experience. Career guidance centers and methodological laboratories, production training centers, apprentice shops, student production brigades, work and recreation camps, and plant occupational clinics (which maintain close contact with the public job placement and information offices) are presently in service, and new ones are being created all the time. Our press has featured this subject on numerous occasions.

A concrete program of development for the career guidance system, taking note of the experience accumulated in the USSR, was outlined in a resolution issued by the CPSU Central Committee and the USSR Council of Ministers entitled "Concerning the further improvement in the instruction and upbringing of general education school pupils, and preparing them for work" [O dal'-neishem sovershenstvovanii obucheniia, vospitaniia uchash-chikhsia obshcheobrazovatel'nykh skhol i podgotovki ikh k trudu]. It covers eighth-grade school-leavers as well as tenth-grade graduates and contains provisions for: a special post of inspector of labor education, training and career guidance (an addition to the staff of regional and district [urban] departments of public education), commissions attached to the executive committees of district soviets, career guidance study and methodological centers in the schools, a broader network of interschool production training centers, and patron enterprises assigned to each school.

The career guidance and consultation available through this system helps reduce the unnecessary personal and social losses that occur when young men and women take their first independent steps, as young people develop occupational self-determination and the ability to stand on their own feet in the work world.

It can be seen that the problems of occupational self-determination for young people in socialist countries are particularly pressing in the context of the scientific and technical revolution. This is because socioeconomic, demographic, and cultural conditions are developing so dynamically, and the personal plans and aspirations of young men and women on the verge of their independent lives are so complex and changeable. Moreover, the more socially developed a society is, the greater the freedom of choice it offers to young people to realize their life-plans, the wider the range of variants open to each person—and the more difficult the choice of occupation, the quest for a vocation and a life-direction. This is why it is so important that Party, planning, and economic organizations and educational personnel devote attention to young people and help them, that research be conducted into personal plans and life-directions, and that proper inferences be drawn from the vast and varied experience that the countries of the socialist community have had in solving the problems of young people.

Notes

1. This research was conducted by members of the USSR Academy of Sciences Institute of the International Workers' Movement, the USSR Academy of Sciences Siberian Section's IIOF, and the Novosibirsk Pedagogical Institute, under the supervision of V. N. Shubkin (D. Philos.). For more detail, see: V. Shubkin, *Sotsiologicheskie opyty*, Moscow, 1970; D. Konstantinovskii and V. N. Shubkin, *Molodezh' i obrazovanie*; V. Shubkin and G. Cheredichenko, ''Social Problems of Occupational Choice (Materials of a Sociological

Study, 'Life-Paths of Youth')," *Rabochii klass i sovremennyi mir*, 1978, no. 2.

2. See the following articles in *Rabochii klass i sovremennyi mir*: F. Gazho, "Social and Occupational Mobility of Youth in the Hungarian People's Republic," 1978, no. 6; V. Dubski, R. Franek, I. Vechernik, "Working Youth: The Role of Education Under Socialism," 1979, no. 3; V. Ademski, S. Kosel', "Youth and Labor in Current Poland," 1980, no. 3; E. Kyneva, K. Gospodinov, "Bulgarian Youth and its Orientation to Continuing Education," 1980, no. 4.

3. K. Marx, F. Engels, *Sochinenie*, vol. 3, p. 25.

4. K. Marx, F. Engels, *Iz rannikh proizvedenii*, Moscow, 1956, pp. 4–5.

5. Sociological research on the social problems of young people was initiated in the Novosibirsk scientific center in the 1960s, under the supervision of V. N. Shubkin. The project continued for over ten years. Graduates from Novosibirsk secondary schools were surveyed. Graduates were asked about their plans immediately on leaving school. In the fall a follow-up study was done to find out what jobs these young men and women had actually obtained. The length of time slated for the project, its mass-based nature and uniform methodology made it possible to create a representative data base on the life-directions of young people, and particularly on the question of occupational prestige, changes in it, and so forth.

6. This table is based on the occupational prestige ranking obtained from Soviet males.

8. Soviet Women

Problems of Work and Daily Life*

E. V. GRUZDEVA and E. S. CHERTIKHINA

A keynote of the latter half of the 1970s and of the 1980s to date is the continuing concern shown by the Soviet government and the Communist Party for the working woman. The Constitution adopted in 1977 not only gave legislative affirmation to the equal rights of men and women, but also provided for the creation of new opportunities for the sexes to achieve social equality, and for suitable ways to combine the occupational, familial/domestic, and maternal roles of women.

The development of these constitutional articles was promoted by Party, government, and trade union resolutions designed to improve yet further the position of working women. Particular mention must be made of a resolution, issued jointly by the USSR Council of Ministers and the All-Union Central Council of Trade Unions on 25 April 1978, which was entitled ''Concerning additional measures to improve the working conditions of women employed by the national economy'' [O dopol 'nitel 'nykh merakh po uluchsheniiu uslovii truda zhenshchin, zaniatykh v narodnom khoziaistve], and aimed at bringing about further improvements in the system of labor protection for women. In order to implement this resolution, the USSR State Labor Committee, together

*Russian text © 1982 by ''Rabochii klass i sovremennyi mir,'' ''Progress'' Publishers. ''Sovetskie zhenshchiny: Problemy truda i byta,'' *Rabochii klass i sovremennyi mir*, 1982, no. 6, pp. 110–117

with the All-Union Central Council of Trade Unions and with the approval of the Ministry of Public Health, ratified on 25 July 1978 an updated list of industries, occupations, and jobs with taxing and hazardous working conditions where the employment of women is forbidden. A resolution adopted by the USSR Council of Ministers and the All-Union Central Council of Trade Unions on 5 December 1981, entitled "Concerning the introduction of new norms for the maximum permissible weight of loads being manually lifted and transferred by women" [O vvedenii novykh norm predel'no dopustimykh nagruzok dlia zhenshchin pri pod"eme i peremeshchenii tiazhestei vruchnuiu], constituted a commitment to protect the interests of mother and child, and to improve women's working conditions. On 21 June 1979, the CPSU Central Committee and the USSR Council of Ministers passed a resolution entitled "Concerning measures for the further improvement of training and skill enhancement of workers in production" [O merakh po dal'neishemu sovershenstvovaniiu podgotovki i povysheniia kvalifikatsii rabochikh na proizvodstve], whose goal was to extend women's opportunities for occupational advancement and which referred to the need to give working women with children eight years old or less the right to temporary leave from their jobs for retraining and skill-enhancement, with a guaranteed average monthly income during the period of instruction. A resolution of the CPSU Central Committee and the USSR Council of Ministers, entitled "Concerning measures to strengthen government assistance to families with children" [O merakh po usileniiu gosudarstvennoi pomoshchi sem'iam, imeiushchim detei] (March 1981), contained provisions for additional measures to increase government assistance to families with children, in order to achieve a rational balance of social and familial upbringing, to ease the circumstances of working mothers, and to create pleasant living conditions and domestic circumstances for their families.

It is symptomatic that documents from recent CPSU congresses have sharply posed the problems of further improvement in women's working and living conditions and of combining mater-

Table 1

Distribution of Workers Surveyed, by Educational Level

	Relative share of each educational group (as a percentage of all respondents)					
	Females			Males		
Education	1968	1978	Differ-ence	1968	1978	Differ-ence
Primary	28	17	−11	28	14	−14
Incomplete secondary	44	37	−7	46	38	−8
General secondary	23	33	+10	18	30	+12
Secondary specialized, higher, incomplete higher	5	13	+8	8	17	+9

nal duties with active participation in production and in community life.[1] At the same time, the fact that the position of women has improved dramatically in the socialist context certainly does not mean that all contradictions in this area of social life have been surmounted. The essence of healthy development under socialism lies not in the absence of contradictions but in their nonantagonistic character.

In this regard, it is interesting to review some findings concerning the work and daily life of working women that were obtained as part of a sociological study in the city of Taganrog, a typical industrial center. These findings are especially valuable because they incorporate the results of two surveys conducted a decade apart, in the late 1960s and the late 1970s (research projects dubbed "Taganrog-1" and "Taganrog-2").[2] A comparative analysis of information gathered at ten-year intervals brings into focus both positive changes in the cultural and occupational growth of working class women and the contradictions that still remain in this field.

It is common knowledge that the general and occupational

Table 2

Educational Level of the USSR's Employed Urban Population (from Findings of 1970 and 1979 All-Union Population Censuses)

Education of USSR's urban population	Female workers			Male workers		
	1970	1979	Differ-ence	1970	1979	Differ-ence
Primary	26	19	−7	28	16	−12
Incomplete secondary	40	33	−13	42	35	−7
General secondary	19	35	+16	19	35	+16
Higher, incomplete higher, secondary specialized	4	9	+5	5	11	+6

Source: see *Vestnik statistiki*, 1981, no. 2, p. 63.

culture of worker cadres are among the indispensible determinants of labor efficiency and quality of work. Data from sociological surveys indicate a significant rise in these indices among working women during the 1970s (Table 1).

It can be seen that the rise in educational levels of women which occurred during those years was largely attributable to the spread of a general secondary education. At the root of this process was the transformation of complete secondary education into a mandatory norm for all Soviet citizens. The stratum of highly educated working women with specialized education increased significantly. The same data attest to the fact that in the 1960s and 1970s the educational levels of men and women moved toward increasing equality. We note that the indices of educational change among workers surveyed during the 1970s reflect a general upward trend in the educational levels of urban workers in the country as a whole (see Table 2).

It is only natural that the rise in female educational levels, along with the ongoing enhancement of material and technical standards in social production, set the stage for an increase in the absolute number and relative share of skilled female worker cadres. This is corroborated by data from the 1978 survey, which show that over half the women in occupations where the work is highly complex and requires specialized instruction prior to the commencement of labor activity were well educated, while women with fairly low educational levels predominated in simple jobs where occupational skills are mastered directly through work experience. Thus, for example, 66% of females working as laboratory technicians, computer operators, inspectors, and so forth (in occupations predominantly associated with information monitoring, processing and storage, which require specialized instruction prior to the commencement of labor activity) had a secondary (general or specialized) or higher education; the remaining 34% had an incomplete secondary education or less. A closely analogous situation (64% and 36% respectively) obtains in service occupations such as senior seamstress, hairdresser, cook, retail clerk, and so on, which require training prior to the commencement of labor activity. Furthermore, among the women surveyed who worked as conductors in urban transit, as nannies, cloakroom attendants in enterprises and institutions, and so on— those engaged in simple manual labor which requires no training prior to the commencement of labor activity, that is—73% had an incomplete secondary education or less, and only 27% had a secondary (specialized or general) or higher education.

Yet, as is now well understood, it would be a mistake to assume that a rise in educational levels automatically and spontaneously solves all the problems relating to improvements in the qualitative characteristics of women's work. The rapid growth of women's education, not matched by a growth in, and by current levels of, occupational training, has given rise to discrepancies between these characteristics of worker cadres among substantial numbers of working women. Women today are engaged for the most part in skilled or low-skilled work, while men mostly hold skilled or highly skilled jobs. True, it should be noted that during the decade between the two sociological surveys, there was an appreciable change in the realtive shares of skilled female worker cadres: the relative share of women employed in low-skilled work fell considerably, while the proportion of skilled and highly skilled female workers almost doubled, from 34% in 1968 to 64% in 1978. However, this index rose from 81% to 88% among male workers. Thus it is apparent that, despite certain changes for the better, the problem of inadequately skilled women's work remains.

However, the point is not only—and not so much—that working women are predominantly employed in the mass-based middle- and low-ranking occupations. As we see it, the problem is an acute one because some significant differences between the type of work done by men and women—as determined by the assimilation of the achievements of the scientific and technical revolution and by the culmination of industrialization processes—may be seen in their respective work-orbits.[2a] The mutually contradictory nature of certain types of work that exist at present is clearly traceable to a distinct developmental imbalance among different branches of the Soviet economy which has arisen because, in the past, "we were forced to concentrate on the number one priority, on that upon which the very existence of the young Soviet state depended."[3] The contradiction, to be sure, is not wholly restricted to the boundary between men's work and women's work; it still inheres, to a certain extent, in the working class as a whole. It is, however, no mere coincidence that it impinges most acutely upon women.

Under the conditions of intensive industrialization the preponderance of women recruited into the ranks of the working class were poorly educated and without occupational training. Despite the enormous positive significance of involving women in industry, this circumstance gave rise to a certain contradiction from the very outset. A significant number of working women, even in industry, were employed in what was, in plain fact, preindustrial work—manual, low-skilled, sometimes physically taxing work— in various forms. That contradiction had certain repercussions which remain with us to this day. Thus, according to data from the 1978 survey, 44% of surveyed female workers were doing extremely simple, manual, more often than not premechanical work, compared to 30% of male workers. Classic factory-industrial and assembly-line work was being done by 36% of the women and 49% of the men, and jobs most palpably influenced by the scientific and technical revolution were held by 20% of both male and female workers.

The imbalance of skills in the female workforce is felt so acutely today not only because female skill levels are so different from those of men but also because industrial and scientific-industrial work are now generally predominant in society. Although manual work of low productivity provides employment for only a certain portion—not the overwhelming majority—of the working class, this type of work is quite widely prevalent among working women. When the bulk of workers were employed in unattractive manual work, the effects were felt less acutely than they are now, when only a small portion of workers find themselves in that situation.

This underlines yet again the extreme urgency of eliminating marginally productive manual work, not only for economic and social reasons but also because of the need to ensure full de facto equality for women, something which necessarily requires the rational utilization of their labor. As production intensifies and the general and occupational culture of most workers grows, the job positions, industries, and kinds of activity which require modest skills and slight occupational expertise will be increasingly experienced as low-prestige spheres of work. Even today, according to data gathered in sociological studies—in Taganrog and elsewhere—most of the low-skilled are older people. Among low-skilled female workers, 46% are over 45 years of age, 42% of low-skilled male workers are over 50. On the other hand, the proportion of young people under 24 in this category does not exceed 15%–16%. Furthermore, young people are increasingly disinclined to take the places of low-skilled retirees. And even in those industries which still have an adequate number of middle-aged and older people (mostly women) who are willing to do low-skilled manual work, this state of affairs cannot be considered normal. It is unlikely that the young women of today, the majority of whom have had a secondary education, will agree to shoulder the burden of unappealing manual labor at some future time when they are in the prime of life. Those branches of social production which will retain a substantial proportion of unattractive work will shortly find themselves in an extremely difficult situation. It is natural, therefore, that the agenda for social development in the 1980s which was drawn up at the Twenty-sixth Party Congress attached particular importance to improvements in conditions of labor activity, to the greatest possible reduction in manual, low-skilled, and physically taxing work, and to easing the conditions under which it must be performed.[4]

The spheres of work activity of male and female worker cadres also predetermine differences in the requirements for specialized occupational training prior to embarking upon a working career. And it is not at all accidental that, as the data from the 1978 Taganrog survey attest, female workers are 73% and male workers are 27% of those employed in occupations which do not require any particular preliminary training, in which work habits are assimilated during an on-the-job apprenticeship of no more than six months' duration. In those jobs where one to two years of specialized occupational training (generally open to those with incomplete secondary education) are required, 45% of the workers are female and 55% are male. As for job positions requiring the kind of full-time, forward-looking instruction which corresponds to the demands of modern production and lasts three to four years, a maximum of 37% of these are held by women and the remaining 63% by men.

Overall, 1.5 times fewer women than men among those surveyed in Taganrog had received occupational training in an educational institution. The data given in Table 3 provide the evidence for this.

The ratio of workers who had received occupational training in the vocational and technical education system, in special courses, or in the secondary specialized education system to those who had been trained directly on the job was 1:1.5 for men, while for women it was 1:3. Certain positive changes associated with the current development of the occupational education system are

Table 3

Occupational Training of Workers (in %)

| | Workers who have had occupational training | | | |
| | on the job | | in the vocational and technical education system, at special courses, in technicums | |
	Females	Males	Females	Males
All workers surveyed	75%	59%	25%	41%
Workers aged 24 or under	64%	51%	36%	49%

occurring in the respective numbers of young people receiving these two forms of training, but it is still the case that a brief on-the-job apprenticeship is far more common as a means of acquiring occupational expertise among young female workers than among their male counterparts.

Not surprisingly, these differences in the means of mastering an occupation result in a considerable gap between the skill levels of jobs filled by men and by women, even at the very outset of their working lives. The occupational grades of people aged 24 or less are given below:

	Women	Men
Grades I and II	42%	14%
Grades III and IV	52%	80%
Grades V and VI	6%	6%

As long as it is still possible to start work without first having had some occupational education—that is, while there are still job positions, occupations, and types of activity whose work operations are simple and modestly skilled—it will be difficult to do away with low-skilled work. Hence, the problem of gradually eliminating nonproductive, low-skilled physical work must be resolved in concert with the further development and improvement of the system of occupational instruction for worker cadres. Data from the Taganrog survey reveal certain changes in the educational and occupational/productive culture of working women, but they also disclose some of the more thorny sides of a continuing problem—namely, the inefficient utilization of labor of a certain proportion of working women. The survey of female workers in Taganrog also revealed their attitude toward their work, toward participation in the affairs of the work place, and toward community activity, as a function of employment in jobs calling for various levels of skill. This analysis of people's feelings with regard to work activity strikes us as very important. It should be said that subjective assessments, being a reflection of public opinion, serve to underscore the urgency of the problem outlined above. It is noteworthy that female workers are highly conscious of the fact that their occupational training lags behind their educational levels.

When asked about the degree of congruence between their work and their education, 80% of female workers responded positively. Nevertheless, one woman in ten remarked that her educational level was higher than was necessary for her job. Fourteen percent of low-skilled female workers but only 3%–4% of skilled and highly skilled female workers held this opinion. The fact that the female workers themselves are aware of this lack of congruence may, in most cases, lead to job dissatisfaction, and often forces a woman to seek work more appropriate to her capacities, thereby aggravating the problem of turnover of worker cadres, an issue which is particularly complicated at a time when labor resources are scarce.

In this regard, special attention should be paid to factors such as female workers' assessments of the nature of their jobs, the degree of interest in them, and, finally, their satisfaction with work. It is gratifying to discover that approximately 80% of women reported themselves satisfied in discharging their daily work duties. But, still, 10% of female workers questioned were not satisfied with their jobs and about the same number was hard put to answer that question at all. There was a clear relationship between the nature of the work and the proportion of women expressing satisfaction with it. A total of 85% of female workers doing skilled and highly skilled work declared themselves satisfied, while two-thirds of low-skilled female workers gave the same response. It is obvious that a worker's assessment of a job will largely hinge upon the content of the job. It is no accident that among female workers performing skilled and highly skilled work operations, 77% found their work interesting, while only 44% of low-skilled female workers felt the same way. Among skilled and highly skilled female workers, 47% considered their work monotonous, compared to 65% among the low-skilled. We see that the proportion of those expressing a positive attitude to work and satisfaction in discharging their daily duties at work is higher where workers are required to have a higher level of occupational culture, and appreciably lower where there is a preponderance of marginally productive, predominantly manual work.

Faced with monotony and lack of substance day after day, female workers frequently perform their labor operations in a purely mechanical manner, relying on habit and ingrained manual dexterity and letting their minds wander. There is nothing odd about the fact that 60% of low-skilled female workers, a third of skilled female workers, and 7% of highly skilled female workers admitted themselves to be potentially prone to this kind of "disengagement" from their work.

The labor and community activity of a significant portion of female workers suffers because they are employed in low-skilled manual jobs. On this level, it is not surprising that 90% of women in skilled jobs and only 70% of those in low-skilled jobs were taking part in socialist emulation campaigns of various kinds, and that 60%–70% of working women with average and high skills and only 30% of low-skilled working women were Communist labor shock workers. As we see, labor activity is fairly intimately linked with the nature and complexity of the work performed: participation in skilled and highly skilled work is manifestly conducive to the assimilation of the best working class qualities—

a high level of consciousness, initiative, and responsibility.

The nature of the work in hand has an equally important influence upon the inculcation of a most important quality of the new type of worker—the feeling of being a master of social production. The extent to which this quality has emerged among female workers engaged in various kinds of work is illustrated by analyzing replies to the question: "Have you participated during the past year in the elaboration and discussion of your enterprise's plan, its collective agreement, or the conditions of a socialist emulation campaign?" Overall, 60% of female workers answered this question in the affirmative. However, the degree of female activity in tackling problems in the workplace or the community is greater for those whose work is more complex: 52% of low-skilled female workers and 68% of skilled and highly skilled female workers had attended formal or informal meetings to discuss these problems.

The same relationship determines the development of the more active forms of participation in the affairs of the labor collective. A provisional indicator of the prevalence of such forms of participation is the relative share of female workers who participate in drawing up their enterprise's obligations and plans, who take the floor at meetings, present their views in the press, put forward suggestions, and so on. Approximately 10% of skilled and highly skilled female workers and a mere 4% of low-skilled female workers fall into this category. Similarly, 48% of women with average and high skills and 28% of low-skilled women carry out long-term or temporary social assignments in their work place or place of residence, or are in elected positions.

On the whole, we are far more likely to encounter lack of satisfaction with and scant interest in the job, and aloofness from the life of the collective, among women doing low-skilled manual work than among women in other worker groups. This state of affairs hampers the free and comprehensive development of the personality in many women, and hinders the growth and manifestation of their capabilities. Documents issued by the Twenty-sixth Party Congress quite rightly emphasized that "the elimination of manual, low-skilled, and physically taxing work is not only an economic problem but a serious social problem. To resolve it means to abolish all substantial obstacles on the way to transforming work into the primary requirement of life for every individual.''[5]

As we know, the attitude toward work, the disposition that comes into being in the course of labor activity, gives a certain tone, as it were, to a person's entire life-activity. It is entirely normal for the exigencies of a high level of work culture to affect not only the occupational development but also the overall development of a worker. It is no accident that in the 1978 Taganrog survey, over half of the skilled female workers and only one-third of the women doing low-skilled work had a complete secondary or specialized (secondary or higher) education. The level of general and occupational culture shapes the nature of workers' nonproduction activity to a significant extent.

Inasmuch as the whole tenor of life outside the production sphere is predominantly familial in nature, the singular features of day-to-day conduct, recreation, entertainment, and consumption of cultural values are largely conditioned by the intellectual atmosphere in the family, which evolves under the influence of its adult members' general cultural development and occupational status. It is interesting to note in this regard that of the skilled workers surveyed in Taganrog approximately one-third lived in families where all (or at least one) of the adult members had a complete secondary or specialized (secondary or higher) education. Only one-fifth of low-skilled workers lived in such families. Data on the nonwork time of Taganrog workers provide clear evidence that the nature of everyday conduct is definitely related to a worker's occupational and general cultural development (see Table 4). It is indicative, for example, that skilled female workers devote somewhat less time to household chores than do women engaged in low-skilled work, and this despite the fact that the group of skilled female workers includes more women with children (who typically do more housework than anyone else). It is entirely possible that a more rigorous adjustment of skill groups

Table 4

Household Chores, Time with Children, Cultural Pastimes, and Recreation of Taganrog Workers Surveyed, as Function of Skill-Level* (Hours per Week)

Types of time outlays	All workers surveyed		Skilled workers		Low skilled workers	
	Females	Males	Females	Males	Females	Males
Household chores	26.9	10.5	25.9	10.4	27.3	11.2
Childcare	4.8	3.1	5.1	3.2	2.8	2.0
Daily cultural life	12.7	19.9	12.7	20.3	12.5	20.0
including:						
reading books, newspapers, magazines	2.2	5.2	2.5	5.3	1.7	4.8
watching television	9.2	12.5	9.0	12.2	9.4	13.9
going to cinemas, theaters, museums, and places of public entertainment	0.6	1.1	0.6	1.1	0.5	1.0
study and self-education	0.4	0.7	0.3	0.6	0.6	0.2
hobbies and creative work not related to occupation	0.3	0.4	0.3	0.5	0.3	0.1
Open-air recreation, sports	1.0	1.9	1.3	2.0	0.6	1.5
Socializing outside the family	5.0	6.8	5.0	6.7	5.0	7.7
Community activity	0.2	0.3	0.2	0.4	0.2	—

*The indices of time expenditures of workers with varying levels of skill are reasonably comparable, since the likelihood that either group would conduct itself, day to day, in a manner typical of the youth lifestyle was approximately equal. In both groups, 10%–15% were unmarried young people; 4%–5% were young childless married couples; 80%–85% of those surveyed were older people or parents with young children. Among the skilled workers of both sexes, people with children somewhat outnumbered those without (in a ratio of approximately 2:1). There were rather more older people among the low skilled workers (among males, 1:1.5; among females, 1:1.1).

for family status and age would uncover even more striking differences in the length of time that skilled and unskilled female workers spend on household chores.

Why is this so? Clearly, a higher skill-ranking does not in itself increase a woman's productivity in the performance of household chores. However, work in a skilled occupation helps shape such practical qualities among women workers as organization, precision, and initiative, and makes their free time more meaningful. It is entirely possible that these traits, acquired and assimilated at work, also manifest themselves in private life and particularly in the woman's desire to rationalize her domestic organization, to go about her household chores in a more orderly and energetic manner, and to increase her productivity in that area. This is why skilled female workers make considerably greater use of modern, labor-saving household appliances than do low-skilled female workers. Thus, 94% of skilled female workers and 89% of low-skilled female workers surveyed in Taganrog in 1978 owned a refrigerator. The percentages for ownership of vacuum cleaners were 56% and 44% respectively, and for washing machines, 82% and 70%. In evaluating these indices, we should bear in mind that these differences in ownership of household devices appear in a context in which the families of Taganrog's female workers, regardless of skill level, are very well equipped with such items. Suffice it to say that for the country as a whole 86% of families possess a refrigerator, 29% possess a vacuum cleaner, and 70% a washing machine.[6] Thus, a characteristic feature of daily life among workers' families in Taganrog is a high degree of reliance upon a number of labor-saving electrical domestic devices. This situation is apparently associated with the fact that the level of material circumstances is virtually identical in all female workers' families, skills notwithstanding. Expressed in terms of per capita income it stands at around 100 to 106 rubles per family member per month. Given the average per capita income level, and the fact that variations in income among families of female workers employed in various sorts of jobs are so slight, these families are all relatively well equipped with household electrical devices. Nonetheless, as can be seen from the data presented above, the households of skilled female workers are somewhat better supplied with household appliances than the families of low-skilled female workers. One is left to surmise that this phenomenon is rooted in the higher level of education and the general and occupational culture which is typical of women engaged in skilled work. The desire to make their domestic life more orderly, to "pack" and "squeeze" the time spent on household chores and to seek increased opportunities to spend their leisure hours in a meaningful manner is more typical of today's skilled female workers than of their low-skilled counterparts.

However, extensive ownership of household electrical appliances is not the only reason why skilled female workers spend somewhat less time on household chores than do women employed in unskilled jobs. Communal amenities are of no small importance in raising the productivity of household chores. The research done in Taganrog indicates that the accommodations of women doing skilled work are somewhat better served in terms of communal amenities than are the living quarters of unskilled female workers and their families. Thus, 44% of unskilled female workers and 47% of skilled female workers surveyed lived in housing with the basic communal amenities (gas, running water, central heating); 29% of unskilled female workers and 26% of highly skilled female workers surveyed had no communal amenities at all in their housing quarters. Apparently, enterprises give first choice of convenient modern housing to skilled workers in an effort to retain them on the payroll. As a result, minimally skilled workers frequently find themselves in less comfortable living quarters. Moreover, as noted above, there is a predominance of older people among low-skilled women workers, who frequently live in antiquated buildings which, as a rule, lack modern urban amenities. Thus, about half of the low-skilled female workers surveyed in Taganrog were over 45 years of age, and approximately half of these lived either in their own homes (which were, as a rule, poorly equipped with household amenities) or in inconvenient communal apartments.

Of course, differences associated with various levels of residential comfort will be increasingly narrowed in the near future, as intensive residential construction continues and older housing resources are refurbished and provided with communal amenities. Between 1960 and 1980 alone, the number of apartments with gas rose from 3.3 million to 55.4 million—almost a seventeen-fold increase which brought 79% of urban housing into the gas-supply network. In addition, 89% of the living space in state and cooperative housing in urban localities has running water; 87% is connected with the sewerage system; and 86% has central heating.[7] In the near future all residential accommodations will have modern household amenities.

The ability to organize their time rationally permits skilled female workers to spend their recreational periods more sensibly and, in a sense, in a more balanced manner. Even by directly comparing the time-budgets of female workers in both skill categories (as presented in Table 4), one sees that women engaged in more complex work spend more time in reading, in active recreation, sports, walking tours, and in excursions into the countryside, and are more selective in their television viewing. Skilled female workers devote approximately 10% of their free time to the cinema or theater, to exhibitions, sports, or organized trips. Low-skilled female workers, however, allot only 5% of their time to these pursuits. A greater interest in reading is seen not only in time-outlays but also in the creation of domestic libraries. Half of the families of skilled female workers own such collections, as opposed to 40% of their low-skilled counterparts. Further evidence is found in the relative share of family subscriptions to newspapers and magazines: 96% of female workers in complex work and 88% of female workers in low content work subscribe to newspapers, and 66% and 58%, respectively, to magazines.

The families of Taganrog's skilled female workers also manifest their desire for a more active and substantive form of leisure by being more likely to own radios, tape recorders, and sports equipment than is the case among families of female workers employed in unskilled jobs. Despite the virtually identical level of per capita income that was mentioned earlier, 63% of the familes of the women surveyed who were employed in complex work owned a radio, compared to 53% of the families of women in low content jobs. For tape recorders, the totals were 52% and 38% respectively; for cameras, 21% and 11%; and for various kinds of sports equipment, 27% and 19%. There is, of course, a strong link between these differences in ownership of cultural items and sporting goods and the presence of children in the family. Transistor radios, like tape recorders, cameras, and various kinds of sporting equipment are, to a great extent, elements of youth culture and are more often than not bought by families with children. There are young children in the families of 67% of the skilled female workers and 54% of the unskilled female workers in Taganrog. It would seem, however, that the general cultural atmosphere in the family and the parents' educational and skill levels are no less important. These factors are often decisive in the intellectual nurturing of children, the shaping of their cultural interests and orientations. In this regard, it is interesting to note that 7% of the families of surveyed female workers employed in skilled work and 5% of the families of female workers in unskilled work in Taganrog owned a piano.

These are not great differences, to be sure. Nonetheless, taken together with the data on ownership of radios and tape recorders, they point to more substantive and cultured ways of spending time among skilled than among unskilled workers.

The level of occupational and productive culture definitely influences the shaping of the worker's intellectual requirements. Thus, female workers engaged in skilled work are typically increasingly drawn toward the cinema and theater. One-third of them had been to the theater in the year preceding the survey (compared to one-fifth of low-skilled female workers). In the month before the survey, 55% of skilled female workers and 45% of low-skilled had been to the cinema.

There is an interesting interconnection between the nature of work and the social circumstances in which a worker's free time is spent. Skilled work and the job satisfaction which it engenders create, in the majority of cases, a climate of congeniality in the work collective, an atmosphere of amicable give and take. It is no accident that one-third of the skilled female workers surveyed reported that they spent free time with their workmates; only one-fifth of unskilled female workers could say the same.

The nature of the day-to-day cultural life and recreation of women engaged in substantive, skilled work attests to the strong impact which the worker's occupational and productive culture has upon his entire mode of life. A high-level general and occupational culture generates a requirement for interesting and varied recreation, a need to transform free time into "space" for personality development.

This does not signify, however, that in life in general, including the daily life of skilled female workers, all problems relating to recreation, personal development, and the upbringing of children have been solved. One sees clearly enough from the time-budget data presented above that the domestic workload of the modern woman, whatever the complexity of her occupational activity, is 2.5 times greater than a man's involvement in household affairs. This obviously does not correspond to social requirements and the ideals of developed socialism. The aggregate workload of a working woman still stands at 70 hours per week. Accordingly, she is less able to pursue an intensive cultural life and her opportunities for occupational upgrading are sharply curtailed, so that ultimately her skills fall substantially behind those of her male counterparts.

The economic and sociocultural development of mature socialism creates favorable opportunities for further improvement in women's work, daily life, and overall mode of life. But these opportunities cannot be spontaneously realized. They cannot become reality without vigorous and purposeful action on the part of state, social and economic organizations, and all clear-thinking members of society.

Notes

1. *Materialy XXVI s"ezda KPSS*, Moscow, 1981, pp. 54, 55, 104–105; *Materialy XXV s"ezda KPSS*, Moscow, 1976, pp. 85, 217; *Materialy XXIV s"ezda KPSS*, Moscow, 1972, pp. 75, 144.

2. These surveys were conducted in 1968 and 1978 by a number of scientific institutions, notably the Social Statistics Laboratory and Section of Social Development of the Working Class (USSR Academy of Sciences, Institute of the International Workers' Movement), under the supervision of L. A. Gordon and E. V. Klopov together with the participation of the authors. The 1968 survey was part of a comprehensive study of social problems in a typical industrial city which was undertaken on the suggestion of the CPSU Central Committee's Propaganda Division. The 1978 survey replicated the earlier one and followed a similar design. The data from the two surveys are wholly comparable.

2a. For more detail on classifying types of labor, see *Sotsial'noe i kul'-turnoe razvitie rabochego klassa v sotsialisticheskom obshchestve (Metodicheskie i metodologicheskie voprosy)*, Moscow, part 1, 1982, pp. 6–72.

3. *Materialy XXIV s"ezda KPSS*, p. 39.

4. *Materialy XXVI s"ezda KPSS*, p. 107.

5. *Ibid.*, p. 57.

6. See *Narodnoe khoziaistvo SSSR v 1980 godu*, p. 406.

7. *Pravda*, 24 June 1981.

Part III

Status Attainment and Social Mobility

9. A Causal Model of Youth Mobility*

A. V. KIRKH and E. A. SAAR

From the socioeconomic perspective three basic elements are involved in the younger generation's initiation into independent life and its subsequent advancement in society: the acquisition of an education and specialized training, socio-occupational mobility, and geographical mobility. The aim of our research was to study the interconnections among these processes, and, on this basis, to construct a model of youth mobility.

This particular problem, and above all the social factors in mobility, have recently been illuminated in a number of special studies.[1] Research has centered on the following topics: the impact of the sociodemographic characteristics of individuals (gender, age, educational level and type of educational institution completed) upon mobility; the social origin and environment from which the young people started out; and the socioeconomic and educational situation in which the mobility occurs.

The first of these aspects has been most thoroughly studied. It is known, however, that educational level, as a factor in social mobility, stems from social-class differences—in particular from the social position of the parents and their material, cultural, and educational levels. Therefore we shall focus our attention upon the latter two groups of factors, supported by our awareness that the social environment and especially the dynamics of the socio-educational situation exert a growing influence on youth mobility.

*Russian text © 1984 by "Nauka" Publishers. "Prichinaia model' mobil'-nosti molodezhi," *Sotsiologicheskie issledovaniia*, 1984, No. 1, pp. 70–73.

Statistical data obtained during the All-Union population censuses of 1959, 1970, and 1979 permit us to conclude that there have been fundamental changes in educational levels of various population groups in the Estonian SSR over the past two decades. With the transition to universal secondary education, the number of years that young people spend in school has increased significantly. In 1970 less than a third of the republic's young men and women had received a secondary education by the age of 19; in 1979, three-quarters had received this kind of education. But among the rural population, the rate of growth in minimum educational levels (eight years of schooling) had slowed down. Two circumstances must be considered here. First, rural inhabitants are, on average, "older" than their urban counterparts, and this aging tendency shows no signs of abating. Second, in recent years the level of migration from rural areas has declined. In 1977, for example, the population of the Estonian countryside showed a 1.1% drop, while in 1982 the reduction was only 0.3%—a difference of 3000 persons.[2] Under existing circumstances the falling growth rates in education levels among rural inhabitants are having a negative effect upon efforts to shape labor resources in rural areas, and upon the socio-occupational aspects of the convergence between town and countryside.

In our analysis of intergenerational mobility we depended upon the findings of a longitudinal study of secondary school graduates in the Estonian SSR conducted over the period from 1966 through 1979.[3] Studies of interaction between the social factors involved in mobility commonly utilize the method of determining the relevant correlational links. But this does not always produce satisfactory results since some indices that characterize mobility do not lend themselves to ranking. We therefore employed the method of path analysis to construct a so-called causal model which permits us to determine the relative importance of each of the factors in the process of social mobility.

Otis Duncan, in the first known attempt to design such a model, took the education and social affiliation of the respondent and his father as basic factors. Since 1967, when Duncan's monograph (written with Peter Blau) appeared, the model has been significantly improved. But the original rationale remains, the aim being to reveal the link between the social characteristics of father and child. However, Western researchers start out with the assumption that the individual enjoys "equality of opportunity" in bourgeois society—and here lies the methodological weakness of this approach, and hence, of the Duncan-Blau socioeconomic index. After all, social status per se is not some sort of a "field" of mobility; it is rather an expression of the respondent's class affiliation.[4]

Bearing all this in mind, we analyzed the interconnections among the social characteristics of young people formed as a result of the educational process and through social and geographical mobility. This model represents a system of equations which express certain characteristics as functions of others. The model is depicted in the form of a schematic which clearly reveals the system of hypotheses that we adopted. The characteristics occupy the vertices of this schematic, and the arrows running between the vertices show the links between the factors.[5]

The figure presents the basic models of intergenerational mobility, with the coefficients of linear correlation and the path coefficients (given in parentheses). The models show the impact of parental education, social position, and place of residence upon the corresponding characteristics of the respondent in 1979, at the time of the survey.[6]

What interpretation may we place upon this model? First let us note that as things presently stand, the significance of the educational factor in achieving social homogeneity is conditioned by social-class differences among the respondents' families. The path coefficients attest to the fact that parental educational level and place of residence largely predetermine the educational path of youth and therefore also affect their future social position (see Table).

Parental place of residence exerts a powerful impact upon the geographical mobility of young people, while at the same time parental social position and education, and even the education of

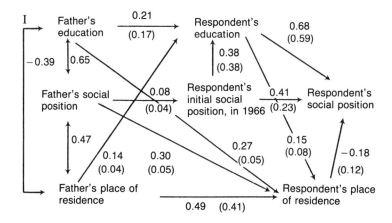

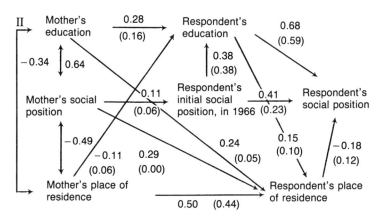

Model of intergenerational social and geographical mobility (data for 1979): I–as function of father's social characteristics; II–as function of mother's social characteristics

the respondents themselves, appear to have virtually no influence upon the respondents' place of residence. In other words, the residential structure is the prime focus of most of the causal links relating to mobility. Intergenerational mobility occurs precisely in and through the type of residential settlement involved and the migrational flow prompted by it. Consequently, in order to forecast the educational level of various groups of young people, it is necessary above all, to have an accurate picture of the migratory process and its unique sociodemographic features in any given

Path Coefficients of Intergenerational Mobility for Various Social Strata

Respondent's socio-occupational position at age 31	Father's educational level	Mother's educational level	Father's social position	Mother's social position	Respondent's social position at age 18	Respondent's education	Coefficient of multiple determination
Skilled worker	0.21*	0.01	0.03	0.01	0.11	0.14	0.03(0.02)
Highly skilled worker	0.02	0.10	0.11	0.01	0.03	0.23	0.06(0.08)
Employee	0.04	0.09	0.10	0.03	0.14	0.47	0.27(0.32)
Uncredentialed practical specialist	0.18	0.06	0.08	0.09	0.23	0.01	0.10(0.08)
Specialist with secondary specialized education	0.06	0.01	0.00	0.01	0.10	0.09	0.01(0.03)
Specialist with higher education	0.03	0.02	0.04	0.04	0.02	0.08	0.01(0.01)

*This figure is presumably a misprint in the original Soviet publication, since the author explicitly refers to a low value for this group.—M.Y.

region. This is extremely pertinent in the case of Estonia, where 60% of the population (according to data for 1979) reported a recent change in place of residence.[7]

An important question concerns the role which the designated factors play in intergenerational mobility within and between the basic social strata. This was decided by reference to the path coefficients of the basic model (see Table). Low values were typically recorded for the skilled worker group. This group must, therefore, be drawn from the most varied social strata. As we expected, the connection between the respondent's education and his present social position was insignificant in this group.

The model is somewhat more informative for highly skilled workers. The direct influence of maternal education and paternal social position is stronger here. And yet, in this group the respondent's present social position is virtually independent of his original social position.

The model is not particularly informative for employees. This is because the employees' stratum is drawn from people who graduated from secondary school within the past two or three years. As a rule, people who enter this group remain at the same educational level.

The path coefficients between both parental education and social position and the respondent's social position are most significant in the group of uncredentialed practical specialists. We can assume that this stratum is drawn from particular types of families whose principal social ambition centers on this kind of a career. For respondents with a secondary specialized and higher education there is virtually no link between the aforementioned factors. These strata must therefore recruit among young people from various social groups.

From all the above we may conclude that the older generation influences the social-class position of young people indirectly— through the factor of education. The children of workers and collective farmers embark upon socially useful work, as a rule, by taking an educational "shortcut"—after completing school or a secondary specialized educational institution. Representatives of the intelligentsia and employees, for their part, encourage the younger generation to proceed on to higher education.

Notes

1. D. I. Ziuzin, "Causes of Low Mobility of the Native Population of The Republics of Central Asia," *Sotsiologicheskie issledovaniia*, 1983, no. 1; V. I. Lukina, S. B. Nekhoroshkov, *Dinamika sotsial'noi struktury naselenii SSSR. Methodologiia i metodika issledovaniia*, Moscow, Finansy i statistika, 1982; F. R. Filippov, "Education and Social Mobility (On Elaborating a System of Indicators)," in *Voprosy sravnitel'nykh mezhdunarodnykh sotsiologicheskikh issledovanii/Materialy III finskosovetskogo simpoziuma po sotsiologii, Turku, oktiabr' 1980 g.*, Moscow, ISI AN SSSR, 1980, pp. 38–47; V. Shubkin, *Nachalo puti. Problemy molodezhi v zerkale sotsiologii i literatury*, Moscow, Molodaia gvardiia, 1979.

2. *Narodnoe khoziaistvo Estonskoi SSR v 1982 g. Statisticheskii ezhegodnik*, Tallin, Eesti paamat, 1983, p. 10; E. Vanatoa, *Estonskaia SSR. Spravochnik*, Tallin, Periodika, 1983, p. 30.

3. The research was conducted by Tartu State University's Laboratory for the Study of Communist Upbringing and the Youth Sociology Section of the Estonian SSR Academy of Sciences Institute of History. In 1966 graduates of daytime and evening general education schools were surveyed (N = 2260 persons). In 1969 third year students in various institutes—the 1966 school leavers (N = 1747)—and young people in employment (N = 502) were surveyed. All of these had been polled during the first stage of the project. In 1973 young specialists (N = 863) were surveyed, followed in 1976 by general education school graduates who started work immediately after leaving school (N = 801). In 1979, 1460 of those who left school in 1966 were polled. They had turned 31 by then and their social standing was basically stable. The authors participated in the 1976 and 1979 studies. For information on the research program and methodology, see *Zhiznennyi put' molodezhi*, Tallin, Izd-vo AN ESSR, 1983.

4. M. Kh. Titma, "Studies of Social Structure in the USA," *Sotsiologicheskie issledovaniia*, 1981, no. 4, p. 205.

5. I. V. Bestuzhev-Lada, V. N. Varygin, V. A. Malakhov, *Modelirovanie v sotsiologicheskikh issledovaniiakh*, Moscow, Nauka, 1978, pp. 77 80.

6. A. Kirkh, E. Saar, "A Model of Intergenerational Social Mobility (A Genetic Study in the Estovian SSR in 1966–1979)," in *Gorod kak sreda zhiznedeiatel'nosti cheloveka*, Vilnius, Izd-vo AN Lit SSR, 1981, part II, pp. 6–10.

7. *Naselenie SSSR. Spravochnik*, Moscow, Politizdat, 1983, p. 53.

10. Generations and Social Self-determination

A Study of Cohorts from 1948 to 1979 in the Estonian SSR*

P. O. KENKMAN, E. A. SAAR, and M. Kh. TITMA

The younger generation's entry into the life of society is a complex social process. This process was studied in the Estonian SSR by sociologists at Tartu State University and the Estonian SSR's Institute of History (project director: M. Kh. Titma).

The project's goal was to shed light on the basic trends in the social mobility of graduates of general educational institutions engaged in finding a stable position in all basic spheres of social life. Young people enter the life of society in stages; each stage undergoes a transformation at the critical point when a solution to one of the problems of self-determination in life is reached. Every stage is characterized by particular social circumstances which have an impact upon young people. The principal interest of this research was to uncover the logic of self-determination in life.

Our project started out with a group of secondary school graduates. The plan was to follow them from the moment they entered the decisive stage of self-determination in life, until they

*Russian text © 1982 by "Nauka" Publishers. "Sotsial'noe samoopredelenie pokolenii (Issledovanie kogorty s 1948 po 1979 g., Estonskaia SSR)," Akademiia nauk SSSR, Institut sotsiologicheskikh issledovanii, *Sovetskaia sotsiologiia*, Vol. II, Moscow, 1982, pp. 82–110.

were 30 years old, which was arbitrarily chosen as the age at which the entire generation achieves social maturity and a stable social position. Our project differed from comparable undertakings in that it focused upon pivotal episodes in the genesis of the phenomenon under study. This type of research may therefore be termed genetic.

The research cycle began in 1966, with a survey of graduates of daytime and evening (shift) general education schools where Estonian was the language of instruction. Of 4,440 graduates, 2,260 (50.9%) were selected for study. The sample was representative of the given aggregate.

The group polled was part of the generation (cohort) that was born mostly in 1948 and the overwhelming majority of which entered the first grade of the general education school in 1955. A total of 18,500 children began their educational careers in that year. This will be our base figure in subsequent discussions of the given cohort.

In 1966, 11 years after beginning first grade, 7,000 people graduated from general education schools. Approximately 60% of them had been taught in Estonian. A total of 9,930 people (54% of the cohort) were receiving secondary education in that year. (In 1966 the transition to universal secondary education was only in the planning stage.) Thus, our total sample encompassed one-third of all those completing the secondary general education school, or slightly under one-quarter of all those who had received a secondary education. Twelve percent of the entire 1948 cohort was included in the first stage of the survey.

Girls comprised 62.7% of those surveyed. This corresponds to the proportions of boys and girls in general education school graduating classes. The sample included 9% of the boys and 16% of the girls in the cohort.

The second stage of this genetic study was conducted in 1969. At that time the 1966 graduates were divided into two groups—students and pupils in secondary specialized educational institutions, on the one hand, and working youth, on the other. Since most young people enter higher educational institutions directly from daytime secondary schools, the majority of the 1966 graduates who went on to become students were in their third year in 1969.

Questions were asked of 1,717 third-year students (78% of all third-year students in daytime classes where the language of instruction was Estonian). The intention was to conduct a comprehensive poll, but there were some omissions because students were absent from the classes in which the questionnaires were administered. The survey covered 427 of the basic contingent who were students in the 1968/69 academic year. This comprised approximately 60% of the secondary school graduates surveyed in 1966 who had since entered daytime divisions of higher educational institutions.

In the same year a survey was conducted of the 1966 graduates who were working in various branches of production, in the service sphere, and in culture. This category accounted for over one-half of all graduates, or 2,560 people. Of these, 502 fell within the basic range of our study. In sum, the two surveys of 1969 encompassed 12% of the cohort, as in 1966.

Three-quarters of the young people studying in higher educational institutions were graduates of secondary general education schools with no work experience.

In our study the period of initial adjustment for a specialist in industry was taken to be two years. Thus in 1973 we surveyed the young people who had made their way into the world of work through higher education. We questioned 863 young specialists— 47% of the aggregate number of specialists with two years of work experience.

One more survey was conducted in 1976 to analyze the paths taken by those secondary school graduates who received no specialized education prior to beginning work. Of the 1,140 secondary school graduates who went directly into production activity, 801 were surveyed (70% of the basic aggregate). The group surveyed in 1976 comprised 35% of all those who had graduated from secondary general education schools in 1966.

Our genetic study culminated in 1979, by which time the bulk of the survey group had turned 30. The aggregate—the group of graduates from general education schools where Estonian was the language of instruction—was studied once more. To derive a "clearer" picture of self-determination among young people, the graduates of evening (shift) educational institutions were excluded from the aggregate at this point. Young people who had completed the same daytime general education schools as those polled in 1966 but who had been omitted from the original sample were now brought into the survey. As a result, 1,460 people were questioned in this culminating stage of the genetic study—which is 43% of our original subject of study (those who graduated from secondary school in 1966).

In accordance with the program of genetic research, all the basic aspects of self-determination in life experienced by young people with secondary education—social, occupational, and sociopolitical self-determination, the creation of a family, the organization of personal life, and the establishment of a sphere of contacts with others—were covered at every stage. In this overview we will examine social self-determination, which is the single most important aspect of self-determination.

1. Social mobility

Social self-determination constitutes the cornerstone of self-determination in life. It expresses itself initially in the attainment of a distinct social position, and thereafter in social mobility.

The process of acquiring a social position begins immediately after the end of secondary school. Three years later one-half of the former graduates are involved in this process, whose culminating stage is reached five years after the completion of secondary education (Table 1). Thereafter it is a question of social mobility out of one group or stratum and into another.

In the 1960s the smallest percentage of secondary school graduates remained in the collective or state farm milieu. Only 2.5% of the graduates became collective farm peasants or state farm workers immediately on leaving school. By the age of 28 the

Table 1

Social Mobility of Secondary School Graduates Aged 18 to 31, in %

Social stratum	18	19	20	21	22
Collective farmers, state farm workers	2.7	2.5	2.0	2.3	2.2
Unskilled workers	12.5	7.8	6.3	4.3	3.5
Skilled workers	11.9	13.6	13.1	12.8	14.5
Highly skilled workers	1.3	1.7	2.5	3.3	4.0
Employees	16.1	13.8	14.5	14.7	15.3
Uncredentialed practical specialists	8.1	7.2	8.1	10.0	10.9
Students and pupils	47.3	53.4	50.9	45.0	37.4
Specialists with secondary specialized education	0.0	0.0	2.6	7.6	9.0
Specialists with higher education	0.0	0.0	0.0	0.0	3.2

relative size of this category had increased, not because their age-mates were leaving workers' jobs in industrial enterprises or employees' positions to become collective farmers and state farm workers, but because agrarian working people are a stable group and because rural living standards rose in the 1970s.

The bulk of the graduates who went into socially useful work immediately upon completing secondary school joined the ranks of workers. At 18 years of age, unskilled workers accounted for one-eighth of the cohort. Their number fell by 5% per year, and eight years after leaving secondary school only a handful remained in this stratum.

A year after the end of secondary education the cohort contained as many skilled workers as unskilled workers. However the skilled worker stratum was a relatively stable group, which grew slowly at the outset and then fell to 8.8% by the time the graduates were 30 years of age.

The number of secondary school graduates in the highly skilled working class stratum was small at first (1.3%). However, it

Table 1 (continued)

Age, in years

23	24	25	26	27	28	29	30	31
2.7	2.9	2.6	2.7	2.9	2.8	2.2	3.3	3.6
2.8	2.6	2.1	1.5	1.6	1.5	1.3	1.5	1.2
14.4	13.0	12.9	12.0	10.9	10.0	9.3	8.8	8.9
4.7	6.1	6.4	6.9	8.0	8.6	8.8	8.9	8.8
14.4	13.8	12.9	11.9	11.6	11.9	11.8	11.3	10.6
11.7	11.8	12.6	12.9	12.1	10.8	10.8	10.5	10.9
19.3	11.1	5.7	3.6	1.7	0.9	0.7	0.1	0.1
10.5	11.2	11.5	11.8	12.3	12.6	12.5	12.5	12.3
19.5	27.5	33.3	36.7	38.9	40.9	42.6	43.1	43.6

gradually grew, so that by approximately 30 years of age it was the same size as the skilled worker stratum, because graduates had moved from the skilled worker stratum to the highly skilled stratum. We may assume that this process will continue.

Immediately after leaving secondary school about one-sixth of the graduates joined the ranks of the employees' category. But the number fell by the age of 26. Uncredentialed practical specialists [*spetsialisti-praktiki*] at first made up the smallest group, but subsequently their relative share came to equal that of employees. Their number also stabilized at around the age of 30, at which time it was somewhat larger than this stratum's overall size in the employed population.

The stratum of middle-level specialists entered the picture two to three years after graduation from school. It reached its maximum size when the graduates were 26 years old. But the relative share of secondary school graduates in this stratum was somewhat less than the relative share of middle-level specialists in the employed population.

Highly skilled specialists were assembled some five or six years after receiving their secondary education. Their number increased as the graduates reached 30.

An analysis of statistical relationships among the social groups of cohorts by years will help us characterize the overall logic of social self-determination. To identify the major deviations in the process of social self-determination we shall take the two strata of specialists with higher education and skilled workers. The mean values of the correlation coefficient between cohort social position in any one year and social position in other years form—for the whole sample—a simple [*monotonnuiu*] curve which rises up to 26 years of age, and then falls. This indicates that, with regard to social mobility, social position at 26 years of age is most decisive in describing initial changes and probable future mobility.

Specialists with higher education typically exhibit a different kind of link. While the peak here comes at the age of 26, this curve exhibits two sharp breaks, the first coming five years after leaving secondary school, and the second at the age of 28, which is difficult to explain at first glance. The fact is, however, that the second phenomenon is a reflection of the first. A specialist's social position by the age of 30 bears very little relation to his position prior to the receipt of his specialist's diploma.

Skilled workers present a completely different picture. This stratum is formed within the first two to three years.

Interconnections in the entire cohort's social position in various years are clearly revealed in a correlational series. Analysis points to three relatively independent time segments: the two years after leaving secondary school, from 20 to 26 years of age, and from 27 to 31. The internal interconnection of annual mobility indices is stronger in the latter period, which points to a stabilization of social position at that age.

One may tentatively identify the first two years as a time for reconnoitering. Then comes the period of initial consolidation of social position, while the third period is characterized by a stabilization of social position. The social self-determination of specialists with higher education exhibits a different chronological pattern. The years of study in a higher educational institution constitute the first stage of social self-determination. The cohort's second stage covers the next six years, and the third stage takes up the final four years. The interconnection of the indices of social position in these three stages grows stronger by 30 years of age, although to a lesser extent than that recorded in the cohort as a whole. The middle period exhibits closer internal integration. An examination of the time series of social mobility for specialists with higher education enables us to determine the reason for this pattern and to more precisely identify the relevant periods.

The correlational series for the skilled worker stratum shows five time segments of social mobility. The first stage covers three years and is the least internally integrated. The second stage lasts for four years. The consolidation of this stratum of the cohort occurs between the ages of 25 and 26. Then there is movement both into and out of this group. Despite the multiplicity of time segments, the process of social mobility into the skilled worker stratum is more stable than the recruitment of specialists with higher education. Interconnection in the entire time series is higher by one order of magnitude, and after the first period— inclusion in the ranks of workers—social position becomes stabilized.

The formation of social strata proceeds by means of a multiplicity of movements. Thus one-quarter of the skilled worker stratum is made up of secondary school graduates and another quarter of its recruits are dropouts from higher educational institutions and technicums, which comes as something of a surprise (Table 2). The former students enter workers' ranks en masse in the second and third year after the end of secondary education. They are the basic source of recruits to the skilled worker contingent during those years, with a slight edge over unskilled workers, who provide one-quarter of this stratum. Both of these recruitment waves occur during the first three years of work.

Next on the list are former employees, who comprise about one-tenth of the skilled workers' stratum. At the ages of 21–23

Table 2

Stratum Distribution of Secondary School Graduates Who Became Skilled Workers by the Age of 31, in %

Social stratum	Age in years												
	18	19	20	21	22	23	24	25	26	27	28	29	30
Collective farmers, state farm workers	1.2	2.6	0.6	1.8	3.3	3.2	3.2	3.2	3.1	3.9	0.5	0.5	0.5
Unskilled workers	26.9	18.0	12.3	13.5	9.1	9.5	11.8	10.2	7.8	5.4	3.2	3.2	2.5
Skilled workers	28.8	36.0	47.3	55.0	58.7	61.1	60.6	65.4	72.7	77.5	85.8	88.2	93.0
Highly skilled workers	1.2	2.0	3.1	0.0	4.0	3.0	3.1	1.0	0.0	0.0	0.0	0.0	0.0
Employees	9.2	8.1	11.3	10.8	10.7	9.5	7.1	7.1	4.7	4.7	3.9	3.0	2.0
Uncredentialed practical specialists	5.0	4.5	3.8	6.3	6.6	4.8	3.9	5.5	5.5	3.1	3.6	2.6	0.0
Students	27.2	28.2	17.8	5.4	1.0	3.3	1.6	0.6	0.0	0.0	0.0	0.0	0.0
Specialists with secondary specialized education	0.0	0.0	3.8	7.2	6.6	5.6	6.3	4.7	3.9	3.1	3.0	2.5	2.0
Specialists with higher education	0.0	0.0	0.0	0.0	0.0	0.0	2.4	2.3	2.3	2.3	0.0	0.0	0.0

years, some of the uncredentialed practical specialists and middle-level specialists move into the ranks of skilled workers. The flow of those joining these ranks is therefore certainly not limited to unskilled workers. It should be stressed that there is virtually no movement from the highly skilled workers' stratum into the stratum of skilled workers with a secondary education.

Two-thirds of the specialists' stratum is recruited from secondary school graduates who went directly into higher education (Table 3). In the four-year period following the completion of secondary school, the higher educational system encompasses 83.4% of those who will one day be specialists with higher education. About one-quarter of specialists with higher education are trained in the correspondence and evening divisions of the higher educational system. These are basically employees and uncredentialed practical specialists.

One-tenth of future specialists are workers, but only remain so for the first two years after graduation. These graduates become workers only on a temporary basis. It is thus safe to state that this stratum is formed directly from secondary school graduates, with only limited contributions from the employees' stratum and the stratum of uncredentialed practical specialists.

In light of the above it is undoubtedly interesting to consider *the probability of social mobility* in the process of cohort self-determination. To establish a general picture of social mobility from the age of 18 to 31 we used Markov chains to ascertain the probability of movement from one stratum to another. As can be seen from Table 4, the greatest probability is that of stabilization of social position once the latter has been attained by a young person. This probability is highest—0.98—in the stratum of specialists with higher education. It is slightly lower—0.82—for middle-level specialists. From here, there is some probability of movement into the stratum of specialists with higher education or the stratum of highly skilled workers.

There is a high probability of movement from the stratum of uncredentialed practical specialists into other strata, primarily into that of specialists with higher education (0.23), and also into

Table 3

Stratum Distribution of Secondary School Graduates Who Became Specialists with Higher Education by the Age of 31, in %

Social stratum	Age in years												
	18	19	20	21	22	23	24	25	26	27	28	29	30
Collective farmers, state farm workers	0.5	0.4	0.3	0.3	0.3	0.0	0.0	0.0	0.0	0.0	0.0	0.0	0.0
Unskilled workers	5.6	3.7	3.4	2.1	0.0	0.0	0.0	0.0	0.0	0.0	0.0	0.0	0.0
Skilled workers	7.0	5.3	3.8	2.8	2.0	1.2	0.0	0.0	0.0	0.0	0.0	0.0	0.0
Highly skilled workers	0.6	0.5	0.5	0.8	0.5	0.6	0.7	0.8	1.2	0.0	0.0	0.0	0.0
Employees	11.8	6.8	5.4	5.4	6.1	5.4	4.8	3.1	2.8	2.3	1.2	0.6	0.0
Uncredentialed practical specialists	7.2	5.2	5.3	5.2	6.9	8.1	7.3	7.0	6.5	5.5	3.2	1.8	0.0
Students	67.3	78.1	81.3	83.4	74.6	37.7	21.6	11.0	6.7	3.8	2.0	1.4	1.3
Specialists with secondary specialized education	0.0	0.0	0.0	0.0	2.5	2.8	3.5	3.5	1.4	1.4	1.5	1.6	0.0
Specialists with higher education	0.0	0.0	0.0	0.0	7.1	44.2	62.2	74.6	81.4	87.0	92.1	94.6	98.7

the middle-level specialists' stratum (0.11). But the likelihood of leaving the specialist ranks is slight (0.09). Employees also constitute a group with a high propensity for mobility, and the range of mobility here is quite wide. There is an almost identical probability of movement into the ranks of uncredentialed practical specialists, of specialists with secondary specialized education, and of specialists with higher education. And there is an equal likelihood of moving into the working class.

The highly skilled workers' stratum is relatively stable (0.67). Here the most probable movement is into the ranks of uncredentialed practical specialists (0.12). The skilled workers' stratum is not particularly stable, the likelihood of movement being significantly higher than the likelihood of remaining a skilled worker. In particular, there is considerable movement into the highest working class stratum (0.17). There is an approximately equal probability of movement into the ranks of employees, uncredentialed practical specialists, and the stratum of specialists with higher education. This is the only stratum that contributes recruits to collective farmers and state farm workers.

The unskilled workers' stratum is the least stable of all (0.18). The likelihood of moving from this stratum into other workers' strata is higher than the likelihood of remaining an unskilled worker. The probability of moving into the ranks of employees or uncredentialed practical specialists is also high. However, the small size of the latter stratum indicates that secondary school graduates do not easily find a place here. Another small contingent is that of collective farmers and state farm workers who are secondary school graduates. It is, however, notable for its relative stability.

Contemporary social conditions render some of the niches of the social structure accessible to secondary school graduates and dictate the likelihood of movement therefrom. We shall examine some of the more important of these. Unquestionably, the national economy's need for labor and the present level of development of the country's social structure are determining features.

Analyzing social mobility by *gender*, we note that the mobility

Table 4

Probability of Social Mobility Within the Cohort

Stratum into which mobility proceeds	Stratum from which mobility proceeds							
	Collective farmers and state farm workers	Unskilled workers	Skilled workers	Highly skilled workers	Nonspecialist employees	Uncre-dentialed practical specialists	Specialists with secondary specialized education	Specialists with higher education
Collective farmers, state farm workers	0.67	0.03	0.06	0.02	0.02	0.00	0.01	0.00
Unskilled workers	0.01	0.18	0.01	0.00	0.02	0.01	0.02	0.00
Skilled workers	0.07	0.26	0.49	0.02	0.04	0.02	0.04	0.01

Highly skilled workers	0.01	0.20	0.17	0.67	0.03	0.02	0.01	0.00
Nonspecialist employees	0.07	0.11	0.09	0.07	0.57	0.04	0.02	0.01
Uncredentialed practical specialists	0.08	0.12	0.08	0.12	0.11	0.54	0.01	0.00
Specialists with secondary specialized education	0.05	0.03	0.03	0.04	0.08	0.11	0.82	0.00
Specialists with higher education	0.04	0.07	0.07	0.06	0.13	0.26	0.07	0.98

Table 5

Changes in Social Position of Cohort, Depending on Sex, in %

	Age in years													
	18		20		22		24		26		28		31	
Social stratum	Males	Females	Males	Females	Males	Females	Males	Females	Males	Females	Males	Females	Males	Females
Collective farmers, state farm workers	3.5	2.0	3.1	2.2	3.3	2.0	3.9	2.3	3.3	3.2	3.6	2.3	4.7	2.8
Unskilled workers	13.7	11.9	4.3	5.8	4.9	2.7	2.6	2.5	1.2	2.6	2.1	3.9	1.0	2.4
Skilled workers	10.0	12.9	8.8	14.9	15.1	14.6	14.4	12.8	13.9	10.7	11.9	8.8	10.4	7.9
Highly skilled workers	1.4	1.9	2.0	2.9	4.5	3.7	8.9	4.6	9.6	5.4	11.5	6.6	12.9	6.5
Employees	3.7	22.8	3.0	19.4	4.7	20.5	5.9	17.7	3.3	16.3	3.8	16.5	1.4	15.5
Uncredentialed practical specialists	4.1	10.2	6.3	8.9	11.0	10.4	10.9	12.7	13.1	12.5	11.2	10.3	11.0	10.7
Students	63.6	38.3	72.5	41.6	49.1	30.8	11.3	10.9	4.0	3.3	0.0	0.0	0.0	0.0
Specialists with secondary specialized education	0.0	0.0	0.0	4.3	4.1	11.6	5.7	13.9	6.2	14.6	6.4	15.9	6.4	15.6
Specialists with higher education	0.0	0.0	0.0	0.0	3.3	3.7	36.4	22.6	45.4	31.4	49.5	35.7	52.2	38.6

of young men is strikingly different from that of young women (Table 5). We shall examine this, using recruitment to the collective farmer and state farm worker complement as our example. A higher percentage of female school graduates remain in agriculture, but in absolute terms males and females are recruited to agriculture in equal measure. Nor is there any particular distinction to be made with regard to recruitment into the ranks of unskilled workers. However the skilled workers' stratum in the initial years is recruited mainly from females. From the age of 22 the males' share begins to pull ahead, although by 30 years of age men and women are equally represented in these groups.

Employees are traditionally female; the formative period comes immediately after secondary school (22.8% of females, 3.7% of males). It is rather surprising that initially most uncredentialed practical specialists are also female. In the year following the completion of secondary school there are almost three times as many girls as boys in this group. But four years after graduation the proportions of boys and girls in the ranks of uncredentialed practical specialists level out, although in absolute terms girls predominate.

The stratum of specialists with secondary specialized education is recruited largely from girls. Less than a quarter of this stratum is male, since fewer boys go on to technicums after finishing secondary school. However the gender composition of the middle-level specialists' group gains some overall balance from pupils who enroll in technicums after eight years of secondary school.

In percentage terms the stratum of specialists with higher education is predominantly recruited from boys. This is most conspicuous in the student body, where boys have a large relative margin. The boys never lose the 14% advantage which emerges immediately after graduation from higher educational institutions, but the relative share of girls in the stratum of specialists with higher education remains high because two-thirds of secondary school graduates are female.

Intergenerational mobility is negligible in this cohort, since the greater portions of young people did not get a complete secondary general education in the 1960s. Mobility is rooted in a succession of social position (Table 6).

Collective farmers and state farm workers form an exceedingly small group which reproduces itself intensively and grows on the strength of mobility from workers' families. Specialists hardly participate at all in recruitment into this stratum: they provide eight times fewer recruits to this group than do collective farmers and state farm workers. The unskilled workers' stratum is also small. By the age of 30 the only secondary school graduates still remaining within it are those who have deviated from the normal process of self-determination in life (and such people also come from intelligentsia families).

Skilled workers come from workers' families that are both heterogeneous and homogeneous in composition. Rural inhabitants are also highly visible recruits into this stratum. And recruitment from employees' families also proceeds intensively, at higher than average rates. Only specialists' families are infrequent participants in this process, providing half as many recruits as the other groups. Highly skilled workers draw most intensively upon the worker milieu, and there is also an especially large number of recruits from heterogeneous "employee—collective farmer" families. In short, people from all strata except "female worker—male employee" families are fairly well represented here. This is an indication that the highly skilled workers' stratum attracts recruits from all strata of society.

Most employees are female. Their ranks are primarily replenished from those types of families which participate to a lesser extent in replenishing the stratum of specialists with higher education. Specialists' families participate least of all in that replenishment process—almost six times less than "female collective farmer—male worker" families.

Uncredentialed practical specialists are drawn most intensively from heterogeneous workers' families. There is no doubt that this reflects the social aspirations of the offspring of these families. A somewhat unexpected discovery is that collective farmers

Table 6

Indices of Links between Respondents' Social Position and Type of Family

Respondent's social position

Family type (social position of mother/father)	Collective and state farm workers	Unskilled workers	Highly skilled workers	Skilled workers	Nonspecialist employees	Uncredentialed practical specialists	Specialists with secondary specialized education	Specialists with higher education
Collective farmers	1.90	1.42	1.28	1.20	1.23	1.38	1.22	0.63
State farm workers	1.92	0.00	1.01	0.88	1.19	0.61	1.12	1.01
Collective farmer/ worker	1.46	0.00	1.72	1.15	1.48	0.69	1.90	0.56
Workers	0.99	3.28	0.91	1.13	1.12	1.04	1.21	0.86
Employee/ worker	1.23	0.00	0.97	1.46	0.83	1.10	0.78	0.98
Specialist/ worker	0.47	0.00	0.93	0.93	1.12	1.18	1.09	1.01
Worker/ employee	0.71	0.00	1.96	0.28	0.72	1.35	0.62	1.09
Employees	0.74	0.00	1.17	0.78	1.00	0.39	1.08	1.19
Worker/ specialist	0.51	0.00	0.81	0.60	1.21	1.77	0.89	0.90
Employee/ specialist	0.26	0.00	0.73	0.94	0.99	0.75	0.69	1.28
Specialists	0.25	0.94	0.50	0.70	0.26	0.96	0.44	1.54

participate extensively in the shaping of this stratum. The stratum of middle-level specialists is recruited from the offspring of collective farm peasant families, and also from workers' families, and much less from other types of families. The stratum of specialists with higher education draws primarily on the offspring of specialists' families and is also a priority goal in the mobility of employees.

But on the whole, differences in social sources are not great and point to greater variation in the choice of life directions, as predicated upon the social milieu, than that established in earlier studies of the student body.[1]

Differences that are contingent upon the residential structure (Table 7) are the same as differences in social-class sources and are, as is known, predominantly socioeconomic in nature. Thus, Tallin—the capital—clearly offers more opportunities for choice in both traditional workers' occupations and in specialists' jobs. From the data in Table 7 it follows that the residents of Tallin provide the bulk of recruits for the ranks of highly skilled workers and specialists (both uncredentialed specialists and specialists with higher education), while the stratum of middle-level specialists is predominantly made up of residents of other areas. Tallin residents play a negligible role in replenishing the collective farmers' and state farm workers' strata.

Tartu (a higher educational center), provides mainly highly skilled specialists. Tartu residents are far less visible in the other specialist strata and among workers. The republic's major towns are multi-functional district centers. Consequently opportunities abound for recruitment to the ranks of uncredentialed practical specialists. The inhabitants of these towns primarily tend to enter the middle-level stratum of specialists. These towns also produce a considerable group of workers.

The republic's small towns provide a somewhat higher than average share of uncredentialed practical specialists and middle-level specialists. These towns also have a distinctively larger proportion of less skilled worker strata. The same is true of urban settlements, except that they play a greater role in supplying collective farmer and state farm worker strata. The villages, naturally enough, provide more collective farmers and state farm workers, and rural girls also set their sights on becoming employees and middle-level specialists. Thus, the idiosyncrasies of the social framework within which any given stratum is molded are dictated by the socioeconomic, educational, and residential structure.

2. Self-determination in the residential structure

One of the fundamental aspects of social self-determination which is often overlooked is the decision made as to place of residence. As society develops, migratory activity increases, and it is only normal that young people should be highly involved in this. The contingent which we studied is rather special in this regard, since its national idiosyncrasies basically limit mobility to within the republic. Therefore it remained virtually untouched by interregional migratory flows.

Both educational level and movement into a social stratum are inescapably tied in with migratory flows within the residential structure. In addition, the residential structure itself generates mobility. To an increasing degree, self-determination depends not only on opportunities but on actual preferences as to place of residence, although the reproduction of population in young people's native residential structures does lie at the root of this aspect of self-determination. This is the starting point for migration.

We shall begin our analysis by examining young people's place of residence from birth to 31 years of age (Table 8). Research has shown that there is a widespread change in place of residence upon admission to and completion of secondary school. Enrollment in first grade has virtually no effect upon the proportion of young people living in the basic sections of the residential structure. But the desire to acquire a secondary education serves to reduce the rural population six-fold, and to increase substantially the proportion of people living in small towns and major cities,

Table 7

Link between Respondent's Social Position and Place of Secondary School Graduation

	Respondent's social position							
Place of secondary school graduation	Collective farmers and state farm workers	Unskilled workers	Skilled workers	Highly skilled workers	Nonspecialist employees	Uncredentialed practical specialists	Specialists with secondary specialized education	Specialists with higher education
Tallin	0.27	0.81	0.69	1.39	1.04	1.14	0.42	1.19
Tartu	0.67	0.00	0.79	0.76	0.96	0.49	0.87	1.32
Major cities	0.74	1.32	1.07	1.11	0.95	1.28	1.26	0.88
Other towns and district centers	1.39	1.55	1.34	0.72	0.96	1.13	1.18	0.87
Urban settlements, central economic units	1.80	1.27	1.21	0.82	1.02	0.63	1.35	0.85
Villages	2.20	0.000	0.68	0.98	1.21	1.01	1.23	0.84

Table 8

Change in Place of Residence of Secondary School Graduates

		Place of Residence				
Age	Capital	Higher educa-tional center	Major city	Small town	Urban settle-ment	Village
At birth	20.5	13.6	16.3	12.7	8.3	28.6
Beginning first grade	20.9	8.8	13.9	13.4	11.9	31.1
Leaving secondary school	24.7	12.6	20.2	21.4	15.8	5.3
18 years old	40.3	25.3	11.2	6.8	8.6	7.8
19 years old	42.0	29.1	8.7	6.4	7.1	6.7
20 years old	39.7	30.8	8.4	6.5	7.7	6.9
21 years old	36.6	29.5	10.6	7.7	8.4	7.2
22 years old	36.3	27.7	11.9	7.5	9.5	7.1
23 years old	34.2	21.4	13.3	9.6	12.6	8.9
24 years old	34.4	17.8	14.7	10.4	13.1	9.6
25 years old	34.7	15.9	15.0	10.9	14.2	9.3
26 years old	33.4	14.8	15.5	11.5	15.1	9.7
27 years old	33.4	14.0	15.4	11.8	15.4	10.0
28 years old	33.4	13.7	15.6	12.0	15.6	9.7
29 years old	33.9	13.7	15.3	12.0	16.1	9.0
30 years old	34.2	13.2	15.6	12.1	15.9	9.0
31 years old	34.2	13.2	15.6	12.4	15.8	8.8

and to a certain extent in urban settlements. The number of people residing in the capital and the major higher educational center increases only negligibly.

The completion of secondary school is a turning point that brings about a change in place of residence. One-third of pupils relocate for this reason. But the change does not stop there. Only 2.5% of people born in a village return home after finishing their secondary education in some other location. This is not even 10% of those "lured" from the villages by school. Thus one may assert that in the 1960s secondary school was a potent factor in rural population migration.

The urban settlements lose far fewer young people with secondary education. They retain over half of their secondary graduates. The percentage of secondary school graduates remaining, moreover, is equal to the percentage of youngsters born there. The small towns lose more young people—over half of those who are educated there. We are dealing here not only with the continuation of educational careers but also a certain lack of clarity in the overall developmental prospects of small towns.

This also applies to the republic's major cities: over half the secondary school graduates stay, although a large number of young people leave to continue their education elsewhere. The higher educational centers—Tartu and the republican capital—are the major recipients of the youth influx. Immediately after leaving secondary school a quarter of the cohort moves to Tartu, which is double the number of those who complete secondary school there. Migration of graduates to the capital is a sizable 15.6%.

At the end of an educational cycle, these initial migratory currents reverse themselves, with youngsters returning to the types of residential settlement from whence they originally came—albeit in depleted numbers. During the year after graduation a certain number of young people are still arriving in Tallin. But thereafter those members of the cohort who have acquired a secondary specialized education start to leave the capital. After a two-year period, therefore, young people begin to quit Tallin. The end of higher education affects the migratory process to a lesser extent. The higher educational institutions of Tartu are of relatively less service to the capital than are Tallin's own higher educational institutions.

Migration to Tartu shows a positive balance for two years after the completion of secondary school. But the end of higher education brings a heavy migrational outflow that reduces by 10% the share of the cohort still remaining in Tartu. The number continues to fall a little in later years, though by the time the graduates are 30 the fraction of this cohort remaining in Tartu is still one-third larger than its share of the overall republican population.

The republic's major cities gain young people in the two years following secondary school graduation, and they also receive a portion of the cohort after graduation from the higher educational system. However by the age of 27 the size of the cohort in these cities stabilizes at a level which is slightly below its relative share in the republican population. This means that they have ceded a portion of their young people to the republic's two principal cities.

Higher education graduates come to the small towns five years after graduation. Subsequently the number of inhabitants here grows slowly, mainly due to migration from urban settlements and from the countryside. There is a steady flow into the urban settlements until the graduates turn 30. Cohort numbers here are sharply increased by higher education graduates. The villages also feel the effect of higher education graduation, albeit to a lesser degree. The villages house 10% of the cohort from the age of 25—which is almost three times less than the number born there. Migration from the villages begins again from the age of 27.

Correlation analysis enables us to delineate more precisely the logic of migration flows, as determined by the respondent's social affiliation. The first set of links is clustered around place of residence prior to completion of secondary school. The internal link in this case is relatively weak and the predictive force of any one year of the three years is only slightly more than one in three. This is understandable, since either parental migration or migration spurred by the need to study elsewhere could occur at this point.

The second set of links clusters around place of residence in the early years after completing school. The link between this period and the subsequent three years is fairly high, the predictive force here being two in three. So these years can be combined in one chronological segment which is determined by the initial place of study and the associated change in place of residence. In the first two years some migrants change their place of residence for reasons other than study. In the subsequent three years there are fewer such cases, which binds these years more firmly together.

When a portion of the cohort completes higher education a new cluster of links forms, which covers the time-segment from 23 to 28 years of age. Place of residence stabilizes for the entire cohort in this period. There then follows a stable period in which migration becomes exceptional, and it is possible to predict the future place of residence with virtual certainty.

The links between place of residence in separate time-segments are particularly interesting. There is good reason here to examine the links between place of residence prior to completion of secondary school and place of residence in the other time-segments of the cohort's life. The strongest links of all are not with the period immediately subsequent to completion of secondary school but with the period in the cohort's life when it has acquired a social position and completed its daytime study. There is an indication of reverse migration here, back to the parental place of residence. This reverse migration continues even when the graduates are thirty years old.

To shed light on the links between these migratory currents we shall examine the link that binds place of birth, place of first-grade enrollment and place of secondary school completion with place of residence during other years covered in the survey. The general logic of residential structure links is as follows: the strongest links are attached to place of residence in the last year of the survey, followed by place of residence at the time of first-grade enrollment, then at the time of secondary school completion, and finally place of birth. This latter's strongest link, however, is with place of first-grade enrollment, and its weakest is with place of secondary school completion.

We shall examine these links in greater detail. The link between place of birth and place of residence grows markedly weaker up to 21 years of age; then the descriptive force of a person's birthplace starts to rise again. But the link between place of residence and place of first-grade enrollment, and place of secondary school completion, grows firmer from the age of 20 years of age—that is, from the time of graduation from secondary specialized educational institutions—and becomes even more so thereafter. It cannot be said that this is solely due to the influence of birthplace—more likely, parental place of residence is the operative factor here. The link between birthplace and place of residence grows stronger, peaking at 27 years of age, and thereafter weakens somewhat.

The link between place of first-grade enrollment (which can be regarded as the place of parental residence) and place of residence in other periods of life grows steadily from age 20 to 24, until it is stronger than the link with the place of residence immediately upon completion of school. This is a pivotal point in the migratory process, when education-related migration becomes less intense than migration to parental place of residence. At 26 years of age, this link is firmer than the links during the first two years after completion of secondary school. In regard to the latter place of residence, parental place of residence acquires a strong predictive potential, and determines place of residence in one case in four.

On this basis we may derive a very definite link between the type of place where a young person grew up and his future place of residence. School tends to accelerate migratory currents. The secondary school has the greatest influence upon the type of residential settlement to which the cohort migrates in the first and second year after completion of secondary school. The impact of parental place of residence grows stronger only after this point. But up to 23 years of age, when most young specialists complete their higher education, the link with place of secondary school completion has almost the same descriptive force with regard to present place of residence as does the link with parental place of residence. But when higher education is over, that link is somewhat less likely to predetermine place of residence than are the links with parental domicile.

We shall now endeavor to present a general description of the migratory process. It is highly specific to the various types of residential settlements involved. The data in Table 9 show that three-quarters of the graduates of secondary schools in Tallin and Tartu remain in those cities, which is explained by the presence of

Table 9

Cohort Migration to Permanent Place of Residence at Age 31, in %

		Type of residential settlement				
Age, in years	Capital	Higher educational center	Major city	Small town	Urban settlement	Village
18	78.0	74.2	45.1	26.7	28.1	36.0
19	79.2	78.2	39.8	26.7	26.5	33.9
20	80.4	82.8	42.3	31.7	32.2	38.3
21	82.0	82.4	55.9	37.4	38.0	47.6
22	82.9	82.5	63.3	42.1	42.9	51.4
23	85.8	86.7	70.3	56.0	60.1	63.2
24	88.8	87.5	78.3	64.4	66.5	77.0
25	91.7	89.6	83.3	71.0	74.8	81.3
26	92.8	90.7	88.3	77.7	82.5	85.3
27	94.0	92.8	90.7	86.2	88.2	92.3
28	96.0	94.9	94.2	88.4	91.8	92.3
29	98.0	97.4	96.1	90.6	96.5	94.6
30	99.4	99.0	99.2	95.6	99.6	98.5
31	100.0	100.0	100.0	100.0	100.0	100.0

their higher educational institutions. The capital has a steady annual growth of population up to 30 years of age which accelerates somewhat around the time of graduation from higher educational institutions. This implies that there are no special factors determining migration to the capital; this is simply a consequence of Tallin's general socioeconomic prominence.

The migratory flow to the higher educational center of Tartu has its own peculiarities. There is an inflow of young people during the first two years, then the population stabilizes for three years. The influx occurs when a portion of the cohort finishes its higher education. But migration increases again after the young specialists have worked for three years, at approximately the age of 30.

The major cities experience a steady population influx, of up to 50% of the cohort. But two years after the completion of secondary school, a portion of the future stable population leaves. Graduates from secondary specialized educational institutions sharply raise—by 13.6%—the cohort numbers in these cities. Higher educational institutions provide a more even supply, and from the age of 26 the resident intake moderates.

Only a quarter of the secondary school graduates who are living in small towns at the age of 31 are permanent residents. The rest have migrated there. Higher educational institutions have a significant impact on that migration: in the first year they replenish the population of these towns by 12.9%. During the three years after graduation, there is an abrupt jump of 8.5%. Then the migratory flow stabilizes, although it is quite intensive among thirty-year-olds.

Similarly, only a little over one-quarter of the cohort resides permanently in urban settlements. The proportion of young people there jumps by 17.2% (the highest index of growth for any one year) on completion of higher education. There is a steady overall rise up to the age of 27, after which migration decreases slightly.

The village is the residential structure's most hermetic unit as regards population influx, with only one-third of the cohort living there. The first influx comes after graduation from secondary specialized educational institutions; subsequently, higher education exerts an impact upon the influx of young people to the villages. A typical feature is that by 24 years of age, four-fifths of the future rural population is already in place. By 27 years of age, the proportion has risen to 92.3%.

This analysis shows how inaccurate it is to present migration as a unidirectional movement from less developed socioeconomic residential settlements to their more developed counterparts. Behind the summary figures, as a rule, there are migratory flows, and counter-flows, even in cases involving a contingent as specific as that of daytime secondary school graduates.

Turning to migration among various social strata we find an even more differentiated picture. Migratory currents are a direct expression of social mobility. This is understandable enough, since the social nature of the division of labor finds its overall

Table 10

Changes in Place of Residence among Secondary School Graduates, Depending on Sex, in %

		Place of Residence					
Age, in years	Sex	Capital	Higher educational center	Major city	Small town	Urban settlement	Village
18	Males	18.4	28.5	6.1	5.5	6.6	4.9
	Females	35.9	23.5	13.9	7.5	9.8	9.4
20	Males	48.5	35.6	3.7	5.1	2.7	4.4
	Females	35.8	28.8	10.5	7.1	9.8	8.0
22	Males	44.7	29.5	8.1	6.2	6.8	4.7
	Females	31.8	26.5	13.1	8.3	11.0	8.3
24	Males	41.7	17.5	12.7	9.5	10.9	7.3
	Females	30.5	17.8	16.1	10.8	14.2	10.9
26	Males	37.6	16.0	13.1	11.0	14.2	8.1
	Females	31.1	14.2	16.9	11.7	15.6	10.5
28	Males	36.7	14.8	13.5	11.7	14.6	8.7
	Females	31.5	13.1	14.8	14.0	16.2	10.4
31	Males	38.0	13.8	13.3	11.9	14.5	8.5
	Females	31.9	13.1	17.0	12.6	16.5	8.9

expression in the residential structure and then in the social strata of socialist society.

The gender-based peculiarities of the distribution of the cohort in the residential structure are not pronounced. The membership of the cohort is, of course, distinctive and rather socially "advanced," which explains its gender imbalance. Research data actually do show some substantial differences between patterns of male and female migration (Table 10).

The capital, and especially its higher educational institutions, attract more boys. In the first year after completion of secondary school there are already 12.9% more boys than girls in the capital. The completion of higher education corrects that imbalance somewhat (up to 24 years of age), but by the age of 30 males still outnumber females by 6% (and shortly before that the figure actually shows an upward trend). In the higher educational center of Tartu there is also a certain disproportion of boys during the first two years, but it declines by the age of 24.

In the republic's major cities, girls outnumber boys substantially in the first year after leaving school (in a 2:1 ratio during the first year, which rises to 3:1 in the second). Graduation from secondary specialized educational institutions equalizes the position somewhat, but more substantial changes occur after the cohort as a whole ends its daytime education. However some excess of girls over boys remains. By the time the graduates are 30, the scales have tipped again, and the difference has increased to 3.7%. For young women wishing to marry this is an unenviable situation.

The small towns lose more boys, but the gap is not as wide as in the major cities. By the age of 26 the differences between the male and female percentages have virtually disappeared. The urban settlements lose a third more boys in the first year, and two years after graduation they are down to 2.7% (which means that there are almost four times fewer boys than girls).

By the age of 22 the position has been somewhat equalized, but the basic turning point comes at the age of 24, after which girls retain a small margin that is bolstered by positive migration on their part.

In the villages girls also have a percentage margin during the first two years, which is retained until the time of graduation from a higher educational institution. At that point there are a larger number of boys in the villages. The gender composition of the cohort in the countryside equalizes in percentage terms as some females migrate from villages at the age of 30.

As we see, secondary school creates some distinctive features in the migratory flows of youth. We shall now examine the impact of social self-determination upon migratory flows and place of residence.

Collective farmers and state farm workers (Table 11) live predominantly in villages and urban settlements. Unskilled workers up to 30 years of age are primarily employed in the capital and major cities. Small as it is, this category is extremely important.

Though the social development of a small portion of the cohort has effectively come to a standstill here, the social conditions in which that portion takes shape are manifestly more developed now than they used to be. None of the unskilled workers in the countryside and very few in urban settlements and small towns are young people with secondary education. The point is that under present circumstances young people have considerable scope for social advancement. This is clearly seen in the fact that the relative shares of sundry kinds of unskilled worker decline in residential settlements as these workers move into other strata.

Skilled workers are the most developed working class stratum in the countryside, in urban settlements, and in small towns. Their movement into the highly skilled workers' stratum is less intensive here than in the capital, where the size of this stratum is declining more or less steadily. This stratum is more numerous in major cities. Here, the relative size of this stratum falls only in the first three years, when its members enter higher educational institutions. Then its numbers rise steadily. In small towns and urban settlements, however, this is a permanent stratum. Here there are five times more twenty-year-old skilled workers than in the republic's major cities, and three times more than in the capital. In the villages, though, the number of skilled workers rises slightly at first, then declines slightly.

The number of highly skilled workers grows steadily as a result of social mobility from other strata, but its representation in various types of residential settlements varies markedly. At the outset—as at the end—the proportion of Tallin residents in this stratum is far above average. Overall, the relative share of Tallin residents in the highly skilled worker stratum grows constantly from the time the graduates turn 21. There is a temporary dip which occurs when highly skilled workers become students. This also alters the relative share of the population in major cities who are highly skilled workers. In the small towns the relative share of the highly skilled worker complement grows at first. This growth slackens off by the age of 21, which reduces slightly the represen-tation of people from this type of residential settlement in this particular working class stratum. Changes in the relative share of rural residents in the highly skilled worker stratum follow the same logic: the share of rural residents in this stratum is seven times less than Tallin residents.

Employees form a distinctive group composed predominantly of women, which has roughly equal representation in various types of residential settlements. There are fewer employees in the capital than in other residential structures, which comes as rather a surprise, since employees are needed to perform the administrative and management activity which is concentrated in metropolitan areas. The growth in the proportion of employees in leading cities becomes especially noticeable as the cohort nears the age of 30. Cadres of employees in small towns and villages are made up of secondary school graduates and remain relatively stable (there being very little evidence of people leaving this stratum to become students). Later, though, as the cohort in the capital and major cities joins the ranks of employees, there is a corresponding fall in the relative share of people from small towns, urban settlements, and villages in this group.

The stratum of uncredentialed practical specialists is a group which in the countryside draws the bulk of its recruits directly from daytime secondary school graduates. In other types of residential settlements anyone wishing to attain this position will need to do more than just graduate from daytime secondary school. So there is a fall in the relative share of rural residents among uncredentialed practical specialists and a rise in the representation of people from the republic's capital and major cities, which therefore acquire a higher-than-average proportion of thirty-year-old uncredentialed practical specialists.

The situation with regard to specialists with secondary specialized education is different. They account for a large proportion of the population in cities other than the capital, where their places are sometimes taken by specialists with higher education. They are negligibly represented in Estonian villages, being preempted there too by a substantial influx of specialists with higher education. However, a year after completion of secondary school,

Table 11

Indices of Links between Type of Residential Settlement and Social Stratum of Cohort at Age 31

Social stratum	Place of residence	Age, in years									
		18	19	20	21	22	23	25	31
Collective farmers and state farm workers	Tallin	0.57	0.66	0.58	0.49	0.51	0.53	0.40	0.36
	Major cities	0.58	0.48	0.45	0.45	0.38	0.25	0.38	0.20
	Other towns, urban settlements	1.47	1.57	1.75	1.86	1.92	1.55	1.24	1.51
	Village	4.27	4.94	4.56	4.72	4.70	4.38	3.97	4.64
Unskilled workers	Tallin	1.16	0.95	0.84	0.73	0.74	0.58	0.96	1.17
	Major cities	0.73	0.70	0.86	1.00	0.84	0.96	1.08	1.15
	Other towns, urban settlements	1.30	1.97	1.41	1.65	1.96	1.80	1.06	0.94
	Village	0.86	1.00	0.97	0.93	0.94	0.75	0.72	0.00
Skilled workers	Tallin	0.80	0.88	0.76	0.66	0.66	0.70	0.69	0.56
	Major cities	0.89	0.79	0.58	0.81	0.87	0.91	0.99	1.07
	Other towns, urban settlements	1.91	2.13	2.50	1.94	1.85	1.50	1.51	1.49
	Village	0.76	0.61	1.13	1.69	1.48	1.28	0.80	0.93

Highly skilled workers	Tallin	1.24	1.29	1.18	1.12	1.21	1.23	1.32	1.33
	Major cities	0.95	0.96	0.79	0.87	0.84	0.91	0.93	1.01
	Other towns, urban settlements	0.69	0.65	0.76	1.17	1.05	0.87	0.86	0.85
	Village	0.62	0.66	0.87	0.73	0.76	0.79	0.46	0.19
Employees	Tallin	0.81	0.78	0.75	0.72	0.72	0.79	0.77	0.75
	Major cities	0.86	0.90	0.77	0.89	0.91	0.97	1.08	1.15
	Other towns, urban settlements	1.52	1.64	1.65	1.60	1.59	1.23	1.12	1.09
	Village	1.64	1.66	1.70	1.69	1.52	1.35	1.29	1.20
Uncredentialed practical specialists	Tallin	0.98	0.96	1.07	1.07	1.13	1.14	1.09	1.11
	Major cities	0.91	0.94	0.80	0.83	0.85	0.94	1.05	1.00
	Other towns, urban settlements	0.97	0.92	0.74	0.96	0.82	0.82	0.76	0.94
	Village	1.62	1.73	1.51	1.67	1.62	1.16	1.29	0.77
Specialists with secondary specialized education	Tallin	1.02	1.07	0.91	0.72	0.75	0.72	0.67	0.68
	Major cities	0.84	0.70	0.70	0.93	0.94	1.05	1.18	1.24
	Other towns, urban settlements	1.41	1.61	1.68	1.81	1.66	1.43	1.24	1.16
	Village	0.86	1.03	1.17	1.03	1.01	0.80	1.16	0.93
Specialists with higher education	Tallin	1.11	1.10	1.16	1.26	1.22	1.19	1.22	1.23
	Major cities	1.19	1.22	1.03	1.19	1.19	1.26	0.98	0.95
	Other towns, urban settlements	0.55	0.38	0.36	0.28	0.37	0.70	0.83	0.83
	Village	0.59	0.37	0.29	0.24	0.28	0.58	0.99	0.84

residents of Tallin are less well represented here because this stratum is becoming more numerous in other types of residential settlements. Specialists with secondary specialized education go to small towns and urban settlements; by 21 years of age cohort representation here is twice the size of that in the major cities. But by 30 years of age the picture changes markedly, since these specialists migrate to the republic's leading cities, which by then contain a much higher share of the cohort.

More of the 1966 secondary school graduates entered the stratum of specialists with higher education than any other. For this reason the capital and the university town of Tartu are prime recipients during the first five years. After graduation from higher education the picture changes. The relative share of 22- and 23-year-olds living in Tallin falls while the villages and small towns make some significant gains. All types of residential settlements except the capital have their maximum share of graduates by the time the latter reach the age of 25. After this, a migration to the capital—low-key though it may be—begins. The concentration of specialists with higher education in the capital comes to exceed their relative share in the cohort as a whole. Their representation in the leading cities is somewhat lower, and in the less developed urban settlements it is lower still.

This analysis has thus confirmed the hypothesis that social mobility, especially into the more developed working class and specialist strata, generates migratory processes.

Our research has pointed up the numerous channels of social mobility, which is initially accomplished through educational institutions and leads to social self-determination in the place of residence. Later, movement is based upon a person's already attained social position.

Note

1. See *Vysshaia shkola kak faktor izmeneniia sotsial'noi struktury razvitogo sotsialisticheskogo obshchestva*, Moscow, 1978; *Sotsial'nye peremeshcheniia v studenchestve*, Vilnius, 1982.

11. The Changing Social Composition and Occupational Orientation of the Student Body in the USSR*

M. N. RUTKEVICH, M. Kh. TITMA, and F. R. FILIPPOV

1. The social sources of student recruitment

Students in higher educational institutions constitute a numerically large and growing complement among Soviet youth. The higher education system in the USSR, in addition to daytime instruction in universities and institutes, also includes evening and correspondence divisions where young people with full-time jobs study. This chapter will deal only with those students who are enrolled in daytime divisions and who are not employed in production—who are not, that is, actual members of any of society's classes or social strata but are "en route" to the social group of the intelligentsia. These students have diverse social origins which, if analyzed, provide us with a picture of the social sources of student recruitment in the Soviet Union.

Changes in the social composition of the student body are intimately linked with its numerical growth, with the expanding

*Russian text © 1982 by "Nauka" Publishers. "Izmeneniia v sotsial'nom sostave i professional'noi orientatsii studenchestva SSSR," Akademiia nauk SSSR, Institut sotsiologicheskikh issledovanii, *Sovetskaia sotsiologiia*, Vol. II, Moscow, 1982, pp. 111–142.

Table 1

Number of Students in Higher Educational Institutions in the USSR (beginning of academic year, in thousands)*

Number of Students	1914/15	1940/41	1960/61	1970/71	1980/81
Total	127	812	2,396	4,581	5,235
In daytime divisions	127	558	1,156	2,241	2,978
As percentage of total population	0.08	0.29	0.54	0.93	1.12

*See *Narodnoe khoziaistvo SSSR v 1980 g.*, Moscow, 1981, pp. 7, 462; *Narodnoe khoziaistvo SSSR v 1960 g.*, Moscow, 1961, pp. 7, 766.

dimensions of higher education in the USSR, whose growth rate is shown in Table 1.

The course of instruction in higher educational institutions lasts for five years. People aged twenty to twenty-four comprised 9.7% of the country's population in 1959, and 7.6% in 1970. From this it follows that the student body (excluding evening students and correspondence students, whose social position is determined by their type of work) forms a significant complement among young people—approximately one in eighteen young people aged between 17 and 25 was a student in 19[6]0, and one in eight in 1970 and 1980.

At issue here, though, is not just the numerical size of this social group but also its social importance. The student body is the future intelligentsia, moreover that stratum of the intelligentsia which is commonly called "specialists with higher education."

Study at higher educational institutions is the critical channel of social movement (social mobility) for young people from all social groups and strata. With the rapid growth in the absolute and relative numbers of specialists in general, and specialists with higher qualifications in particular, the latter group is undergoing a process of expanded reproduction. The growth rates of the stratum of specialists with higher education employed in the national economy are presented below.[1]

Year	Absolute numbers, in thousands	Year	Absolute numbers in thousands
1913	136	1960	3,545
1928	233	1970	6,853
1941	909	1981	12,600

It should be obvious that, since this stratum has been almost doubling in size every ten years of late, the problem of the social sources from which it draws its recruits now requires the closest possible analysis. The following two factors are decisive in bringing about the increasingly even recruitment of the student body for all social groups.

1. The convergence between social groups in material conditions of existence. While in 1940 the average wages of engineering and technical personnel in industry were 215 (taking workers' wages as 100), this coefficient had fallen to 146 in 1965, and 116 in 1979.[2] An analogous tendency has been operating in other branches of the economy. Simultaneously, the income of collective farmers has converged markedly with the wages of workers and employees. Factoring in the income from private household plots, the rural population as a whole differs only negligibly from its urban counterpart. The real income of collective farmers grew from 75% of the real income of workers and employees in 1965 (per family member) to 89% in 1979.[3] In some parts of the country—in Estonia for instance—the average income of collective-farm workers is higher than that of workers with comparable skills in state enterprises.

2. The implementation of universal complete secondary education has been a crucial step in overcoming cultural distinctions between young people belonging by birth and upbringing to different social groups and living in different areas (countryside or

town). By the end of the 1970s, after finishing incomplete secondary school (eight years of schooling), almost all youngsters of both sexes went on to complete their secondary education in a variety of ways: in ten-year general education schools (eleven-year in the Baltic republics); in technicums and other secondary specialized educational institutions; in the so-called ''secondary vocational and technical education training schools'' (which award a work rating along with a secondary education completion certificate); and, finally, in evening (shift) schools. This latter route, which is designed for young people in full-time work, is difficult and demanding. This is why not all who choose this route manage to complete the course of secondary school instruction, despite the substantial perquisites provided by their enterprises and assiduous monitoring on the part of social organizations.

Both these above-mentioned achievements—achievements of historic scope—in the drive toward total social equality are having an increasingly tangible impact upon equalizing opportunities for a higher education among the younger generation. The social composition of those entering higher educational institutions and of the whole student body (not counting those studying at evening and correspondence faculties, where the social categories which predominate depend on the type of specialization being pursued) are steadily converging with the social composition of the population. Changes in the latter are shown most clearly in the population censuses. (Table 2).

Data on the social origins of students accepted into first-year courses of daytime instruction are presented in Table 3.

Here we may observe an obvious tendency toward gradual convergence between the relative share of students from workers' families and the relative share of the working class in the overall population of the country. The slight drop in the relative share of students coming from the collective-farm peasantry is explained by the decline in the overall numbers of this class in Soviet society and a corresponding decrease in its relative share in the country's population.

Table 2

Changes in the Social Class Composition of the Soviet Population
(including nonworking family members), in %*

Social group	1939	1959	1970	1979
Workers	33.5	49.5	56.8	60.0
Employees	16.7	18.8	22.7	25.1
Collective farm peasantry and cooperative artisans	47.2	31.4	20.5	14.9
Individual peasants and noncooperative artisans	2.6	0.3	0.0	0.0

*Narodnoe khoziaistvo SSSR v 1979 g., pp. 8–9; Vestnik statistiki, 1981, no. 1, p. 66.

The "outflow coefficient" into higher education for the various social groups of the population (the relation between the relative share of those coming from a given social group among first-year entrants and the relative share of that group in the overall population) also attests to the gradual convergence between the social composition of the student body and that of the population. In the years between the two censuses in the 1970s this index has gone from 0.71 to 0.74 for workers, from 2.19 to 2.10 for employees and specialists, and from 0.36 to 0.46 for collective farmers. This latter case reflects the influence of differences in the quality of general educational training available to urban and rural schoolchildren. But of special importance is the rise in the share of students of working-class origin, which is connected with the rise in working-class educational and cultural levels.

In the highly urbanized and industrially developed areas of the USSR the percentage of students of working-class origin is substantially above the countrywide average. Table 4 presents data on the social composition of the student body in the daytime divisions of higher educational institutions in Sverdlovsk—one of the Soviet Union's largest industrial cities and the focus of systematic sociological research into the problem of the student body for the past 20 years.

Table 3

The Social Composition of Students Accepted into the First Year of Daytime Instruction, in %*

Social origin	Academic year					
	1970/71	1971/72	1972/73	1973/74	1975/76	1979/80
Workers	37.7	39.8	42.4	44.4	45.5	47.3
Collective farmers	9.0	9.9	8.8	6.5	7.5	6.5
Employees	53.3	50.3	48.8	49.1	47.0	46.2

* See M. N. Ruthevich and F. R. Filippov, editors, *Vysshaia shkola kak faktor izmeneniia sotsial'noi struktury razvitogo sotsialisticheskogo obshchestva*, Moscow, 1978, p. 110; L. Ia. Rubina, *Sovetskoe studenchestvo*, Moscow, 1981, p. 56.

It should, however, be borne in mind that an influx of young people from contiguous (or sometimes even distant) areas will affect the social composition of the student body in any given city, so that there cannot always be a precise correspondence between changes in the social composition of students and changes in the social composition of the population in the area centering on the given city. But from the general direction of these changes it is obvious that the relative share of students of working-class origin is increasing signficantly among those entering higher educational institutions in industrial areas.

The proportions typically found in first-year classes continue basically unchanged during the entire course of higher educational instruction. Virtually every student who enters the first year leaves with a diploma, unless prevented from doing so by unforeseen circumstances (illness or a change in family circumstances). Some students drop out because they are unprepared for study in a higher educational institution. But this does not exert a major influence upon the social composition of the student body.

Thus according to the results of research conducted in six areas of the USSR in 1973–1974 there was a drop of only five percentage points over the whole period of instruction at higher educa-

Table 4

Composition of First-year Student Body in Sverdlovsk Higher Educational Institutions (Daytime Instruction) by Social Origin, in %*

Social origin of students	Academic year				
	1971/72	1973/74	1975/76	1977/78	1979/80
Workers	47.6	49.7	49.2	56.1	55.1
Collective farmers	2.8	2.4	2.1	1.9	1.1
Office personnel	49.6	47.9	48.7	42.0	43.8

*See L. Ia. Rubina, *Sovetskoe studenchestvo*, p. 56.

tional institutions for students of working-class origin. For students of collective-farm peasant origin there was a drop of one percentage point. In the higher educational institutions of Sverdlovsk the percentage of workers' children (according to paternal social position) falls by six points between the first and final years, which is close to the average for all the areas surveyed.

The increasing convergence among Soviet society's basic social groups in supplying new recruits for the intelligentsia is one of the most important indices of the growth in real, de facto equality under mature socialism. Inasmuch as social differences still exist in socialist society (between the working class and the collective-farm peasantry, between inhabitants of town and countryside, between those employed in physical work and those in mental work), these differences have an impact upon the composition of student contingents. But these differences are not decisive in nature: the actual fact is that all social groups of the population have broad access to higher education.

It behooves us, however, to concretize this general conclusion, to uncover contradictions in objective social processes, and to evaluate the effect which the subjective factor has on these processes. This factor, in its turn, must be examined fairly broadly, in a perspective that ranges from the socio-occupational orientation of young people (as an expression of their plans, which reflect the interests of society through the prism of personal interests), to steps taken to regulate the composition of the student body (as determined by government-level decisions, by economic and social measures to assist various categories of students, and so forth).

The socio-occupational orientation of young people increased greatly in scope during the 1970s. In addition to the extensive information that young people are given about society's requirements for personnel in various occupations and about working conditions in the various branches of the national economy, there is now a widespread network of production training centers, especially in large cities, where young people gain a practical familiarity with various occupations and acquire rudimentary work habits. In the 1980/81 academic year 98% of daytime secondary schools were providing their pupils with in-depth labor instruction.[4] Young workers and collective farmers are given a certain amount of preferential treatment in admissions to higher education. Since the end of the 1960s preparatory divisions in higher educational institutions have been working to make good the gaps in their knowledge. Some students are studying on assignment (with travel authorization) from their enterprises or collective farms and are receiving enhanced stipends. The state gives financial aid to female students with children.

All these measures (and many others) have one common aim— to mitigate the vestigial inequality of opportunity for receiving a higher education. This inequality stems from the incomplete equality in work and in the remuneration for work that is inherent in socialism. Inequality also exists in the educational and cultural levels of various social groups within the population, and this affects the quality of knowledge exhibited by rural youth, as opposed to its urban counterpart, and by young people from families where mental, as opposed to physical, work is done.

In striving to achieve equality in social position and to erode social-class differences, socialism is certainly not striving to level the physical and spiritual capacities of individuals. Socialism utilizes existing inequalities in social position as a means to achieve equality. Thus the more precisely pay is pegged to the amount of work done, the degree of responsibility borne, the results of work and its conditions (in an enterprise, a branch of the economy, a given territory, and so forth), the greater the incentive for effort in the given job position, and the greater the motivation toward skill enhancement, toward acceptance of responsibility for the work done by the collective (through promotion to a supervisory position of whatever rank), and so on.

What we are talking about here is the training of highly skilled specialists for labor activity—the right, that is, to undertake in the immediate future high-grade executor-type job responsibilities, and, to a significant extent, executive-type responsibilities too, since as things presently stand, supervisors in all economic and cultural branches and in the sphere of management are, as a rule, recruited from specialists.

In such circumstances the general contradiction mentioned above takes on a specific form. Socialist society is vitally interested in increasing the rate at which intellectual potential in science, technology, and art is developed. There are capable and talented people everywhere, but only under certain conditions will they be discovered and developed, especially at an early age. Inequality in the material and cultural levels of various population categories and of the families within them, and in access to cultural values in various population centers (which still persists under socialism), affects the extent to which the capacities of children and adolescents are revealed and, more particularly, the level of training available to young people to prepare them for self-determination in life. The goal which socialist society has adopted involves the swiftest possible advancement toward ever-increasing social equality, a determination to uncover the capabilities of every single citizen to the fullest possible extent. But today's admissions policies for higher educational institutions must work from the level of capabilities actually revealed and sometimes even from the level of factual knowledge, which, as we know, by no means always and completely corresponds to capacity levels.

This contradiction will be resolved primarily by the ongoing equalization of material and cultural living conditions among working people. But in addition, special measures are being formulated with the objective of providing assistance for working and rural youth. These measures include the aforementioned preparatory courses.

Thus there is in society a contradiction between current needs, which demand the most rapid possible utilization of young people's existing spiritual potential, irrespective of the diverse conditions under which that potential evolved, and prospective needs, which demand that the capabilities and talents of every citizen starting out in life be revealed in full. The accelerated development of the productive forces, of science and culture is imperative today in order to assure peak personal performance by all citizens in the future. By accepting the best prepared people into higher education institutions today, society is striving to bring about that accelerated development—and by the same token to continue the advance toward the ultimate "equalization of opportunity."

2. The social composition of the student body

From the abundance of sociological studies begun in the early 1960s (in Sverdlovsk and Novosibirsk), we shall turn first of all to the results of a uniquely extensive research project conducted in the USSR in the 1970s.

The USSR Academy of Sciences Institute of Sociological Research supervised a study (conducted in 1973 and 1974 in six areas of the Soviet Union, and in 1977 and 1978 in 13 cities in the European RSFSR and in the republics of Estonia, Latvia, and Lithuania) to determine the impact of higher education upon the social structure of Soviet society. The program and methodology were identical in both projects, which ensured that the results would be sufficiently comparable.[5]

In addition to students, the first project surveyed secondary school pupils who still faced, so to speak, "a long haul" to higher education. This allowed researchers to study an array of factors affecting the social sources of intelligentsia recruitment. The second project surveyed university students (in humanities and natural science faculties) and students in technical, agricultural, economic, pedagogical, and medical institutes—that is, in the most common specializations. Both samples include students in their first year and in graduating classes, which made it possible to trace the dynamics of a number of social characteristics of the student body over the period spent in higher education.

The populations in the areas chosen for the first project— Moscow and Moscow region, Krasnodar territory, Odessa, Novosibirsk and Sverdlovsk regions, and the Estonian SSR—were quite typical in terms of social composition. Thus the survey covered both areas where the working class was largely preponderant within the employed population (Moscow region—66.6%, Sverdlovsk region—70.5%, Novosibirsk region—72.3%, Estonian SSR—60.8%), and areas with a significant proportion of collective farm peasantry (Krasnodar territory—21.5%, Odessa region, 27.7%) and intelligentsia (Moscow—50.3%).[6] The overall sample totaled 7,200 first-year students and 7,955 graduating students (not to mention the 29,700 schoolchildren).

The second project, conducted in the European part of the Russian Federation, covered the north-west (Leningrad), the Transvolga (Astrakan', Gor'kii, Kazan', and Saransk), the northern Caucasus (Groznyi and Krasnodar), the central Black Earth Region (Voronezh), the Urals (Sverdlovsk and Nizhnii Tagil), and the central part of the country (Vladimir, Ivanovo, and Orekhovo-Zuevo). Virtually all the large cities in the Baltic republics—Tallin and Tartu in Estonia, Riga and Daugavpils in Latvia, Vil'nius and Kaunas in Lithuania—were included in the sample. Thus, three cities with one million inhabitants and a high density of scientific establishment and higher educational institutions (Leningrad, Gor'kii, and Sverdlovsk), the three Baltic republic capitals, eight regional and autonomous republican centers, and five industrial centers were included. The sample totaled 15,650 persons.

In the first phase the basic research task was to study the

specific mechanisms of interaction between the higher educational system as a whole and the social structure of Soviet society. The plan in the second phase was to compare the student body's specific occupational complements and their role in supplying recruits for the corresponding socio-occupational groups of the Soviet intelligentsia. The basic procedure was to take a serial sample of roughly equal size (about 50 people) for each specialty. The series were made up by random sampling techniques, and within each a comprehensive poll was taken, using questionnaires designed along identical lines for all the groups, studied, with ranked scales, usually four-point scales that were, as a rule, equal in length and had equal intervals. Questions on the type of secondary education which the respondents had received and the place where they had completed secondary school ensured that the data on general educational training collected from both projects would be comparable.

Both projects were based upon the theoretical conception that there is an interaction between the social structure of society, the educational system, and the life-plans of young people. In accordance with this conception a system of objective and subjective indices was drawn up to trace the processes of social movement (social mobility) among youth. In the context of socialist society one of the channels of this social mobiltiy is higher education. In this respect both projects were a continuation of investigations into problems raised by the authors in previous works.[7]

We begin by assuming that when young people enter the sphere of work they take over positions in the social (and occupational) structure which have fallen vacant and also fill new positions which society has created. Thus the development of the social structure and its reproduction interact with the replacement of generations, whose entry into working life is mediated by the educational system (including higher education). Society's present and imminent needs are reflected in the life-plans of young people, in their social and occupational positions), and also in their value orientations (that is, in the preference for one or another system of values, including those attaching to education and future occupation).

At the empirical level the objective and subjective aspects of social mobility were identified with the help of the following indices: the social position of respondent's parents (both father and mother, which shed light upon the degree of social homogeneity and heterogeneity of families) and their educational levels; respondent's birthplace, location of respondent's first school and graduating school, type of secondary education; respondent's personal social position prior to entering higher education, and the kind of job he had (in cases where he had been working independently prior to beginning his higher educational studies), the degree of congruence between his work activity and the specialty acquired in the higher educational institution; the degree of preparedness for higher educational study (by self-evaluation, by the mark on the secondary school leaving certificate grade, and the average grade in higher education entrance and continuation examinations); the time when the decision to go on to higher education and take up a particular specialty was made; participation in the higher educational institution's scientific research work, in the activity of student social organizations and self-management bodies, in cultural life and sports; and the type of job and work location sought upon completion of higher education. This sytem of indices, in our view, elicits a sufficient amount of necessary information on the social processes under study.

The results, once processed, shed light upon the degree of integration of the student body (as one of the social groups in Soviet society), and made it possible to discern several differentiating factors, determine the extent of their influence upon the student body's social identity, and examine certain trends in the social mobility of young people through the higher educational system, and the problems associated with them. Let us examine the data from the two projects.

Table 5 presents government statistical data for the USSR showing changes in the number of students in higher educational institution in the principal specialties. In the 1973/74 academic year 52% of all higher education students were in specialties related to industry, construction, agriculture, transport, and com-

Table 5

Changes in Number of Students in the USSR, 1973–1980*

Indicator	Academic year		
	1973/74	1977/78	1979/80
Number of higher educational institutions	834	861	870
Students in these institutions (thousands)	4,671	5,037	5,186
Including:			
enrolled in daytime divisions	246†	2,789	2,932
as percentage of total number of students	52.7	55.4	56.5
Number of students by groups of specialties (thousands):			
industry, construction, agriculture and forestry, exploitation of natural resources, transport	2,423.2	2,639.6	2,736.8
economics and law	663.0	719.9	733.8
healthcare and physical education	339.8	361.0	372.8
university specialization	350.0	378.5	386.5
specializations in pedagogical higher educational institutions and cultural institutes	854.4	896.1	913.7
art	40.9	41.5	42.3
Students accepted (thousands)	937.7	1,017.1	1,043.0
in daytime divisions	544.7	613.2	637.7
In percentages	58.1	60.3	61.1

*Narodnoe khoziaistvo SSSR v 1973 g., pp. 711–712, 717; Narodnoe khoziaistvo SSSR v 1977 g., Moscow, 1978, pp. 495–496, 501; Narodnoe khoziaistvo SSSR v. 1979 g., 1980, pp. 492–493, 498. (Author's calculations.)

†This figure seems incorrect and is presumably misprinted in the Russian text.

munications; in 1979/80 this percentage had risen to 55%. Thus the absolute and relative number of student in engineering and technical sciences, economics, veterinary science, and similar specialties, which implies future work as specialists in the sphere of material production has shown an appreciable increase.

The number of specialists with higher education employed in the Soviet national economy rose from 8.4 million in 1973 to 11.1 million in 1979, or by 37%.[8] Changes in the structure of

Table 6

Changes in the Structure of the Soviet Intelligentsia, in %*

Basic intelligentsia complements	Proportion of total number employed in predominantly mental work	
	1970	1977
Supervisory cadres	6.5	5.8
Engineering-technical, agrotechnical and zootechnical personnel	28.9	30.9
Medical personnel	8.7	8.9
Scientific and pedagogical personnel	19.7	19.5
Juridical staff	0.3	0.4

*Narodnoe khoziaistvo SSSR za 60 let, p. 475. (Author's calculations.)

employment in predominantly mental work are shown in Table 6, whose most salient feature is a rise in the relative share of engineering-technical, agrotechnical and zootechnical personnel.

Hence in the period between the two projects changes had occurred not only in the proportions among the occupational complements within the student body but also in the corresponding complements of specialists with higher education, which invites the conclusion that there is a connection between these two processes, and that they move in parallel directions stimulated by developments in the scientific and technical revolution and improvements in the organization of production.

As noted above, the USSR completed the transition to universal compulsory secondary education in the mid-1970s. As a result, the social base for recruitment to higher education widened considerably. Of the total number of people receiving a complete secondary education the relative share of graduates from rural schools—boys and girls who completed their school education in outlying districts—rose significantly, as did the proportion of graduates from evening schools and secondary vocational and technical training schools (Table 7).

Thus the socio-educational situation in the USSR as a whole

Table 7

Numbers and Composition of Secondary Educational Institution Students and Graduates in the USSR*

Type of secondary educational institution	1973/74 academic year	1977/78 academic year
Daytime secondary school:		
number of students in grades 9 and 10 (millions)	5.6	6.1
in cities	3.2	3.3
in rural localities	2.4	2.8
students in grades 9 and 10 as percentage of overall number of school students	12.6	15.0
in cities	14.0	15.2
in rural localities	11.8	14.8
Number of those completing daytime secondary school (millions)	2.3	3.0
Evening secondary school:		
number of students in grades 9 thru 11 (millions)	4.3	4.5
students in grades 9 thru 11 as percentage of overall number of evening school students	88.0	94.0
number of those completing evening secondary school (millions)	0.8	1.2
Secondary vocational and technical training schools:		
number of students (millions)	0.7	2.1
number of those completing training school (millions)	0.09	0.5
Secondary specialized educational institutions:		
number of graduates (millions)	1.1	1.2

*Narodnoe khoziaistvo SSSR v 1973 g., pp. 597, 703, 704, 718; Narodnoe khoziaistvo SSSR v 1979 g., pp. 400, 487, 488, 499.

has undergone momentous changes. At the Twenty-sixth CPSU Congress Leonid I. Brezhnev laid heavy emphasis upon this fact. He noted that ". . . in the productive activity of millions of workers and collective farmers, physical and mental work are ever more closely intertwined. Many of them are involved in rationalization and innovative activity, are authors of articles and books, are state and community activists. They are, in the fullest sense, highly cultured, intellectual people."[9]

These changes in the socio-educational situation naturally affected the social nature of the student body. Juxtaposing the results of the two projects with changes in the social structure of Soviet society as a whole (including the structure of the intelligentsia) and in levels of public education, we may conclude that higher education in the Soviet Union is becoming increasingly democratized and access to it is widening.

The 1977–1978 research program made it possible to identify differences in the social composition of respondents in higher educational institutions of differing kinds (Table 8). These differences are an "extension," as it were, of the socio-occupational differentiation of the corresponding complements among the intelligentsia, as predicated upon the special nature and content of their work and the demands they make upon the particular type of higher education. From this standpoint the sociological researcher sees the higher educational system not as an undivided whole, but as a complex totality of subsystems which are oriented toward the corresponding socio-occupational groups ("complements") among the intelligentsia.

The preponderance of people of working-class origins in technical and pedagogical institutes is explained, on the one hand, by the greater capacity of workers' children to adapt to the conditions of modern industrial production and, on the other hand, by the fact that technical and pedagogical institutes have a mass character and are found in most parts of the country. The relatively high percentage of collective farmers' children in agricultural and pedagogical institutes is similarly explained, and in addition a certain amount of preferential treatment is extended to them when they enroll in these institutes.

A factor analysis of data from the 1977–1978 project brings the following particular features to light. The strongest differentiating factors (12% and above) are: paternal and maternal socio-occupational group (14.9% each), the student's own occupational complement (14%), and parental place of residence—large city,

Table 8

Social Position of Respondents' Fathers at Time of Entering Higher Education, 1977–1978, in %*

	Type of higher education						
	University						
Social position of respondents' fathers	Humanities	Natural sciences	Technical studies	Agriculture	Economics	Pedagogy	Medicine
Workers	32.2	31.2	40.3	30.9	32.4	39.0	26.0
Employees	7.7	5.6	7.3	8.0	4.3	6.8	8.7
Specialists	49.2	51.5	39.9	21.4	54.1	32.8	52.1
Collective farmers	3.8	5.6	5.6	33.6	3.6	13.6	2.7

* Those not replying, etc., omitted.

small city, urban settlement, or village—(12.3%). The following are the least effective differentiating factors: respondent's social position prior to enrolling in higher education (9.1%) and respondents's level of performance (8.6%).[10] Analysis revealed a similar relationship among differentiating factors for the value orientations of the student body, about which more later.

According to data from the 1977–1978 project, the type of jobs held by parents had a powerful impact upon the distribution of young people in educational institutions of various kinds. Thus the children of collective-farm peasants and workers in state agricultural enterprises (state farms) are heavily concentrated in agricultural institutes (46.2%), the children of doctors and other medical personnel are largely found in medical institutes (38.9%), and the children of scientific workers and the creative intelligentsia are highly visible in the universities (55.6%). At the same time there are virtually no children of medical personnel in technical institutes (0.8%), while the children of industrial and construction workers and of the productive technical intelligentsia equally represented there (26.6% and 21.8% respectively).

All this attests to a certain developmental tendency in the social structure of socialist society—specifically, that as the basic social differences between classes and social groups are surmounted there is an obvious increase in the relative significance of social differences between strata and complements within those classes and groups. Occupational differences also become more pronounced.

These, then, are the results obtained by comparing several objective social characteristics of the student body, recorded five years apart.

A juxtaposition of the subjective characteristics of the contingents under study—chiefly young people's orientations and life-plans—also proved to be of great value.

3. The socio-occupational and value orientations of students

Both stages of the research confirmed our hypothesis concerning the priority of social orientation (the choice of future social position) over occupational orientation (choice of specific occupation and specialty). A comparison of research results invites the conclusion that there has been a certain change in young people's social orientation, indicating that the choice of higher education as a means of attaining a desired social position is now made earlier in life. Thus in 1973, 4.3% of the respondents reported making that choice before starting school; in 1977 this figure had risen to 19.1%. In 1973, 24% of the respondents had made the choice while in incomplete secondary school (grades one through seven), compared to 17% in 1977. In 1973, 24% made the choice in eighth grade, compared to 12.5% in 1977. And in 1973, 19% decided after completing secondary school, compared to 10% in 1977. Hence, young people adopted an orientation toward higher education earlier in their lives in the late 1970s than they did in the first half of the decade.

The greatest change in this respect was observed among the

are about children of workers and the intelligentsia, while the children of collective farmers exhibited the smallest change. The explanation—here as elsewhere—is that the quality of general educational training is of increasing importance for those wishing to get into higher education, and the quality of the training provided to rural youth remains lower than that available to urban youth. The earliest orientation toward higher education was reported by respondents in pedagogical and medical institutes and in the humanities faculties of universities.

The 1977–1978 project analyzed the link between the orientation toward higher education and the impact of fathers, agemates, school-teachers, and so forth, upon the respondents' socio-occupational choice. The influence of teachers was most closely connected with the students' chosen occupational complement (coefficient of correlation 0.233), while the influence of fathers was most closely connected with the respondents' educational levels (0.148) and chosen kind of work (0.173).

In the intricate system of subjective social characteristics of the student body, a special place must be reserved for value-based attitudes toward higher education and future occupation, and also toward future social position (status values). A large and self-contained section of both projects was concerned with comparing the students' value-based characteristics. Student value-orientations could not, naturally enough, remain untouched by the general changes in the socio-educational situation and in the Soviet social structure. Yet for all that, value orientations were discovered to be relatively stable.[11]

Both phases of the research revealed that the value-based attitude which was most strongly differentiated among students was that which relates to various facets of the mode of life ("'life orientation'") and incorporates value-based aspects of socio-occupational orientation. When data from the two phases were compared, it was found that the analysis of educational and occupational values done during the first stage was relatively less informative than the broader analysis of mode of life values. Our analysis made use of data from the All-Union sample, as well as from the Estonian group (the latter was used basically as a control since it was subject to stricter comparability).

Data on respondents' value orientations with regard to education are given in Table 9. The values of education are determined by its social functions: general-humanistic (indicator: significance of educational level), social (indicator: significance of given social "position"), and occupational (indicator: significance of occupational training). The value orientation of Estonian students with regard to education's occupational functions was relatively stable in both phases of the project. As for the overall group, the significance of education's value as a means of acquiring an occupational specialty was slightly lower in the second phase than in the first. This can be attributed to regional idiosyncrasies. Students rated the general-humanistic function of education somewhat lower in 1973 than in 1977. But it is especially important that this rating did not fall significantly between the first year and the graduating year. The social function of education was reflected in two value indicators—material compensation and the respondent's future social position. Analysis of the data shows that social standing was rated lower than the value of material recompense that was paired with it.

Factor analysis of the links between evaluations of the significance of education made by first-year and graduating students produced almost identical results. But the graduating students singled out general educational development as a discrete factor in the evaluation of higher education.

An analysis of the data for both 1973 and 1977 shows that the specific occupational complement within the student body is most important in differentiating student social characteristics, followed by gender, year of study, area, and respondent's social origin. However, differences in the significance of the various aspects of education are not all that great, and the consciousness of the student body is relatively homogeneous.

However, subsequent analysis showed that education is only relatively independent as an object of student evaluation. Education and work share similar evaluational bases, so that research

Table 9

Value-based Attitudes of Student Body toward Higher Education

Educational values	Score	RSFSR						ESSR					
		1973		1977				1973		1977			
		FS		FS		GS		FS		FS		GS	
		%	x̄	%	x̄	%	x̄	%	x̄	%	x̄	%	x̄
Occupational training	4	69		49		43.4		70.5		81.6		69.9	
	3	23		32.1		35		23.6		16.0		26.9	
	2	3	1.3	11.7	1.8	13.2	1.9	2.8	1.3	1.5	1.2	2.7	1.3
	1	1.6		5.2		6.7		1.4		0.8		0.6	
Educational level	4	38.2		41.8		40.3		41.1		72.5		69.5	
	3	49.9		37.1		38.1		46.9		22		26.2	
	2	10.6	1.7	15.5	1.9	15.4	1.9	11.2	1.7	4.5	1.3	3.5	1.3
	1	1.3		3.5		4.6		0.7		1		0.8	
Social position	4	22.7		8.2		7.0		24.9		8.6		9.0	
	3	35.7		16.5		16.9		47.5		32.6		40.0	
	2	21.1	2.3	26.4	3.2	25	3.2	15.3	2.1	33.4	2.7	35.1	2.6
	1	16.3		44.5		45.8		9.5		20.8		17.9	
Material compensation	4	15.9		8.3		7		12.1		13		19	
	3	25.9		16.8		18.4		24.5		42.6		42.2	
	2	32.5	2.6	28.1	3.2	27.3	3.2	35.0	2.8	30.2	3.2	24.7	2.3
	1	32.5		42.8		43.4		26		14.2		14.2	

Notes: 4—very important, 3—fairly important, 2—fairly unimportant, 1—completely unimportant; x̄—average score on the scale; FS—first-year students, GS—graduating students.

limited to the educational values of the student body can have only limited meaning. In actual fact, the socio-occupational orientation of the student body manifests itself in a single value-basis which combines evaluations of education and evaluations of work. This is natural enough, for education is only a step on the way to acquiring a stable social position and occupation.

Value-based attitudes toward occupation

The student body's indices of occupational values, it must be said, were generally stable. The most substantial changes were those occurring in the evaluation of creativity as a value-basis for work activity (Table 10). As we can see, the percentage of those who considered this requirement "highly essential" fell by 20 points. This considerable change in evaluations is explained in some measure by the fact that the 1977 sample was drawn from higher educational institutions in various cities, not just in higher educational centers (as was the case in 1973).

While a comparative analysis at the level of a simple distribution revealed some appreciable changes in the student body's value-bases with regard to work, more detailed conclusions emerged when factor analysis was applied separately to the 1973 and 1977 data.

As can be seen from Table 11, the orientations of first-year and graduating students in higher educational institutions differed somewhat in 1973.

First-year students have two independent bases for evaluation of occupational activity (Table 10). The first is the factor which is formed around the following indicators: career growth (0.70), success in life (0.62), good pay (0.61), position in society (0.58), and social recognition (0.51).[12] This may be termed the career growth factor, and the relevant value orientation is formed as an integrated entity. The crux of this factor is the desire for social recognition, which is achieved through career growth. This basis for evaluating labor activity is even more clear-cut in the assessments of higher educational institution graduating students. Here

Table 10

Evaluation of Demands Made by First-year and Graduating Students upon their Occupation*

| Demands made upon occupation | | Average evaluation on the scale | | Percentages of respondents rating the given demand as | | | |
| | | | | Highly essential | | Completely inessential | |
		USSR, 1973	RSFSR, 1977	USSR, 1973	RSFSR, 1977	USSR, 1973	RSFSR, 1977
Creativity	FS	1.9	—	47.6	23.1	1.1	4.0
	GS	1.9	—	47.2	27	—	4.6
Self-affirmation	FS	1.3	—	68.4	51.2	0.3	0.9
	GS	1.7	—	42.2	50.2	0	0.8
Usefulness to society	FS	1.4	1.3	63.3	65.8	0.8	0.9
	GS	1.5	1.6	56.0	53.9	—	1.7
Respect of associates	FS	1.8	1.7	41.8	47.8	4.6	1.6
	GS	1.9	1.8	37.3	42.2	—	1.9
Interaction in the work process	FS	1.7	1.6	50.0	51.9	1.6	1.7
	GS	1.8	1.7	40.3	43.9	2.5	2.7
Career growth	FS	2.9	2.8	6.5	8.1	22.6	24.8
	GS	2.7	2.8	12.3	7.6	—	24.6
Good pay	FS	2.4	2.4	14.0	15.5	8.8	8.3
	GS	1.2	2.2	27.2	18.3	—	6.6

*FS—first year students, GS—graduating students; USSR—6 areas, RSFSR—13 cities in the European RSFSR. A four-point scale was used.

this first factor is more forcefully described by the follwing indicators: position in society (0.66), career growth (0.65), success in life (0.64), social recognition (0.59), repute (0.54), and authority among associates (0.53).

The relative importance of indicators of social position increases appreciably. On the whole this is the most direct expression of the drive to acquire a particular social position. It is, however, essential to realize that this drive is associated with social recognition and that its social content differs completely from that of its counterpart in bourgeois society, where this kind of position is construed as an entree into "the elite." Thus the

Table 11

Factor Analysis of Evaluations of Work Significance, Made by First-year and Graduating Students (All-Union Total, 1973)*

Indicators of value of diverse facets of work	First-year students		Graduating students		
	Factor 1	Factor 2	Factor 1	Factor 2	Factor 3
Potential for creativity	−0.08	0.28	0.02	−0.32	−0.12
Self-affirmation	−0.06	0.49	−0.02	−0.33	0.03
Self-improvement	−0.03	0.51	0.01	−0.39	0.11
Usefulness to society	−0.11	0.57	−0.01	−0.48	0.03
Good pay	0.61	−0.14	0.49	0.11	0.34
Respect of acquaintances	0.48	0.27	0.46	−0.25	0.15
Career growth	0.70	−0.07	0.65	0.08	0.09
Position in society	0.58	0.29	0.66	0.03	0.14
Occupational growth	0.12	0.33	0.27	−0.33	−0.13
Independence	0.05	0.39	0.09	−0.42	0.03
Potential for interaction	0.10	0.45	0.09	−0.51	0.14
Success in life	0.62	0.11	0.64	−0.17	0.16
Social recognition	0.51	0.35	0.59	−0.40	0.06
Free time	0.41	−0.06	0.09	−0.01	0.69
Authority among associates	—	—	0.53	−0.39	0.19
Repute	—	—	0.54	−0.06	−0.06
Material wellbeing	—	—	0.48	0.17	0.52
Comprehensive development	0.12	0.44	—	—	—
Descriptive power of factors	28.5%		32.3%		

* A more complete list of indicators was used in this research project to characterize the significance of diverse facets of work.

most fully formed orientation here is the orientation toward career growth, which includes the indicators of compensation for work. This signifies that compensation for work—an aspect of the evaluation of work singled out in theory—is indeed the basis of a value orientation.

The second factor identified in the evaluations of first-year students comprises the following indicators: the possibility of being useful to society (0.57), self-improvement (0.51), self-affirmation (0.49), the potential for interaction (0.45), and comprehensive development (0.44). By and large, this can be labeled the factor of self-expression through work. Indicators of the first factor here acquire negative values, and indicators which describe the second factor are found as negative values in the first factor. Hence these two basic approaches to labor activity are not only independent but are also in opposition to one another.

The contrasting nature of these two approaches intensifies during the years spent in higher education. Among graduating students they are wholly antipodal. The second factor may be more fully described at this point since among graduating students it included a larger number of indicators, namely: the potential for interaction at work, independence at work, usefulness to society, social recognition, and also all the indicators of self-expression in occupational activity. In the course of their studies some of the students become more aware of the social usefulness of their future labor activity and of the importance of the advantages that typically accrue to intellectual-type work (relative independence at work, dealing with people instead of with an inanimate environment). Self-expression in labor activity plays a smaller role in this orientation for graduating students than it does for first-year students.

A third basis for evaluation of labor activity among graduating students is a factor which is defined by the following indicators: free time to do other things, potential for the satisfaction of spiritual needs, and material well-being. This factor describes an attitude toward work as a means of ensuring other forms of life-activity and of achieving other good things in life. This approach to labor was found largely among seniors; first-year students did not exhibit it.

In 1977 three factors were identified in the responses of first-year and graduating students (Table 12). The first, which describes an orientation toward the social consequences of occupational activity, runs counter to the other two. This suggests that in the student consciousness there is a distinction between the social consequences and the substantive characteristics of occupational activity. An orientation toward the substantive characteristics of work leads to an underestimation of its social consequences, and, conversely, an orientation toward the social consequences of la-

Table 12

Factor Analysis of Evaluations of Significance of Work Made by First-year Students (RSFSR, 1977)

Indicator of value of diverse facets of work	Factor 1	Factor 2	Factor 3
Potential for creativity	0.02	0.05	−0.82
Self-affirmation	−0.02	−0.26	−0.73
Usefulness to society	−0.09	−0.60	−0.49
Material wellbeing	0.72	0.02	0.00
Authority among associates	0.52	−0.49	−0.02
Occupational growth	0.83	0.04	−0.01
Social recognition	0.71	−0.09	−0.08
Interesting work	0.15	−0.20	−0.54
Success in life	0.80	−0.01	−0.01
Usefulness to people	−0.01	−0.73	−0.23
Potential for interaction	0.08	−0.76	−0.03
Descriptive power of factors	24.1%	16.5%	16.7%

bor activity detracts from the significance of its substantive characteristics. As we see, this corresponds to the singularities of the value orientation among graduating students in higher educational institutions also observed in 1973. However, the distinguishing feature of the student body in 1977 was that the two orientations toward the substantive characteristics of labor were more strongly expressed. We can also see that ''commanding authority among associates'' was a borderline indicator. Its significance derived both from personal altruism and the aspiration for social recognition. This is also associated with the personal orientation toward self-expression in occupational activity. On the whole, it can be said that the value-bases of the attitude toward labor are undergoing a process of individualization.

For the purpose of a deeper analysis of the links between the student body's value-based attitudes to labor and its social characteristics, factor analysis was used to produce some new factor indicators. When these were calculated for each respondent, a total of six factor orientations clearly emerged. It was also possible to compute the average factor loadings for each of the indicators in various student groups (Table 13) and the degree of variability in the factor indicators as a function of the basic objective characteristics of the student body (Table 14). The attitude toward education and occupation is most strongly differentiated depending on the complement to which the student belongs, with regional differences coming second. The value orientations of these young people are least affected by year of study, which attests to the high stability of these orientations.

The significance of material compensation is basically contingent upon year of study. Material welfare invariably becomes more important as independent working life draws closer, so that this value-basis is stronger among students about to graduate from higher education. The opposite is the case with respect to the significance of occupational training as a basis for evaluating education. As occupational training is acquired, its importance decreases. The significance of the intelligentsia's cultural status also falls somewhat during the years spent in higher education. And the significance of social usefulness as a criterion for the evaluation of work and education also falls somewhat. These three value-bases are associated with chosing a specialty, deciding which educational route to take. Subsequently their immediate relevance fades.

The respondent's gender is more significant in differentiating these three value-bases. Girls have quite a strong orientation toward the intelligentsia's cultural status, which is clearly associated with their greater interest in self-improvement. The social usefulness of work and education also means more to them. At the same time, though, they are less strongly oriented toward social advancement, and they attach slightly less importance to material compensation than boys.

Overall, the analysis of the value-based attitudes toward occupational activity held by students who are future recruits to the various ranks of the intelligentsia leads to the conclusion that the foundations of these attitudes are laid during higher education and are actively influenced by differences between the types of mental work which define the intelligentsia's internal structure. The value-based attitude toward the various facets of mode of life (the "life orientation") determines the hierarchy of people's attitudes toward various kinds of life activity. Life orientation is, therefore, highly important to the study of subjective aspects of mode of life. In that sense, the student body's life orientation foreshadows the formation of the corresponding orientation in the various groups of the intelligentsia.

As one of the components of consciousness, life orientation incorporates the three levels—the emotional (social sentiments), the cognitive (a conscious tilt toward given forms of life activity), and the behavioral (a willingness to engage in one or another kind of activity)—that characterize any value orientation.[13] In analyzing the empirical data, it is important to note that initially these three levels can exist relatively independently of each other.

The following method was used to measure life orientiations. A four-point scale was used to reveal the respondents' evaluations of the signficance of various aspects of life activity on two or three levels. A factor analysis was then done to determine precisely which orientations served as bases for the factor indicators that permitted us to determine the dependence of these orientations upon value-based attitudes toward education and work, as well as upon objective indices.

This analysis revealed that the respondents evaluated their studies (which were linked to mastery of a specialty) quite highly on the cognitive level, although their readiness for these studies— the behavioral level—was far lower. There was close similarity in the data on this score in both phases of the project and from both basic groups (first-year and graduating students).

Occupation-related work activity and family life play a larger role than community activity. A comparison of data from both polls found that these evaluations are tending to converge. The converegence was stronger among both Estonian graduating students and first-year students than it was for students in the country as a whole.

Table 13

Average Factor Loadings by Occupational Values Among Basic Student Contingents in the Baltic States*

Respondent characteristics	Factors					
	Social advancement	Self-expression in work	Material compensation	Cultural status	Social usefulness	Occupational training
Language of instruction						
Lithuanian	0.07	0.07	−0.02	−0.13	0.05	−0.13
Latvian	0.03	−0.01	−0.02	0.13	−0.09	0.18
Estonian	−0.44	−0.04	0.26	0.17	−0.29	0.22
Russian	0.21	−0.10	−0.14	0.02	0.20	0.04
Gender						
male	0.17	−0.02	0.08	−0.24	−0.16	0.01
female	−0.16	0.02	−0.07	0.21	0.14	−0.01

Year of study						
first	-0.04	0.00	-0.11	0.05	0.05	0.11
graduating	0.06	0.00	0.15	-0.06	-0.06	-0.14
Type of higher educational institution						
humanities (university)	-0.24	0.20	0.11	0.31	0.04	-0.08
economics	0.02	-0.21	0.28	0.22	-0.01	-0.31
engineering	0.18	-0.09	0.09	-0.15	-0.10	-0.13
agriculture	-0.02	-0.23	0.02	-0.09	0.16	0.09
pedagogy	-0.30	0.16	-0.13	0.14	0.10	0.08
medicine	0.04	0.14	-0.34	0.00	0.27	0.44
creative (art, music)	-0.12	0.53	-0.12	0.00	-0.52	0.25

*The standard errors of factor loadings at the $p < 0.05$ level for the following variables were: gender ± 0.045; year of study ± 0.045; type of higher educational institution ± 0.079; language ± 0.081

Table 14

Differentiating Impact of Basic Social Characteristics of Students upon Value-based Attitudes toward Work and Occupation (RSFSR)

Social and demographic description of student body	Altruistic interaction			Self-expression			Career growth			
	Useful-ness to society	Useful-ness to people	Interaction at work	Content of work	Creative nature	Respect	Advance-ment	Recog-nition	Success	Pay
Student body complement	0.14	0.15	0.13	0.12	0.14	0.12	0.20	0.11	0.18	0.14
Gender							0.22	0.15	0.18	0.10
Age					0.11	0.11	0.12	0.10	0.11	0.10
Area	0.11	0.11	0.12				0.12		0.12	
Father's level of education						0.11				
Father's socio-occupational group		0.14	0.11	0.12	0.12		0.12		0.11	0.11
Income level of parental family			0.10				0.10			
Intended place of residence		0.11	0.10				0.12			0.11
Intended place of work	0.14	0.14	0.14	0.10	0.13	0.10	0.14		0.12	0.11

The respondents rated hobbies positively on the whole, although there are certain important aspects of this which should not be overlooked. First, all the data point to a drop in the significance of hobbies by the student's final year. Second, in the Baltic group hobbies were more important to the Estonian contingent, most of whose members looked favorably upon them. Third, this kind of activity is most highly rated on the emotional level—not on the cognitive level, as was the case for the first two forms of activity.

Students were also positive about media-related pastimes. This is the one case where the behavioral component of the evaluation almost parallels the other two components. The data gathered in Estonia during 1977 actually showed an increase in the significance of this component, reaching a level equal to the All-Union data collected in 1973.

The active leisure-time pursuit of athletics was also rated highest on the emotional level (as were hobbies). The rating drops substantially during the years spent in higher education, though the Estonian contingent rated athletics as significant on all levels of evaluation. In 1977, however, the evaluations converged somewhat.

Interaction with a favorite person is part of activity that is characteristic of this period of youth. It is, therefore, extremely significant for young people—as significant as occupational training and socializing with friends. Since Estonian students are a year older (having completed eleven grades of school instead of ten), their evaluations are naturally higher. But one cannot fail to notice that this activity is highly rated on the cognitive level, not the emotional level. This signifies that the attitude toward family life is consciously worked out, and not simply molded by the emotional satisfaction gained from interacting with a favorite person. The older age-groups accord a greater significance to the family. Along with occupational training this is the record form of activity receiving the highest rating by students graduating from higher educational institutions. Yet it must be stated that the significance of this activity fell slightly among students over the course of the 1970s (as seen from a comparison of data from the two polls).

Socializing with friends is an especially characteristic pastime for young people. As the data of both projects show, this also corresponds with the interests of students, who give a maximum rating to socializing with a circle of friends. The evaluations on all three levels are fairly close. By the final year, the evaluations have fallen slightly: socializing with a small group is now about equal in significance with occupational training and interacting with a favorite person.

Despite the fact that some of the social characteristics differ in the groups under comparison—which naturally means that a total congruence of evaluations was never to be expected—all in all, a comparison of student value orientations makes it quite clear that there is not a great deal of difference between respondents' approaches to educational and occupational values. Ratings were highest on the cognitive level and slightly lower on the emotional level, and on the behavioral level they were geared to the student's mode of life.

Factor analysis furnishes some additional conclusions on the structure of life orientations. Five factor orientations that were elicited from first-year students in both contingents in 1973 bespeak a substantial differentiation in evaluations of life activity. The first factor is described by the following indicators: entertainment (0.65); mass media (0.56, 0.54), and socializing with a circle of friends (0.5, 0.4, 0.4); and socializing (0,63). Only the mass media indicator is conspicuously positive when included with the other factors; the rest receive predominantly negative scores. This orientation is formed on an emotional level—under the direct impact of socializing, that is.

The second factor is characterized by an orientation toward interests which subsequently serves as a basis for the orientation toward either occupation or cultural consumption. The third factor characterizes the Estonian contingent's orientation toward cultural consumption, and is most strongly manifested on the emotional level. The All-Union contingent does not exhibit this factor at all. The fourth factor characterizes an orientation toward young love, which subsequently is transformed into an orientation toward family life.

The following indicators comprise the Estonian contingent's fifth (the All-Union contingent's third) factor: community activity (0.73; 0.63) and occupational activity (0.32; 0.29). A decisive role in shaping this orientation is played by goal-oriented specialist upbringing which engenders a conscious perception of work as pivotal to our society's mode of life (first-year students rate work training above the other spheres of activity). The cognitive component is paramount here.

The maximum gap between conscious and emotional evaluations of the significance of occupational training is 0.6 points. This is explained by the fact that the first-year student's orientation toward labor activity is comparatively inchoate. The weight of individual indicators within the factor indicates that this orientation is most fully formed in those first-year students who accord a great deal of significance to community activity.

As was the case with occupational values, the complement to which a student belongs is most important in differentiating life orientations. The following discussion of these differences draws upon data from the All-Union samples and data gathered in the Baltic states in 1977. Future medical personnel accord most significance on all levels to the value of occupational training, except in the RSFSR in 1977. Data from the Baltic states show especially large differences between student complements on the behavioral level (with an 0.3-point rift between medical personnel and the complement immediately following). This tells us that, as a component of the value-basis of life activity, occupational training is highly integrated. The engineering complement within the student body is less strongly oriented toward occupational training. Here, however, there is a gap between the data gathered far the country as a whole and that collected in the Baltic states in 1973, which can be explained by the fact that the higher educational contingent is formed under differing circumstances in various parts of the country.

A rather stronger orientation toward occupational training is seen among future agricultural specialists, and in the Baltic states among future teachers. Deeper analysis reveals the role played here by the fact that the rural schools' top graduates, who are firmly oriented toward occupational training, find their way into this complement. Among all the groups under comparison, students in the agricultural higher educational institutions rate community activity more highly, while engineers, on the other, rate it lower. Medical students mark occupational activity down even further, and incorporate into it the meaningful elements of community activity.

Cultural consumption is one of the components of an inclination toward social activism. As might have been supposed, the signficance of cultural consumption is higher among student complements where women are in the majority. Furthermore, in all contingents and on all levels of measurement, this evaluation is higher among future teachers and people training in the humanities. By the final year the importance of cultural consumption has risen for people in the humanities, while for engineers and agricultural specialists, conversely, it is considerably less important than before. Hence the distinctions in life orientation profiles. Engineers and agricultural specialists judge cultural consumption to be part of their orientation toward social activism in the broad sense. It is not a self-contained orientation for them, as it typically is for the contingent of future teachers and the humanities-based intelligentsia.

Athletics means more to boys—hence the great significance of athletics to students in agricultural and engineering higher educational institutions in all groups. The humanities students and the medical complement accord much less significance to this kind of activity. Education students also give a below-average rating to athletic activities. A factor analysis of evaluations elicited from the engineering complement and future agricultural specialists shows that an orientation toward athletics is part of their life orientations.

Hobbies tend to denote some kind of physical activity for boys, while for girls they tend to be cultural. Accordingly, this indicator is subsumed under the orientation toward cultural consumption among students in the humanities and education, while for the engineering complement and the agricultural specialists it is part of their orientation toward athletics. Yet differences in the significance accorded to hobbies are not substantial. They rank somewhat higher for education students, while for future agricultural specialists they plummet downward during the course of their studies.

Each individual value construct cannot, as a matter of principle, play a large role in the description of a concrete orientation (which is characterized by a correlation between evaluations of the corresponding activity and the orientation toward the given sphere of activity).

The life orientation can be most fully delineated only by means of the integral system of value constructs which comprise it. Therefore the basic task in studying the value-content of life orientations relates less to conducting research into the link between individual value constructs and life orientations than to pointing up the structure and general bearing of the value-content, seen as an integral system of value constructs. Individual value constructs and the correlations between them can only serve in such a case as indicators of this system, as a basis for a more or less coherent overall construct. This is why we must apply ourselves directly to available material on socio-occupational orientation.

Our analysis of the dynamics of student value orientations, based upon a juxtaposition of data from two research projects, has both theoretical and practical significance. It permits us to draw a concrete picture of the intellectual life of Soviet student youth, to shed light on a number of important links that define the values which students attach to their present and future positions, to their upcoming occupational and community activity, and to the most important facets of their mode of life.

The practical significance of this analysis lies in the fact that it offers broader opportunities to improve students' style of life, both from the standpoint of Soviet society's requirements for specialists with higher qualifications and from the perspective of the requirements and interests of the individual. This increases our chances of further strengthening the unity of sociological theory and socialist practice.

All in all, this two-part study of the impact of the higher educational system upon the social structure of socialist society— a project of unprecedented scope and a five-year time span— created a significant groundwork for the further development of educational sociology in the USSR. The basic concern here was the interaction occurring between the educational system and the social structure of Soviet society. The second phase of the research, being a joint effort between several socialist countries, fostered broader and stronger scholarly contacts, and threw light upon an array of important common developmental regularities in socialist society and upon the unique ways in which these regularities are manifested in each country.

Notes

1. *SSSR v tsifrakh v 1981 g.*, Moscow, 1982, p. 164.
2. See *Narodnoe khoziaistvo SSSR v 1979 g.*, p. 394. (Author's calculation.)
3. *Narodnoe khoziaistvo SSSR za 60 let*, Moscow, 1977, p. 487; *Narodnoe khoziaistvo SSSR v 1979 g.*, pp. 4–6.
4. *Narodnoe khoziaistvo SSSR v 1980 g.*, Moscow, 1981, p. 458.
5. The findings of the first project are summarized in the co-authored monograph, *Vysshaia shkola kak faktor izmeneniia sotsial'noi struktury razvitogo sotsialisticheskogo obshchestva* (Moscow, 1978). The second phase was a component part of an international research project jointly conducted by scholarly institutions in Bulgaria, Hungary, the USSR, and several other countries, under the aegis of the Advisory Commission on Multilateral Cooperation between the Academies of Sciences in socialist countries. The project was entitled "The Evolution of the Social Structure of Socialist Society. Social Planning and Forecasting" See F. R. Filippov, "The Replenishment of the Socialist Intelligentsia: The Results of an International Study," *Sotsiologicheskie issledovaniia*, 1980, no. 2, pp. 87–98; *Youth and Higher Education*, Sofia, 1982.
6. Data for 1970 from *Itogi Vsesoiuznoi perepisi naseleniia 1970 g.*, Moscow, 1974, vol. V. pp. 16–21, 24–25.
7. M. N. Rutkevich, editor, *Zhiznennye plany molodezhi*, Sverdlovsk,

1966; M. N. Rutkevich and F. R. Filippov, *Sotsial'nye peremeshcheniia*, Moscow, 1970; M. Kh. Titma, *Vybor professii kak sotsial'naia problema*, Moscow, 1975; F. R. Filippov, *Vseobshchee srednee obrazovanie v SSSR: Sotsiologicheskie problemy*, , Moscow, 1976; M. N. Rutkevich, *Intelligentsia v razvitom sotsialisticheskom obshchestve*, Moscow, 1977; F. R. Filippov, Sotsiologiia obrazovaniia, Moscow, 1980.

8. *Narodnoe khoziaistvo SSSR v 1973 g.*, Moscow, 1974, p. 591; *Narodnoe khoziaistvo SSSR v 1979 g.*, p. 397.

9. *Materialy XXVI s"ezda KPSS*, Moscow, 1981, p. 53.

10. Calculations by Iu. P. Eidukas.

11. T. S. Baranova and Iu. P. Eidukas participated in the analysis of respondents' value orientations.

12. Factor loadings are given in parentheses.

13. For more detail, see *Vysshaia skhola kak faktor izmeneniia sotsial'noi struktury* . . . .

12. The Dynamics of Social Mobility in the USSR*

N. A. AITOV

Social mobility is one of the crucial developmental characteristics of the social structure. Social mobility is here defined as the transition of individuals from one social group to another or from one stratum within a social group to another. It connotes a change in the individual's social affiliation.

These changes in social affiliation can occur between generations (when a child's social position is different from that of his parents) or within a generation (when an individual's social position alters in the course of his working life). In principle, they can be vertical (transition to a group or stratum which is higher or lower on the ladder of the social hierarchy) or horizontal (transition to an equivalently placed stratum or group). In the context of socialism, however, the ladder of the social hierarchy is by no means always easy to formulate: one indicator places one social group above another, while another indicator reverses that position. Only within classes or social groups—between strata that are identified by the degree of complexity in work performed—can a reasonably clear-cut hierarchy be discerned. Thus there is no question that worker-intelligentsia and highly skilled workers stand higher than all the other working class strata with respect to

*Russian © 1982 by ''Nauka'' Publishers. ''Dinamika sotsial'nykh pere-meshchenii v SSSR,'' Akademiia nauk SSSR, Institut sotsiologicheskikh issledovanii, *Sovetskaia sotsiologiia*, Vol. II, pp. 197–210.

their educational level, occupational training, income, cultural requirements, political activism, and other indicators. Therefore only mobility within social groups can be identified as vertical (upward or downward) or horizontal. But it is very difficult to attach such labels to social mobility between the working class, the peasantry, the intelligentsia, and nonspecialist employees.

What, then, are the regularities of social mobility? As we see it, no single set of regularities applicable to every society exists, though there are regularities of social mobility for a given socio-economic formation or even for a particular stage in a formation's development. We shall explore here the particularities and regularities of social mobility in developed socialist society.

The first particularity lies in the fact that developed socialist society comprises only classes and social groups of working people. Consequently, social mobility consists exclusively of movement between social groups of working people. While the classes in developed socialist society exhibit specific traits by virtue of their respective relations to the means of production, they also possess one common unifying trait: they are all co-owners, joint proprietors of the means of production belonging to the whole people. Though they may move from one social group to another, people always remain owner of that universal public property. Hence, social mobility does not change their social position totally, as is the case under capitalism; the change is only partial. This explains the relative ease (and therefore the mass character) of social mobility under socialism.

The second important particularity of social mobility in the context of developed socialism lies in the fact that an individual's transition to another group entails no material sacrifice. While under capitalism a worker's son has to pay for higher educational instruction (and, consequently, for an entree into the intelligentsia), under socialism the state meets the bill for education. Under socialism children are less likely to be firmly attached to their parents' social group than they are under capitalism.

The next particularity of social mobility under socialism is that most of such mobility is voluntary in nature. Under capitalism the transition from the urban petite bourgeoisie, the peasantry, or bourgeois strata to the ranks of the working class, for example, is frequently occasioned by financial ruin.

The bulk of mobility under socialism occurs on a voluntary basis. Everyone chooses the direction his own social mobility will take. Of course, desires and reality do not always coincide, but in the majority of cases this lack of correspondence stems from subjective factors—the individual's energy, determination, and capabilities. Thus in a developed socialist society a person's freedom of choice in controlling his own fate is much greater than in a capitalist context.

The corollary of this is that socialist society is far more ''open'' than its capitalist counterpart. This openness is made possible by the fact that all social groups and strata in socialist society have converged, and the basic essential distinctions between them have been surmounted, so that only the less deep-rooted distinctions remain.

1. Intergenerational mobility and changes in social position

Socialist society's social groups stand in an identical relationship to the means of production. It is worth noting that the ratio between the incomes of the 10% most highly paid and the 10% lowest paid personnel in the USSR, which stood at 4.4:1 in 1956, had fallen to 3:1 by the end of 1975.[1] In 1977 there were 700 people with higher or secondary (complete or incomplete) education per 1,000 people doing predominantly physical work, and 970 per 1,000 people doing predominantly mental work.[2] The mode of life of all social groups in the USSR is converging through their joint efforts at work, through living in the same types of homes, being treated in the same clinics and making use of the same social infrastructure. This convergence serves to accelerate the process of social mobility. We shall endeavor to trace this tendency by drawing on material from a special research project which we conducted in Magnitogorsk in 1976 and

Table 1

Influence of Social Origin upon Respondent's Social Position at Commencement of Labor Activity, in %

Social position of respondent's father	Social position of respondent				
	Worker	Intelligentsia	Non-specialist employee	Collective farmer	Total
Worker	72.7	15.4	9.4	1.5	100.0
Intelligentsia	43.5	45.0	8.8	2.7	100.0
Nonspecialist employee	56.8	22.1	16.0	5.1	100.0
Collective farmer	55.0	12.4	7.3	15.3	100.0

which covered about 3,000 members of the city's employed population.

Let us examine mobility between generations—the influence which paternal social position exerts upon the respondent's social position at the commencement of his labor activity (Table 1).

From Table 1 it can be seen that there is considerable social mobility between the generations; 42.9% of all respondents had moved out of the paternal social group.

An analysis of answers given to our question on the social position of the respondents' children reveals the dynamics of the process much more clearly. Basically, we are able here to compare intergenerational social mobility of two different generations— that of the respondents and that of their adult children (Table 2).

In comparing Tables 1 and 2, which depict the social mobility of the respondents and of their children (with respect to parental social position in both cases), one cannot fail to see that the intensity and frequency of social mobility has increased sharply in one generation's lifetime. This is particularly true of workers. About three-quarters of people from worker families in the parental generation became workers. In the children's generation, this fraction was halved. The proportion of workers' children

Table 2

Influence of Respondent's Social Position upon Social Position of Respondent's Children, in %

	Social position of respondent's children								
Social position of respondent	Worker	Intelligentsia	Employee	Member of armed services	Collective farmer	Student	Pupil in urban vocational and technical training school	Not working	Total
Worker	35.2	12.9	16.1	5.7	0.2	9.0	18.1	2.8	100.0
Intelligentsia	20.8	30.1	12.4	6.0	0.5	16.2	12.2	1.8	100.0
Employee	35.8	27.1	16.6	6.4	0.0	6.4	5.0	2.7	100.0

becoming intelligentsia or students (the intelligentsia-to-be) increased by almost 1.5 times. The proportion of workers' children becoming nonspecialist employees rose substantially.

The proportion of children from the intelligentsia who joined the intelligentsia or the student body remained almost unchanged. The outflow of the intelligentsia into the worker category declined, while a greater proportion became nonspecialist employees.

Considerably more children of nonspecialist employees moved into the intelligentsia, because fewer were becoming workers.

In the course of the change in generations among Magnitogorsk residents, intergenerational social mobility—especially movement into the intelligentsia from other groups—increased sharply. The reasons for this are, first, a sharp rise in the number of specialists (from 190,000 specialists with higher or secondary specialized education employed in the national economy in 1913,

Table 3

Relationship between Education of Respondent's Father and Respondent

Father's educational level	Respondent's average educational level, number of grades	Educational growth, number of grades
Illiterate, marginally literate	8.9	+ 8.9
Grades 1 thru 4	9.8	+ 7.3
Grades 5 thru 7	10.7	+ 4.7
Grades 8 and 9	11.2	+ 2.7
Secondary	11.7	+ 1.7
Secondary specialized	12.6	+ 0.6
Higher	12.7	- 2.3

Note: We relied on the following equivalences in our calculations: complete technicum education = 12 grades of school; incomplete higher education = 12.5 grades; higher education = 15 grades; completed graduate study = 18 grades.

to 28.6 million in 1980)[3]; and, second, the Soviet educational system's democratic nature, its absence of fees and universal accessibility. It is no accident that our respondents' education differed enormously from that of their [fathers] (Table 3).

The data in Table 3 indicate that the educational level of the least educated portion of the population is rising more intensively than the rest. As a result, the gap in educational levels of groups at either end of the spectrum (the most and the least educated) is rapidly closing. Thus the parental generation's maximum 15-fold gap had narrowed to a 1.43-fold gap in the children's generation. Thus over the lifetime of one generation under socialism the disparity was reduced to less than a tenth of what it had been. Of course, parental education still influences the education of offspring (as Marx and Engels wrote, "The children's capacity for development depends upon the development of their parents"),[4] but, since it is not a decisive factor (Table 4), all the signs point to a substantial rise in the future incidence of social mobility.

Table 4

Relationship between Educational Levels of Parents and Children at Commencement of Labor Activity, for Inhabitants of Kazan' and Al'met'evsk, in %

Age-range of children's generation, in years	Education, in %	Kazan'			Al'met'evsk		
		Children	Fathers	Mothers	Children	Fathers	Mothers
Below 30	Higher and secondary specialized	27	17	15	28	10	9
	Average number of years of schooling	10.2	7.2	5.8	9.9	6.3	5.6
30–39	Higher and secondary specialized	31	16	12	24	5	3
	Average number of years of schooling	9.9	5.1	3.8	9.1	3.5	2.3
40–49	Higher and secondary specialized	26	10	5	12	3	1
	Average number of years of schooling	8.0	4.1	2.4	7.3	2.8	1.4
50–59	Higher and secondary specialized	24	8	5	18	4	1
	Average number of years of schooling	8.6	3.7	2.4	7.7	2.2	0.7

E. K. Vasil'eva gathered similar data on the extent to which parents' education influences the education of their children.[5] Thus two research projects, conducted independently of each other in different locations, at different times, and following different methodologies, produced approximately identical results.

In the socialist context the most common form of social mobility is that which occurs not between generations but within them. This mobility is predicated upon the extensive educational and occupational opportunities offered by the Soviet government. As social groups continue to converge and the distinctions between them are eroded, social mobility is experienced more frequently. Our research has furnished data which supports this assertion. Respondents were questioned on their social affiliation at the commencement of their labor activity, in 1950 (25 years prior to

Table 5

Respondent's Social Position at Commencement of Labor Activity and at Time of Study, in %

Social affiliation at commencement of labor activity	Social position at time of poll			
	Worker	Intelligentsia	Non-specialist employee	Total
Worker	72.3	21.3	6.4	100.0
Intelligentsia	10.8	82.5	6.7	100.0
Nonspecialist employee	30.9	29.6	39.5	100.0
Collective farmer	69.2	17.9	12.9	100.0

this study), and in 1970 (five years before).

Table 5 presents data characterizing social mobility from the commencement of labor activity up to the time of the study.

While only 72.7% of workers had inherited their parents' social position at the commencement of their labor activity (see Table 1), intragenerational social mobility reduced this figure to not quite 52%. The other half joined the ranks of the intelligentsia and nonspecialist employees. As for children of the intelligentsia, in the final analysis slightly more than one-third inherited their parents' social position. A mere handful of the children of nonspecialist employees remained in that social stratum.

These patterns of mobility are to a large extent determined by changes in the urban social structure. While 19.3% of the respondents were members of the intelligentsia at the commencement of their labor activity, this proportion had risen to 34.6% by the time of the study. This parallels the dynamics of technical progress in Magnitogorsk.

It is interesting to examine social mobility between working class strata, where we can be quite precise in speaking of movement "up" or "down" the ladder of the social hierarchy. Among those who commenced their labor activity in the category of the worker-intelligentsia or highly skilled workers, 63.2% were still there by the time of the study. Twelve percent had transferred into less developed working-class strata, and 24.8% had moved into the ranks of the intelligentsia or had become employees. The transfer to the ranks of less-skilled workers is explained by the fact that previously, when technical progress was slower, it was possible to master a complex line of work through a sheer buildup of work experience. In the context of today's scientific and technical progress, some specialties can only be firmly mastered through the acquisition of in-depth knowledge. The socio-occupational status of workers doing complex jobs but lacking an appropriate education becomes unstable,[6] and this generates mobility into the less developed strata of the working class.

Among skilled workers, 58.8% remained in that stratum; 10.5% moved into less developed strata of the working class; 3% became worker-intelligentsia or highly skilled workers, and 22.3% moved into other social groups within the urban population.

Among low-skilled workers, 28.3% remained so; 41.6% shifted into more developed strata; 4.5% became unskilled workers, and 25.6% moved into other social groups within the urban population.

Among those who commenced their labor activity as unskilled workers, only 12.7% remained so up to the time of the study. Over half (55.3%) shifted into more developed working-class strata, and 32.0% completed the social movement into the intelligentsia or nonspecialist employee stratum.

This analysis of social mobility of various strata within the working class leads us to the following conclusions.

First, the proportion of workers moving into more developed working-class strata is four times greater than the proportion shifting into less developed working-class strata. Consequently, the social structure of the Soviet working class is undergoing considerable improvement; the incidence of upward social mobility sharply exceeds that of downward mobility.

Second, the least stable strata within the working class are those containing low-skilled and unskilled workers. This is not surprising: 35.2% of low-skilled workers and 22.7% of unskilled workers had been educated to, or beyond, the secondary school level. If people with an incomplete secondary education (eight or nine grades) are included, then more than one-half of these workers are highly educated. And a high educational level invariably engenders a specific orientation toward complex, interesting, substantive work. The transition to universal secondary education in this country eliminated almost all the sources from which the social strata of workers doing simple work had previously been recruited. These strata had earlier been drawn from poorly educated migrants from the countryside. Now, as many research projects have confirmed, almost 90% of migrants from rural areas are young people up to 30 years of age, with secondary education as a rule, who have no desire to do unskilled work in the cities (since one of the main motives for leaving the countryside is an urge to find complex, interesting work).

Capitalist countries still have a reserve of "second-grade" individuals (foreign workers in the Common Market countries, "the colored" in the USA) from which these strata can be recruited. Under socialism, real de facto equality has been implemented for all nations and nationalities, and therefore the eradication of the objective requirement for low-skilled and unskilled labor is a more urgent problem here than in the capitalist countries. It is no accident that the decisions of the Twenty-sixth CPSU Congress paid special attention to this question.[7]

Finally, the analysis of our data shows that the social group of nonspecialist employees is highly unstable. Only about one-third of those who commenced their labor activity in this social group remained in at the time of the study. The rest had moved in almost equal proportions into the intelligentsia and the working class.

In speaking of nonspecialist employees we are actually referring to those doing simple mental labor which can be performed without higher or secondary specialized education. This includes cashiers, retail clerks, ordinary laboratory assistants, clerical workers, bookkeepers, the rank-and-file militia, and so on. The

Table 6

Respondent's Social Position in 1950 and 1976, in %

Social position in 1950	Social position in 1976			
	Worker	Intelligentsia	Non-specialist employee	Total
Worker	80.5	13.1	6.4	100.0
Intelligentsia	9.3	85.7	5.0	100.0
Nonspecialist employee	25.9	27.9	46.2	100.0
Collective farmer	75.6	5.4	19.0	100.0

majority of these people are employed in the nonproductive branches of the economy, and they perform ancillary, auxiliary functions in the productive branches. As research done by ourselves and others shows, occupational prestige is extremely low in this social group. As a result, the turnover of personnel among nonspecialist employees is fairly high, and almost always takes the form of social mobility.

2. The dynamic of change in social mobility

We have examined social mobility without reference to the dimension of time, using concepts such as "generation" and "labor activity," whose quantitative definition leaves something to be desired. Now, in order to discern the dynamics of social mobility, we shall examine the extent of that mobility over the 25 years (Table 6) and five years (Table 7) prior to our study.

Overall, 27.6% of the respondents shifted from one social group to another between 1950 and 1976, and 29.7% did so between 1970 and 1976. The incidence of social mobility was thus far higher over the more recent five-year period than over the twenty-five–year period. The rate was, in fact, five times faster.

Table 7

Respondent's Social Position in 1970 and 1976, in %

Social position in 1970	Social position in 1979			Total
	Worker	Intelligentsia	Non-specialist employee	
Worker	88.7	7.3	4.0	100.0
Intelligentsia	5.7	88.1	6.2	100.0
Nonspecialist employee	19.2	15.5	65.3	100.0
Collective farmer	71.4	16.3	12.3	100.0

It should be noted that the social mobility occurring over the two timespans (25 years and five years) represents the movement of two different generations. The social mobility recorded for the 25-year period is that of people who were already working in 1950. By 1976 they were at least 40 years of age. This is the paternal generation—the generation with relatively low educational levels. The social mobility recorded for the five years prior to the study mostly involved the youth of the 1970s—that is, the children of the earlier generation. In the contemporary context, as a rule, mobility occurs at a relatively early age. This is associated with changes in education (which people basically acquire up to the age of 30), with relocation from countryside to city (52.5% of the migrants among those polled had moved to the city by the age of 18), and with skill enhancement and a transfer to more complex work (which is a less daunting prospect at an earlier age).

The rapid rise in social mobility recorded in recent times is linked, moreover, with changes in the social structure of the employed population under the impact of the scientific and technical revolution—the swift growth, that is, in the relative share of the intelligentsia and workers employed in the more complex kinds of jobs (members of the worker-intelligentsia and highly skilled workers). The change in respondents' educational levels

Table 8

Respondent's Educational Level, in %

Education	1950	1976
Illiterate, marginally literate	6.1	0.2
Grades 1 thru 4	27.0	3.8
Grades 5 thru 7	37.7	17.8
Grades 8 and 9	12.1	12.7
General secondary	5.3	18.2
Secondary specialized	6.1	21.4
Incomplete higher	2.5	1.3
Higher	3.2	24.6
Total	100.0	100.0

is also a highly significant factor (Table 8).

In 1950, only 17.1% of the individuals had received a general secondary education or more, while 25 years later the figure stood at 65.5%; while in 1950 those with a secondary education formed an islet in a sea of low-educated people, by the end of the 1970s they accounted for two-thirds of our sample group.

It must be said that the data in Table 8 do not give a complete picture of educational change in the employed population, since they do not show how educational levels of the employed altered over those years when older, marginally educated people went into retirement.

When asked about their most recent episode of social mobility, 48.2% of those questioned attributed it to a rise in educational level, 24.9% to a change in place of residence (usually relocation from countryside to city, apparently), 7.9% to the birth of a child (some women seek work that is convenient, rather than congenial, to them after having a baby), 4.2% to their state of health, and 14.9% to other reasons. (We shall return to those "other reasons" later.) Almost three-quarters of all social mobility, therefore, occurs under the impact of two basic factors—a rise in education and migration from countryside to city. It is relevant that those who attributed their social mobility to educational enhancement had completed an average of 12.7 grades; those who attributed it to a change in place of residence had averaged 8.75 grades; those who attributed it to the birth of a child had completed 9.3 grades; those who attributed it to health reasons had completed 9.5 grades; and the rest had completed 9.8 grades. Hence education and migration appear to be the basic factors in social mobility for various categories of people.

We shall now examine in greater detail the processes of social mobility during those five- and 25-year periods. Since we lack the data to compare the position of large social groups (workers, intelligentsia, nonspecialist employees) within the urban population, we shall assume that shifts between these groups represent horizontal movement. Movement between strata of the working class (upward or downward), we shall term vertical.

An analysis of Table 9 leads to several important conclusions.

First, though there was a fivefold acceleration in overall social mobility in the 1970–1976 period, the rates of transfer from the worker-intelligentsia and highly skilled worker strata into other strata were significantly lower. This is bound up with a change in the composition of these working-class strata. While in 1950 they consisted predominantly of low-educated workers with long work experience who had mastered their specialty by trial and error, there is now a preponderance of highly educated workers, frequently with diplomas from higher educational institutions, technicums, and secondary urban vocational and technical training schools, who are capable of rapid adjustment to new machinery and technology, and who are thus less susceptible to instability in personal socio-occupational status than was the case in the 1950s. This stratum as a whole is now more stable.

The social mobility of skilled workers has undergone comparable changes.

There has been a sharp increase in the outflow from the uncredentialed practical intelligentsia group—which contains people without specialized education who are working as engineers,

Table 9

Nature of Social Mobility, 1950–1976 and 1970–1976, in %*

Respondent's social position in 1950 and 1970	Mobility between 1950 and 1970			Mobility between 1970 and 1976		
	Horizontal	Vertical		Horizontal	Vertical	
		Upward	Downward		Upward	Downward
Worker	13.7	—	—	11.2	—	—
Worker-intelligentsia and highly skilled worker	39.9	—	27.2	14.9	—	17.2
Skilled worker	18.9	1.6	17.7	11.9	1.9	8.9
Low skilled worker	12.5	30.6	9.7	6.6	13.3	4.3
Unskilled worker	17.0	49.1	—	12.2	36.0	—
Intelligentsia	14.3	—	—	11.8	—	—
Including:						
Educated specialists	10.2	—	—	6.5	—	—
Uncredentialed practical specialists	31.3	28.0	—	17.3	32.6	—
Nonspecialist employee	53.8	—	—	34.9	—	—
Collective farmers	100.0	—	—	100.0	—	—

*The proportion of individuals experiencing various forms of social mobility from the given social category, as a percentage of the number of respondents in that category.

teachers, managers, and so forth. About one-third of these acquired an education and transferred into the ranks of the specialist intelligentsia, while a significant portion of them became workers and nonspecialist employees.

Social mobility out of the group of intelligentsia with specialized education deserves a special examination. The processes here are extremely varied and have diverse repercussions.

First, this includes engineers and technicians moving into the ranks of the worker-intelligentsia. On the historical plane this is a positive process that is prompted by the scientific and technical revolution, which has made the ordinary worker's job so sophisticated that he needs the education of an engineer or a technician in order to attend to certain machinery.

Second, this involves members of the intelligentsia shifting into workers' ranks where jobs do not require higher or secondary specialized education, because of sundry shortcomings in the payment of labor. Thus in 1955 the average salary of an industrial engineer was 1.68 times an ordinary worker's wage. A construction engineer earned twice as much as a worker. In 1977 these figures had fallen, respectively, to 1.21 times and 1.08 times more.

Third, this involves some educated specialists becoming workers or nonspecialist employees because they could not cope with a specialist's job. The high moral and professional demands made upon people in leadership positions in this country (whatever their ranking) are a matter of record. People who do not meet these demands take up other work. In many cases a person who has begun to work in his specialty gradually realizes that he has made a mistake in choosing that particular specialty and turns away from it. These are the "other reasons" which were mentioned previously.

The fastest rise in social mobility is seen in the unskilled worker stratum and the group of nonspecialist employees, which signifies that problems associated with the mechanization and automation of the work done by these groups will have to be solved.

The last question which we would like to raise in this chapter concerns equality and inequality in social mobility.

As we know, socialist society does not yet enjoy full social equality. However, the remnants of inequality here are quantitatively and qualitatively different from inequality under capitalism. The qualitative distinctions lie in the fact that in the context of the bourgeois order inequality is predicated upon the amount of capital—if any—that a person possesses. Under socialism, inequality is predicated upon the socioeconomic heterogeneity of work. But since differences in work cannot be as great as differences in the possession of capital, the quantitative measure of social inequality is sigificantly less under socialism than under capitalism. Unquestionably, social mobility cannot fail to be affected by the existence of residual social inequality.

On the whole, however, social mobility is to a far greater extent illustrative of the equality which predominates under socialism. First, this equality is seen in the tremendous ''openness'' of Soviet society, in the scope which social mobility has attained under socialism. Second, it is seen in the increasing rates of social mobility which we noted earlier. The strengthening of social integration is the chief developmental tendency in the social structure of Soviet society.

Notes

1. *Kommunist*, 1976, no. 4, p. 94.
2. *Narodnoe khoziaistvo SSSR za 60 let*, Moscow, 1977, p. 56.
3. *Narodnoe khoziaistvo SSSR v 1980 g.*, Moscow, 1981, p. 367.
4. K. Marx, F. Engels, *Sochinenie*, 2nd. ed., Vol. 3, p. 426.
5. E. K. Vasil'eva, *Sotsial'no-ekonomicheskaia struktura naseleniia SSSR*, Moscow, 1978, p. 122.
6. On the phenomenon of unstable socio-occupational status, see: N. A. Aitov, *NTR i sotsial'noe planirovanie*, Moscow, 1978, pp. 52–61.
7. *Materialy XXVI s"ezda KPSS*, Moscow, 1981, p. 137.

Selected Bibliography

Aitov, N.A. "Some Debatable Questions in the Study of the Soviet Intelligentsia." *Sotsiologicheskie issledovaniia*, 3, 1979.

——————. *Sovetskii rabochii*. Moscow, 1981.

Akademiia nauk SSSR, Institut sotsiologicheskikh issledovanii. *Formirovanie sotsial'noi odnorodnosti sotsialisticheskogo obshchestva*. Moscow, 1981.

——————. *Sotsial'naia i professional'naia orientatsiia molodezhi i problemy kommunisticheskogo vospitaniia*. Tallin, 1977.

——————. *Sotsial'naia i professional'naia orientatsiia molodezhi v usloviiakh razvitogo sotsialisticheskogo obshchestva v SSSR*. Tallin, 1977.

——————. *Sotsial'naia struktura razvitogo sotsialisticheskogo obshchestva v SSSR*. Moscow, 1976.

——————. *Vysshaia shkola kak faktor izmeneniia sotsial'noi struktury razvitogo sotsialisticheskogo obshchestva*. Moscow, 1978.

Bueva, L. P., editor. *Sotsial'naia struktura sotsialisticheskogo obshchestva i vsestoronnee razvitie lichnosti*, Moscow, 1983.

Filippov, F. R. "The Role of Higher Education in Changing the Social Structure of Soviet Society (Results of an All-Union Study)." *Sotsiologicheskie issledovaniia*, 2, 1977.

——————. "The Study of the Social Structure of Soviet Society." *Sotsiologicheskie issledovaniia*, "From the Editors." *Sotsiologicheskie issledovaniia*, 4, 1980.

Geliuta, A. M. and Staroverov, V. I. *Sotsial'nyi oblik rabochego-intelligenta*. Moscow, 1977.

Igitkhanian, E. D. and Kirkh, A. V. "Important Problems in the Development of the Social Structure of Soviet Society." *Sotsiologicheskie issledovaniia*, 1, 1982.

Kapto, A. S. "The Social Structure of Society and A Differentiated Approach to the Organization of Upbringing." *Sotsiologicheskie issledovaniia*, 4, 1981.

Kirkh, A. V. "An Experiment in Measuring the Intergenerational Mobility of Youth." *Sotsiologicheskie issledovaniia*, 4, 1984.

—————— and Saar, E. "Modelling Intergenerational Educational and Social Mobility." *Izvestiia akademii nauk Estonskoi SSR*, Vol. 32, Obshchestvennye nauki, 2, 1983.

Komarova, V. B. "The Realization of Life Plans and Social Mobility of

Graduates of Rural Secondary Schools." *Sotsiologicheskie issledovaniia*, 3, 1980.

Kogan, L. N. "The Convergence of Social Groups in the Sphere of Socialist Culture." *Sotsiologicheskie issledovaniia*, 2, 1977.

Kogan, L. N. "The Intelligentsia in the Period of Developed Socialism." *Sotsiologicheskie issledovaniia*, 4, 1979.

Lukina, V. I. and Nekhoroshkov, S. B. *Dinamika sotsial'noi struktury naseleniia SSSR. Metodologiia i metodika issledovaniia*. Moscow, 1982.

Mokliak, N. N. *Sotsial'no-professional'nye peremeshcheniia na sotsialisticheskom predpriiatii*. Kiev, 1977.

Osipov, G. V. et al. "The Working Class and the Engineering-Technical Intelligentsia in the USSR: Indicators of Social Development," in Akademiia nauk SSSR, Institut sotsiologicheskikh issledovanii. *Sovetskaia sotsiologiia*, Vol. II. Moscow, 1982.

Ovsiannikov, A. A. "Differentiation of Consumption Behavior." *Sotsiologicheskie issledovaniia*, 3, 1982.

Pavlova, I. I. "On the Social Sources of Recruitment of the Soviet Intelligentsia." *Sotsiologicheskie issledovaniia*, 3, 1982.

Popova, I. M. and Moin, V. B. "Prestige and Attractiveness of Occupations." *Sotsiologicheskie issledovaniia*, 4, 1979.

Pribaltiiskoe otdelenie Sovetskoi sotsiologicheskoi assotsiatsii, and Akademiia nauk Litovskoi SSR, otdel filosofii, prava i sotsiologii pri institut istorii. *Sotsiologicheskie problemy vzaimodeistviia lichnosti i sotsial'nykh grupp v usloviiakh razvitogo sotsialisticheskogo obshchestva*. Vil'nius, 1977.

Roots Kh. and Sygel U. "The Social Structure of the Estonian SSR Under Mature Socialism: Some Results and Problems of Study." *Izvetiia Akademii nauk Estonskoi SSR, Tom 31, Obshchestvennye nauki*, 4, 1982.

Rubina, L. Ia. "Changes in the Social Composition of the Student Body." *Sotsiologicheskie issledovaniia*, 1982.

————. *Sovetskoi studenchestvo*. Moscow, 1981.

Rutkevich, M. N. *Intelligentsiia v razvitom sotsialisticheskom obshchestve*. Moscow, 1977.

————. "On the Conception of Social Structure." *Sotsiologicheskie issledovaniia*, 4, 1978.

————. "The Convergence Between the Working Class and the Engineering-Technical Intelligentsia." *Sotsiologicheskie issledovaniia*, 4, 1980.

————. "The Social Class Structure of Socialist Society and Its Expression in a System of Concepts." *Sotsiologicheskie issledovaniia*, 1, 1979.

Sankova, K. A. "The Dynamics of Socially Heterogeneous Marriages Among the Urban Population." *Sotsiologicheskie issledovaniia*, 4, 1981.

Seniavskii, S. L. *Sotsial'nai struktura sovetskogo obshchestva v usloviiakh razvitogo sotsializma (1961–1980 gg.)*. Moscow, 1982.

Sheremet, I. I. "The Social Composition of the Student Body." *Sotsiologicheskie issledovaniia*, 2, 1977.

Shkaratan, O. I., Eremicheva, G. V., Kanygin, G. V. and Riabikova, I. V.

''The Character of Non-Production Activity and Social Differentiation of Urban Residents.'' *Sotsiologicheskie issledovaniia*, 4, 1979.

Shkaratan, O. I., Filippova, O. V. and Demidova, L. G. ''Social Stratum and Occupation.'' *Sotsiologicheskie issledovaniia*, 3, 1980.

Shubkin, V. N. ''Education and the Life-Paths of Youth,'' in Akademiia nauk SSSR, Institut sotsiologicheskikh isledovanii. *Sovetskaia sotsiologiia*, Vol. II. Moscow, 1982.

————. *Nachalo puti. Problemy molodezh v zerkale sotsiologii i literatury.* Moscow, 1979.

Slesarev, G. A. *Demograficheskie protsessy i sotsial'naia struktura sotsialisticheskogo obshchestva.* Moscow, 1978.

Soskin, S. N. *Sotsial'naia struktura sela i narodnoe obrazovanie.* Alma-Ata, 1979.

Staroverov, V. I. ''Changing Trends in the Social Structure of the Rural Population of the USSR at the Stage of Developed Socialism.'' *Sotsiologicheskie issledovaniia*, 1977.

————. *Sotsial'naia struktura sel'skogo naseleniia SSSR na etape razvitogo sotsializma.* Moscow, 1978.

Stepanian, Ts. A. ''The Indisputable and the Debatable in Discussions of the Social Structure of Soviet Society.'' *Sotsiologicheskie issledovaniia*, 4, 1980.

————. ''The Soviet Intelligentsia and the Main Paths of its Formation.'' *Voprosy filosofii*, 1, 1979.

Titma, M. Ka. ''A Discussion on Problems of Social Structure.'' *Sotsiologicheskie issledovaniia*, 1, 1979.

Tsurkanu, N. V. *Sotsial'naia struktura kollektiva agropromyshlennogo predpriiatiia.* Kishinev, 1980.

Vasil'eva, E. K. *Sotsial'no-ekonomicheskaia struktura naseleniia SSSR.*

Zavtur, AA. *Sotsial'naia struktura Moldavii: stanovlenie sotsial'no-politicheskogo edinstva.* Kishinev, 1977.

Ziuzin, D. I. ''Causes of the Low Mobility of the Native Population of the Central Asian Republics.'' *Sotsiologicheskie issledovaniia*, 1, 1983.

About the Editor

MURRAY YANOWITCH is Professor of Economics at Hofstra University. He is the author of *Social and Economic Inequality in the Soviet Union* (1979) and *Work in the Soviet Union* (1985) and editor of *Soviet Work Attitudes* (1979) and (with Wesley A. Fisher) *Social Stratification and Mobility in the USSR* (1973).